OCEANSIDE PUBLIC LIBRARY
615 FOURTH STREET
OCEANSIDE, CALIF. 92054

D0032159

SOYINKA

COLLECTED PLAYS

2

822
SOY
(v.2)

WOLE
SOYINKA

——

COLLECTED PLAYS

2

Oxford   New York

OXFORD UNIVERSITY PRESS

OCEANSIDE PUBLIC LIBRARY
615 FOURTH STREET
OCEANSIDE CALIF 92054

Oxford University Press, Walton Street, Oxford OX2 6DP

Oxford New York Toronto
Delhi Bombay Calcutta Madras Karachi
Petaling Jaya Singapore Hong Kong Tokyo
Nairobi Dar es Salaam Cape Town
Melbourne Auckland

and associated companies in
Beirut Berlin Ibadan Nicosia

ISBN 0–19–281164–9

© Wole Soyinka 1963, 1964, 1967, 1971, 1973, 1974

The Lion and the Jewel, first published by Oxford University Press, 1963
Kongi's Harvest, first published by Oxford University Press, 1967
The Trials of Brother Jero, first published by Oxford University Press, 1964
Jero's Metamorphosis, first published by Eyre Methuen Ltd., 1973
Madmen and Specialists, first published by Eyre Methuen Ltd., 1971,
and reprinted with their permission
Madmen and Specialists, first published in the U.S. by Farrar, Straus & Giroux,
Inc., 1971, and reprinted in the U.S. with their permission

This edition first published 1974 as an Oxford University Press paperback
Reprinted 1976, 1981, 1982, 1986

All rights reserved. No part of this publication may be reproduced,
stored in a retrieval system, or transmitted, in any form or by any means,
electronic, mechanical, photocopying, recording, or otherwise, without
the prior permission of Oxford University Press

This book is sold subject to the condition that it shall not, by way
of trade or otherwise, be lent, re-sold, hired out or otherwise circulated
without the publisher's prior consent in any form of binding or cover
other than that in which it is published and without a similar condition
including this condition being imposed on the subsequent purchaser

Printed in Great Britain by
J. W. Arrowsmith Ltd
Bristol

MAY 2 7 1987

CONTENTS

THE LION
AND
THE JEWEL

Characters

SIDI the village belle
LAKUNLE school teacher
BAROKA the 'Bale' of Ilujinle
SADIKU his head wife
THE FAVOURITE
VILLAGE GIRLS

A WRESTLER
A SURVEYOR
SCHOOLBOYS
ATTENDANTS ON THE 'BALE'
Musicians, Dancers, Mummers,
Prisoners, Traders, the Village

MORNING

A clearing on the edge of the market, dominated by an immense odan tree. It is the village centre. The wall of the bush school flanks the stage on the right, and a rude window opens on to the stage from the wall. There is a chant of the 'Arithmetic Times' issuing from this window. It begins a short while before the action begins. Sidi enters from left, carrying a small pail of water on her head. She is a slim girl with plaited hair. A true village belle. She balances the pail on her head with accustomed ease. Around her is wrapped the familiar broad cloth which is folded just above her breasts, leaving the shoulders bare.

Almost as soon as she appears on the stage, the schoolmaster's face also appears at the window. (The chanting continues—'Three times two are six', 'Three times three are nine', etc.) The teacher Lakunle, disappears. He is replaced by two of his pupils, aged roughly eleven, who make a buzzing noise at Sidi, repeatedly clapping their hands across the mouth. Lakunle now reappears below the window and makes for Sidi, stopping only to give the boys admonitory whacks on the head before they can duck. They vanish with a howl and he shuts the window on them. The chanting dies away. The schoolmaster is nearly twenty-three. He is dressed in an old-style English suit, threadbare but not ragged, clean but not ironed, obviously a size or two too small. His tie is done in a very small knot, disappearing beneath a shiny black waistcoat. He wears twenty-three-inch-bottom trousers, and blanco-white tennis shoes.

LAKUNLE: Let me take it.

SIDI: No.

LAKUNLE: Let me. [*Seizes the pail. Some water spills on him.*]

SIDI [*delighted.*]:
There. Wet for your pains.
Have you no shame?

LAKUNLE: That is what the stewpot said to the fire.
Have you no shame—at your age
Licking my bottom? But she was tickled
Just the same.

SIDI: The school teacher is full of stories
This morning. And now, if the lesson
Is over, may I have the pail?

LAKUNLE: No. I have told you not to carry loads
    On your head. But you are as stubborn
    As an illiterate goat. It is bad for the spine.
    And it shortens your neck, so that very soon
    You will have no neck at all. Do you wish to look
    Squashed like my pupils' drawings?

SIDI: Why should that worry me? Haven't you sworn
    That my looks do not affect your love?
    Yesterday, dragging your knees in the dust
    You said, Sidi, if you were crooked or fat,
    And your skin was scaly like a . . .

LAKUNLE: Stop!

SIDI: I only repeat what you said.

LAKUNLE: Yes, and I will stand by every word I spoke.
    But must you throw away your neck on that account?
    Sidi, it is so unwomanly. Only spiders
    Carry loads the way you do.

SIDI [*huffily, exposing the neck to advantage.*]:
    Well, it is my neck, not your spider.

LAKUNLE [*looks, and gets suddenly agitated.*]:
    And look at that! Look, look at that!
    [*Makes a general sweep in the direction of her breasts.*]
    Who was it talked of shame just now?
    How often must I tell you, Sidi, that
    A grown-up girl must cover up her . . .
    Her . . . shoulders? I can see quite . . . quite
    A good portion of—that! And so I imagine
    Can every man in the village. Idlers
    All of them, good-for-nothing shameless men
    Casting their lustful eyes where
    They have no business . . . .

SIDI: Are you at that again? Why, I've done the fold
    So high and so tight, I can hardly breathe.
    And all because you keep at me so much.
    I have to leave my arms so I can use them . . .
    Or don't you know that?

LAKUNLE: You could wear something.
    Most modest women do. But you, no.
    You must run about naked in the streets.

Does it not worry you . . . the bad names,
The lewd jokes, the tongue-licking noises
Which girls, uncovered like you,
Draw after them?

SIDI: This is too much. Is it you, Lakunle,
Telling me that I make myself common talk?
When the whole world knows of the madman
Of Ilujinle, who calls himself a teacher!
Is it Sidi who makes the men choke
In their cups, or you, with your big loud words
And no meaning? You and your ragged books
Dragging your feet to every threshold
And rushing them out again as curses
Greet you instead of welcome. Is it Sidi
They call a fool—even the children—
Or you with your fine airs and little sense!

LAKUNLE [*first indignant, then recovers composure.*]:
For that, what is a jewel to pigs?
If now I am misunderstood by you
And your race of savages, I rise above taunts
And remain unruffled.

SIDI [*furious, shakes both fists at him.*]:
O . . . oh, you make me want to pulp your brain.

LAKUNLE [*retreats a little, but puts her aside with a very lofty gesture.*]:
A natural feeling, arising out of envy;
For, as a woman, you have a smaller brain
Than mine.

SIDI [*madder still.*]:
Again! I'd like to know
Just what gives you these thoughts
Of manly conceit.

LAKUNLE [*very, very patronizing.*]:
No, no. I have fallen for that trick before.
You can no longer draw me into arguments
Which go above your head.

SIDI [*can't find the right words, chokes back.*]:
Give me the pail now. And if you ever dare
To stop me in the streets again . . .

LAKUNLE: Now, now, Sidi . . .

SIDI: Give it or I'll . . .

LAKUNLE [*holds on to her.*]:
> Please, don't be angry with me.
> I didn't mean you in particular.
> And anyway, it isn't what I say.
> The scientists have proved it. It's in my books.
> Women have a smaller brain than men
> That's why they are called the weaker sex.

SIDI [*throws him off.*]:
> The weaker sex, is it?
> Is it a weaker breed who pounds the yam
> Or bends all day to plant the millet
> With a child strapped to her back?

LAKUNLE: That is all part of what I say.
> But don't you worry. In a year or two
> You will have machines which will do
> Your pounding, which will grind your pepper
> Without it getting in your eyes.

SIDI: O-oh. You really mean to turn
> The whole world upside down.

LAKUNLE: The world? Oh, that. Well, maybe later.
> Charity, they say, begins at home.
> For now, it is this village I shall turn
> Inside out. Beginning with that crafty rogue,
> Your past master of self-indulgence—Baroka.

SIDI: Are you still on about the Bale?
> What has he done to you?

LAKUNLE: He'll find out. Soon enough, I'll let him know.

SIDI: These thoughts of future wonders—do you buy them
> Or merely go mad and dream of them?

LAKUNLE: A prophet has honour except
> In his own home. Wise men have been called mad
> Before me and after, many more shall be
> So abused. But to answer you, the measure
> Is not entirely of my own coinage.
> What I boast is known in Lagos, that city
> Of magic, in Badagry where Saro women bathe
> In gold, even in smaller towns less than
> Twelve miles from here . . . .

SIDI: Well go there. Go to these places where
       Women would understand you
       If you told them of your plans with which
       You oppress me daily. Do you not know
       What name they give you here?
       Have you lost shame completely that jeers
       Pass you over.

LAKUNLE: No. I have told you no. Shame belongs
         Only to the ignorant.

SIDI: Well, I am going.
       Shall I take the pail or not?

LAKUNLE: Not till you swear to marry me.
         [*Takes her hand, instantly soulful.*]
         Sidi, a man must prepare to fight alone.
         But it helps if he has a woman
         To stand by him, a woman who . . .
         Can understand . . . like you.

SIDI: I do?

LAKUNLE: Sidi, my love will open your mind
         Like the chaste leaf in the morning, when
         The sun first touches it.

SIDI: If you start that I will run away.
       I had enough of that nonsense yesterday.

LAKUNLE: Nonsense? Nonsense? Do you hear?
         Does anybody listen? Can the stones
         Bear to listen to this? Do you call it
         Nonsense that I poured the waters of my soul
         To wash your feet?

SIDI: You did what!

LAKUNLE: Wasted! Wasted! Sidi, my heart
         Bursts into flowers with my love.
         But you, you and the dead of this village
         Trample it with feet of ignorance.

SIDI [*shakes her head in bafflement.*]:
       If the snail finds splinters in his shell
       He changes house. Why do you stay?

LAKUNLE: Faith. Because I have faith.
         Oh Sidi, vow to me your own undying love
         And I will scorn the jibes of these bush minds

Who know no better. Swear, Sidi,
Swear you will be my wife and I will
Stand against earth, heaven, and the nine
Hells . . . .

SIDI: Now there you go again.
One little thing
And you must chirrup like a cockatoo.
You talk and talk and deafen me
With words which always sound the same
And make no meaning.
I've told you, and I say it again
I shall marry you today, next week
Or any day you name.
But my bride-price must first be paid.
Aha, now you turn away.
But I tell you, Lakunle, I must have
The full bride-price. Will you make me
A laughing-stock? Well, do as you please.
But Sidi will not make herself
A cheap bowl for the village spit.

LAKUNLE: On my head let fall their scorn.

SIDI: They will say I was no virgin
That I was forced to sell my shame
And marry you without a price.

LAKUNLE: A savage custom, barbaric, out-dated,
Rejected, denounced, accursed,
Excommunicated, archaic, degrading,
Humiliating, unspeakable, redundant.
Retrogressive, remarkable, unpalatable.

SIDI: Is the bag empty? Why did you stop?

LAKUNLE: I own only the Shorter Companion
Dictionary, but I have ordered
The Longer One—you wait!

SIDI: Just pay the price.

LAKUNLE [with a sudden shout.]:
An ignoble custom, infamous, ignominious
Shaming our heritage before the world.
Sidi, I do not seek a wife
To fetch and carry,

To cook and scrub,
To bring forth children by the gross. . . .

SIDI: Heaven forgive you! Do you now scorn
Child-bearing in a wife?

LAKUNLE: Of course I do not. I only mean . . .
Oh Sidi, I want to wed
Because I love,
I seek a life-companion . . .
[*Pulpit-declamatory.*]
'And the man shall take the woman
And the two shall be together
As one flesh.'
Sidi, I seek a friend in need.
An equal partner in my race of life.

SIDI [*attentive no more. Deeply engrossed in counting the beads on her neck.*]:
Then pay the price.

LAKUNLE: Ignorant girl, can you not understand?
To pay the price would be
To buy a heifer off the market stall.
You'd be my chattel, my mere property.
No, Sidi! [*Very tenderly.*]
When we are wed, you shall not walk or sit
Tethered, as it were, to my dirtied heels.
Together we shall sit at table
—Not on the floor—and eat,
Not with fingers, but with knives
And forks, and breakable plates
Like civilized beings.
I will not have you wait on me
Till I have dined my fill.
No wife of mine, no lawful wedded wife
Shall eat the leavings off my plate—
That is for the children.
I want to walk beside you in the street,
Side by side and arm in arm
Just like the Lagos couples I have seen
High-heeled shoes for the lady, red paint
On her lips. And her hair is stretched
Like a magazine photo. I will teach you

The waltz and we'll both learn the foxtrot
And we'll spend the week-end in night clubs at Ibadan.
Oh I must show you the grandeur of towns
We'll live there if you like or merely pay visits.
So choose. Be a modern wife, look me in the eye
And give me a little kiss—like this.
[*Kisses her.*]

SIDI [*backs away.*]:
No, don't! I tell you I dislike
This strange unhealthy mouthing you perform.
Every time, your action deceives me
Making me think that you merely wish
To whisper something in my ear.
Then comes this licking of my lips with yours.
It's so unclean. And then,
The sound you make—'Pyout!'
Are you being rude to me?

LAKUNLE [*wearily.*]: It's never any use.
Bush girl you are, bush girl you'll always be;
Uncivilized and primitive—bush girl!
I kissed you as all educated men—
And Christians—kiss their wives.
It is the way of civilized romance.

SIDI [*lightly.*]: A way you mean, to avoid
Payment of lawful bride-price
A cheating way, mean and miserly.

LAKUNLE [*violently.*]: It is not.
[*Sidi bursts out laughing. Lakunle changes his tone to a soulful one, both eyes dreamily shut.*]
Romance is the sweetening of the soul
With fragrance offered by the stricken heart.

SIDI [*looks at him in wonder for a while.*]:
Away with you. The village says you're mad,
And I begin to understand.
I wonder that they let you run the school.
You and your talk. You'll ruin your pupils too
And then they'll utter madness just like you.
[*Noise offstage.*]
There are people coming

Give me the bucket or they'll jeer.
[*Enter a crowd of youths and drummers, the girls being in various stages of excitement.*]

FIRST GIRL: Sidi, he has returned. He came back just as
he said he would.

SIDI: Who has?

FIRST GIRL: The stranger. The man from the outside world.
The clown who fell in the river for you.
[*They all burst out laughing.*]

SIDI: The one who rode on the devil's own horse?

SECOND GIRL: Yes, the same. The stranger with the one-eyed box.
[*She demonstrates the action of a camera amidst admiring titters.*]

THIRD GIRL: And he brought his new horse right into the village
square this time. This one has only two feet. You should
have seen him. B-r-r-r-r.
[*Runs round the platform driving an imaginary motor-bike.*]

SIDI: And has he brought . . . ?

FIRST GIRL: The images? He brought them all. There was hardly
any part of the village which does not show in the book.
[*Clicks the imaginary shutter.*]

SIDI: The book? Did you see the book?
Had he the precious book
That would bestow upon me
Beauty beyond the dreams of a goddess?
For so he said.
The book which would announce
This beauty to the world—
Have you seen it?

THIRD GIRL: Yes, yes, he did. But the Bale is still feasting his eyes
on the images. Oh, Sidi, he was right. You *are* beautiful. On the
cover of the book is an image of you from here [*touches the top
of her head.*] to here [*her stomach.*]. And in the middle leaves,
from the beginning of one leaf right across to the end of
another, is one of you from head to toe. Do you remember it?
It was the one for which he made you stretch your arms
towards the sun. [*Rapturously.*] Oh, Sidi, you looked as if, at
that moment, the sun himself had been your lover. [*They all
gasp with pretended shock at this blasphemy and one slaps her
playfully on the buttocks.*]

FIRST GIRL: The Bale is jealous, but he pretends to be proud of you.
And when this man tells him how famous you are in the
capital, he pretends to be pleased, saying how much honour and
fame you have brought to the village.

SIDI [*with amazement.*]: Is not Baroka's image in the book at all?

SECOND GIRL [*contemptuous.*]: Oh yes, it is. But it would have been
much better for the Bale if the stranger had omitted him
altogether. His image is in a little corner somewhere in the
book, and even that corner he shares with one of the village
latrines.

SIDI: Is that the truth? Swear! Ask Ogun to
Strike you dead.

GIRL: Ogun strike me dead if I lie.

SIDI: If that is true, then I am more esteemed
Than Bale Baroka,
The Lion of Ilujinle.
This means that I am greater than
The Fox of the Undergrowth,
The living god among men . . .

LAKUNLE [*peevishly.*]: And devil among women.

SIDI: Be silent, you.
You are merely filled with spite.

LAKUNLE: I know him what he is. This is
Divine justice that a mere woman
Should outstrip him in the end.

SIDI: Be quiet;
Or I swear I'll never speak to you again.
[*Affects sudden coyness.*]
In fact, I am not so sure I'll want to wed you now.

LAKUNLE: Sidi!

SIDI: Well, why should I?
Known as I am to the whole wide world,
I would demean my worth to wed
A mere village school teacher.

LAKUNLE [*in agony.*]: Sidi!

SIDI: And one who is too mean
To pay the bride-price like a man.

LAKUNLE: Oh, Sidi, don't!

SIDI [*plunging into an enjoyment of Lakunle's misery.*]:

Well, don't you know?
Sidi is more important even than the Bale.
More famous than that panther of the trees.
He is beneath me now—
Your fearless rake, the scourge of womanhood!
But now,
He shares the corner of the leaf
With the lowest of the low—
With the dug-out village latrine!
While I—How many leaves did my own image take?

FIRST GIRL: Two in the middle and . . .

SIDI: No, no. Let the school teacher count!
How many were there, teacher-man?

LAKUNLE: Three leaves.

SIDI [*threateningly*.]: One leaf for every heart that I shall break.
Beware!
[*Leaps suddenly into the air.*]
Hurray! I'm beautiful!
Hurray for the wandering stranger!

CROWD: Hurray for the Lagos man!

SIDI [*wildly excited*.]: I know. Let us dance the dance of the lost
Traveller.

SHOUTS: Yes, let's.

SIDI: Who will dance the devil-horse?
You, you, you, and you.
[*The four girls fall out.*]
A python. Who will dance the snake?
Ha ha! Your eyes are shifty and your ways are sly.
[*The selected youth is pushed out amidst jeers.*]
The stranger. We've got to have the being
From the mad outer world . . . . You there,
No, you have never felt the surge
Of burning liquor in your milky veins.
Who can we pick that knows the walk of drunks?
You? . . . No, the thought itself
Would knock you out as sure as wine. . . . Ah!
[*Turns round slowly to where Lakunle is standing with a kindly,
fatherly smile for the children at play.*]
Come on book-worm, you'll play his part.

LAKUNLE: No, no. I've never been drunk in all my life.

SIDI: We know. But your father drank so much,
He must have drunk your share, and that
Of his great grandsons.

LAKUNLE [*tries to escape.*]: I won't take part.

SIDI: You must.

LAKUNLE: I cannot stay. It's nearly time to take
Primary four in Geography.

SIDI [*goes over to the window and throws it open.*]:
Did you think your pupils would remain in school
Now that the stranger has returned?
The village is on holiday, you fool.

LAKUNLE [*as they drag him towards the platform.*]:
No, no. I won't. This foolery bores me.
It is a game of idiots. I have work of more importance.

SIDI [*bending down over Lakunle who has been seated forcibly on the platform.*]:
You are dressed like him
You look like him
You speak his tongue
You think like him
You're just as clumsy
In your Lagos ways—
You'll do for him!

[*This chant is taken up by all and they begin to dance round Lakunle, speaking the words in a fast rhythm. The drummers join in after the first time, keeping up a steady beat as the others whirl round their victim. They go faster and faster and chant faster and faster with each round. By the sixth or seventh, Lakunle has obviously had enough.*]

LAKUNLE [*raising his voice above the din.*]: All right! I'll do it.
Come now, let's get it over with.

[*A terrific shout and a clap of drums. Lakunle enters into the spirit of the dance with enthusiasm. He takes over from Sidi, stations his cast all over the stage as the jungle, leaves the right topstage clear for the four girls who are to dance the motor-car. A mime follows of the visitor's entry into Ilujinle, and his short stay among the villagers. The four girls crouch on the floor, as four wheels of a car. Lakunle directs their spacing, then takes his place in the middle, and sits on air. He alone does not dance. He does realistic miming. Soft throbbing*]

drums, gradually swelling in volume, and the four 'wheels' begin to
rotate the upper halves of their bodies in perpendicular circles.
Lakunle clowning the driving motions, obviously enjoying this fully.
The drums gain tempo, faster, faster, faster. A sudden crash of drums
and the girls quiver and dance the stall. Another effort at rhythm
fails, and the stalling wheels' give a corresponding shudder, finally,
and let their faces fall on to their laps. Lakunle tampers with a
number of controls, climbs out of the car and looks underneath it.
His lips indicate that he is swearing violently.
Examines the wheels, pressing them to test the pressure, betrays the
devil in him by seizing his chance to pinch the girls' bottoms. One
yells and bites him on the ankle. He climbs hurriedly back into the
car, makes a final attempt to re-start it, gives it up and decides to
abandon it. Picks up his camera and his helmet, pockets a flask of
whisky from which he takes a swig, before beginning the trek.
The drums resume beating, a different, darker tone and rhythm,
varying with the journey. Full use of 'gangan' and 'iya ilu'. The
'trees' perform a subdued and unobtrusive dance on the same spot.
Details as a snake slithering out of the branches and poising over
Lakunle's head when he leans against a tree for a rest. He flees,
restoring his nerves shortly after by a swig. A monkey drops suddenly
in his path and gibbers at him before scampering off. A roar comes
from somewhere, etc. His nerves go rapidly and he recuperates
himself by copious draughts. He is soon tipsy, battles violently with
the undergrowth and curses silently as he swats the flies off his
tortured body.
Suddenly, from somewhere in the bush comes the sound of a girl
singing. The Traveller shakes his head but the sound persists.
Convinced he is suffering from sun-stroke, he drinks again. His last
drop, so he tosses the bottle in the direction of the sound, only to be
rewarded by a splash, a scream and a torrent of abuse, and finally,
silence again. He tip-toes, clears away the obstructing growth, blinks
hard, and rubs his eyes. Whatever he has seen still remains. He
whistles softly, unhitches his camera, and begins to jockey himself into
a good position for a take. Backwards and forwards, and his eyes are
so closely glued to the lens that he puts forward a careless foot and
disappears completely. There is a loud splash and the invisible singer
alters her next tone to a sustained scream. Quickened rhythm and
shortly afterwards, amidst sounds of splashes, Sidi appears on the stage,

with a piece of cloth only partially covering her.

Lakunle follows a little later, more slowly, trying to wring out the water from his clothes. He has lost all his appendages except the camera. Sidi has run right across the stage, and returns a short while later, accompanied by the villagers. The same cast has disappeared and re-forms behind Sidi as the villagers. They are in an ugly mood, and in spite of his protests, haul him off to the town centre, in front of the 'odan' tree.

Everything comes to a sudden stop as Baroka the Bale, wiry, goateed, tougher than his sixty-two years, himself emerges at this point from behind the tree. All go down, prostrate or kneeling with the greetings of 'Kabiyesi', 'Baba' etc. All except Lakunle who begins to sneak off.]

BAROKA: Akowe. Teacher wa. Misita Lakunle.

[*As the others take up the cry 'Misita Lakunle' he is forced to stop. He returns and bows deeply from the waist.*]

LAKUNLE: A good morning to you sir.

BAROKA: Guru morin guru morin, ngh-hn! That is
All we get from 'alakowe'. You call at his house
Hoping he sends for beer, but all you get is
Guru morin. Will guru morin wet my throat?
Well, well our man of knowledge, I hope you have no
Query for an old man today.

LAKUNLE: No complaints.

BAROKA: And we are not feuding in something
I have forgotten.

LAKUNLE: Feuding sir? I see no cause at all.

BAROKA: Well, the play was much alive until I came.
And now everything stops, and you were leaving
Us. After all, I knew the story and I came in
Right on cue. It makes me feel as if I was
Chief Baseje.

LAKUNLE: One hardly thinks the Bale would have the time
For such childish nonsense.

BAROKA: A-ah Mister Lakunle. Without these things you call
Nonsense, a Bale's life would be pretty dull.
Well, now that you say I am welcome, shall we
Resume your play?
[*Turns suddenly to his attendants.*]
Seize him!

LAKUNLE [*momentarily baffled.*]: What for? What have I done?

BAROKA: You tried to steal our village maidenhead
Have you forgotten? If he has, serve him a slap
To wake his brain.

[*An uplifted arm being proffered, Lakunle quickly recollects and nods his head vigorously. So the play is back in performance. The villagers gather round threatening, clamouring for his blood. Lakunle tries bluff, indignation, appeasement in turn. At a sudden signal from the Bale, they throw him down prostrate on his face. Only then does the Chief begin to show him sympathy, appear to understand the stranger's plight, and pacify the villagers on his behalf. He orders dry clothes for him, seats him on his right, and orders a feast in his honour. The stranger springs up every second to take photographs of the party, but most of the time his attention is fixed on Sidi dancing with abandon. Eventually he whispers to the Chief, who nods in consent, and Sidi is sent for. The stranger arranges Sidi in all sorts of magazine postures and takes innumerable photographs of her. Drinks are pressed upon him; he refuses at first, eventually tries the local brew with scepticism, appears to relish it, and drinks profusely. Before long, however, he leaves the party to be sick. They clap him on the back as he goes out, and two drummers who insist on dancing round him nearly cause the calamity to happen on the spot. However, he rushes out with his hand held to his mouth. Lakunle's exit seems to signify the end of the mime. He returns almost at once and the others discard their roles.*]

SIDI [*delightedly.*]: What did I say? You played him to the bone,
A court jester would have been the life for you,
Instead of school.

[*Points contemptuously to the school.*]

BAROKA: And where would the village be, robbed of
Such wisdom as Mister Lakunle dispenses
Daily? Who would tell us where we go wrong?
Eh, Mister Lakunle?

SIDI [*hardly listening, still in the full grip of her excitement.*]:
Who comes with me to find the man?
But Lakunle, you'll have to come and find sense
In his clipping tongue. You see book-man
We cannot really do
Without your head.

[*Lakunle begins to protest, but they crowd him and try to bear him down. Suddenly he breaks free and takes to his heels with all the women in full pursuit. Baroka is left sitting by himself—his wrestler, who accompanied him on his entry, stands a respectful distance away —staring at the flock of women in flight. From the folds of his 'agbada' he brings out his copy of the magazine and admires the heroine of the publication. Nods slowly to himself.*]

BAROKA: Yes, yes . . . it is five full months since last
I took a wife . . . five full months . . .

A road by the market. Enter Sidi, happily engrossed in the pictures of herself in the magazine. Lakunle follows one or two paces behind carrying a bundle of firewood which Sidi has set out to obtain. They are met in the centre by Sadiku, who has entered from the opposite side. Sadiku is an old woman, with a shawl over her head.

SADIKU: Fortune is with me. I was going to your house to see you.

SIDI [*startled out of her occupation.*]: What! Oh, it is you, Sadiku.

SADIKU: The Lion sent me. He wishes you well.

SIDI: Thank him for me.

[*Then excitedly.*]

Have you seen these?

Have you seen these images of me

Wrought by the man from the capital city?

Have you felt the gloss? [*Caresses the page.*]

Smoother by far than the parrot's breast.

SADIKU: I have. I saw them as soon as the city man came. . . . Sidi,
 I bring a message from my lord. [*Jerks her head at Lakunle.*]
 Shall we draw aside a little?

SIDI: Him? Pay no more heed to that
 Than you would a eunuch.

SADIKU: Then, in as few words as it takes to tell, Baroka wants
 you for a wife.

LAKUNLE [*bounds forward, dropping the wood.*]:
 What! The greedy dog!
 Insatiate camel of a foolish, doting race;
 Is he at his tricks again?

SIDI: Be quiet, 'Kunle. You get so tiresome.
 The message is for me, not you.

LAKUNLE [*down on his knees at once. Covers Sidi's hands with kisses.*]:
 My Ruth, my Rachel, Esther, Bathsheba
 Thou sum of fabled perfections
 From Genesis to the Revelations
 Listen not to the voice of this infidel. . . .

SIDI [*snatches her hand away.*]:
>
> Now that's your other game;
> Giving me funny names you pick up
> In your wretched books.
> My name is Sidi. And now, let me be.
> My name is Sidi, and I am beautiful.
> The stranger took my beauty
> And placed it in my hands.
> Here, here it is. I need no funny names
> To tell me of my fame.
> Loveliness beyond the jewels of a throne—
> That is what he said.

SADIKU [*gleefully.*]: Well, will you be Baroka's own jewel?
> Will you be his sweetest princess, soothing him on weary
> nights? What answer shall I give my lord?

SIDI [*wags her finger playfully at the woman.*]:
> Ha ha. Sadiku of the honey tongue.
> Sadiku, head of the Lion's wives.
> You'll make no prey of Sidi with your wooing tongue
> Not this Sidi whose fame has spread to Lagos
> And beyond the seas.
>
> [*Lakunle beams with satisfaction and rises.*]

SADIKU: Sidi, have you considered what a life of bliss awaits you?
> Baroka swears to take no other wife after you. Do you know
> what it is to be the Bale's last wife? I'll tell you. When he dies—
> and that should not be long; even the Lion has to die sometime
> —well, when he does, it means that you will have the honour
> of being the senior wife of the new Bale. And just think, until
> Baroka dies, you shall be his favourite. No living in the
> outhouses for you, my girl. Your place will always be in the
> palace; first as the latest bride, and afterwards, as the head of the
> new harem. . . . It is a rich life, Sidi. I know. I have been in
> that position for forty-one years.

SIDI: You waste your breath.
> Why did Baroka not request my hand
> Before the stranger
> Brought his book of images?
> Why did the Lion not bestow his gift
> Before my face was lauded to the world?

Can you not see? Because he sees my worth
Increased and multiplied above his own;
Because he can already hear
The ballad-makers and their songs
In praise of Sidi, the incomparable,
While the Lion is forgotten.
He seeks to have me as his property
Where I must fade beneath his jealous hold.
Ah, Sadiku,
The school-man here has taught me certain things
And my images have taught me all the rest.
Baroka merely seeks to raise his manhood
Above my beauty.
He seeks new fame
As the one man who has possessed
The jewel of Ilujinle!

SADIKU [*shocked, bewildered, incapable of making any sense of Sidi's
    words.*]: But Sidi, are you well? Such nonsense never passed
    your lips before. Did you not sound strange, even in your own
    hearing? [*Rushes suddenly at Lakunle.*] Is this your doing, you
    popinjay? Have you driven the poor girl mad at last? Such
    rubbish . . . I will beat your head for this!

LAKUNLE [*retreating in panic.*]: Keep away from me, old hag.

SIDI: Sadiku, let him be.
    Tell your lord that I can read his mind,
    That I will none of him.
    Look—judge for yourself.
    [*Opens the magazine and points out the pictures.*]
    He's old. I never knew till now,
    He was that old . . .
    [*During the rest of her speech, Sidi runs her hand over the surface of
    the relevant part of the photographs, tracing the contours with her
    fingers.*]
        . . . To think I took
    No notice of my velvet skin.
    How smooth it is!
    And no man ever thought
    To praise the fulness of my breasts. . . .

LAKUNLE [*laden with guilt and full of apology.*]:

Well, Sidi, I did think . . .
But somehow it was not the proper thing.
SIDI [*ignores the interruption.*]:
See I hold them to the warm caress
[*Unconsciously pushes out her chest.*]
Of a desire-filled sun.
[*Smiles mischievously.*]
There's a deceitful message in my eyes
Beckoning insatiate men to certain doom.
And teeth that flash the sign of happiness,
Strong and evenly, beaming full of life.
Be just, Sadiku,
Compare my image and your lord's—
An age of difference!
See how the water glistens on my face
Like the dew-moistened leaves on a Harmattan morning
But he—his face is like a leather piece
Torn rudely from the saddle of his horse,
[*Sadiku gasps.*]
Sprinkled with the musty ashes
From a pipe that is long over-smoked.
And this goat-like tuft
Which I once thought was manly;
It is like scattered twists of grass—
Not even green—
But charred and lifeless, as after a forest fire!
Sadiku, I am young and brimming; he is spent.
I am the twinkle of a jewel
But he is the hind quarters of a lion!
SADIKU [*recovering at last from helpless amazement.*]: May Sango
restore your wits. For most surely some angry god has taken
possession of you. [*Turns around and walks away. Stops again as
she remembers something else.*] Your ranting put this clean out of
my head. My lord says that if you would not be his wife,
would you at least come to supper at his house tonight. There
is a small feast in your honour. He wishes to tell you how happy
he is that the great capital city has done so much honour to a
daughter of Ilujinle. You have brought great fame to your
people.

SIDI: Ho ho! Do you think that I was only born
Yesterday?
The tales of Baroka's little suppers,
I know all.
Tell your lord that Sidi does not sup with
Married men.

SADIKU: They are lies, lies. You must not believe everything
you hear. Sidi, would I deceive you? I swear to you . . .

SIDI: Can you deny that
Every woman who has supped with him one night,
Becomes his wife or concubine the next?

LAKUNLE: Is it for nothing he is called the Fox?

SADIKU [advancing on him.]: You keep out of this, or so Sango be
my witness . . .

LAKUNLE [retreats just a little, but continues to talk.]:
His wiliness is known even in the larger towns.
Did you never hear
Of how he foiled the Public Works attempt
To build the railway through Ilujinle.

SADIKU: Nobody knows the truth of that. It is all hearsay.

SIDI: I love hearsays. Lakunle, tell me all.

LAKUNLE: Did you not know it? Well sit down and listen.
My father told me, before he died. And few men
Know of this trick—oh he's a die-hard rogue
Sworn against our progress . . . yes . . . it was . . . somewhere here
The track should have been laid just along
The outskirts. Well, the workers came, in fact
It was prisoners who were brought to do
The harder part . . . to break the jungle's back . . .
[Enter the prisoners, guarded by two warders. A white surveyor
examines his map (khaki helmet, spats, etc.). The foreman runs up
with his camp stool, table etc., erects the umbrella over him and
unpacks the usual box of bush comforts—soda siphon, whisky bottle,
and geometric sandwiches. His map consulted, he directs the sweat
team to where to work. They begin felling, matchet swinging, log
dragging, all to the rhythm of the work gang's metal percussion (rod
on gong or rude triangle, etc.). The two performers are also the song
leaders and the others fill the chorus. 'N'ijo itoro', 'Amuda el 'ebe
l'aiya', 'Gbe je on'ipa' etc.]

LAKUNLE: They marked the route with stakes, ate
          Through the jungle and began the tracks. Trade,
          Progress, adventure, success, civilization,
          Fame, international conspicuousity . . . it was
          All within the grasp of Ilujinle. . . .
          [*The wrestler enters, stands horrified at the sight and flees. Returns
          later with the Bale himself who soon assesses the situation.
          They disappear. The work continues, the surveyor occupies himself
          with the fly-whisk and whisky. Shortly after, a bull-roarer is heard.
          The prisoners falter a little, pick up again. The bull-roarer continues
          on its way, nearer and farther, moving in circles, so that it appears to
          come from all round them. The foreman is the first to break and then
          the rest is chaos. Sole survivor of the rout is the surveyor who is too
          surprised to move.
          Baroka enters a few minutes later accompanied by some attendants
          and preceded by a young girl bearing a calabash bowl. The surveyor,
          angry and threatening, is prevailed upon to open his gift. From it he
          reveals a wad of pound notes and kola nuts. Mutual understanding is
          established. The surveyor frowns heavily, rubs his chin, and consults
          his map. Re-examines the contents of the bowl, shakes his head.
          Baroka adds more money, and a coop of hens. A goat follows, and
          more money. This time 'truth' dawns on him at last, he has made a
          mistake. The track really should go the other way. What an
          unfortunate error, discovered just in time! No, no, no possibility of a
          mistake this time, the track should be much further away. In fact
          (scooping up the soil) the earth is most unsuitable, couldn't possibly
          support the weight of a railway engine. A gourd of palm wine is
          brought to seal the agreement and a cola-nut is broken. Baroka's men
          help the surveyor pack and they leave with their arms round each
          other followed by the surveyor's booty.*]
LAKUNLE [*as the last of the procession disappears, shakes his fist at them,
          stamping on the ground.*]:
          Voluptuous beast! He loves this life too well
          To bear to part from it. And motor roads
          And railways would do just that, forcing
          Civilization at his door. He foresaw it
          And he barred the gates, securing fast
          His dogs and horses, his wives and all his
          Concubines . . . ah, yes . . . all those concubines.

Baroka has such a selective eye, none suits him
But the best. . . .
[*His eyes truly light up. Sidi and Sadiku snigger, tip-toe offstage.*]
    . . . Yes, one must grant him that.
Ah, I sometimes wish I led his kind of life.
Such luscious bosoms make his nightly pillow.
I am sure he keeps a time-table just as
I do at school. Only way to ensure fair play.
He must be healthy to keep going as he does.
I don't know what the women see in him. His eyes
Are small and always red with wine. He must
Possess some secret. . . . No! I do not envy him!
Just the one woman for me. Alone I stand
For progress, with Sidi my chosen soul-mate, the one
Woman of my life. . . . Sidi! Sidi where are you?
[*Rushes out after them, returns to fetch the discarded firewood and
runs out again.*]

[*Baroka in bed, naked except for baggy trousers, calf-length. It is a
rich bedroom covered in animal skins and rugs. Weapons round the
wall. Also a strange machine, a most peculiar contraption with a
long lever. Kneeling beside the bed is Baroka's current Favourite,
engaged in plucking the hairs from his armpit. She does this by first
massaging the spot around the selected hair very gently with her
forefinger. Then, with hardly a break, she pulls out the hair between
her finger and the thumb with a sudden sharp movement. Baroka
twitches slightly with each pull. Then an aspirated 'A-ah', and a look
of complete beatitude spreads all over his face.*]

FAVOURITE: Do I improve my lord?
BAROKA: You are still somewhat over-gentle with the pull
    As if you feared to hurt the panther of the trees.
    Be sharp and sweet
    Like the swift sting of a vicious wasp
    For there the pleasure lies—the cooling aftermath.
FAVOURITE: I'll learn, my lord.
BAROKA: You have not time, my dear.
    Tonight I hope to take another wife.
    And the honour of this task, you know,

Belongs by right to my latest choice.
But—A-ah—Now that was sharp.
It had in it the scorpion's sudden sting
Without its poison.
It was an angry pull; you tried to hurt
For I had made you wrathful with my boast.
But now your anger flows in my blood stream.
How sweet it is! A-ah! That was sweeter still.
I think perhaps that I shall let you stay,
The sole out-puller of my sweat-bathed hairs.
Ach!
[*Sits up suddenly and rubs the sore point angrily.*]
        Now that had far more pain than pleasure
Vengeful creature, you did not caress
The area of extraction long enough!
[*Enter Sadiku. She goes down on her knees at once and bows her head
into her lap.*]
Aha! Here comes Sadiku.
Do you bring some balm,
To soothe the smart of my misused armpit?
Away, you enemy!
[*Exit the Favourite.*]

SADIKU: My lord . . .

BAROKA: You have my leave to speak.
        What did she say?

SADIKU: She will not my lord. I did my best, but she will have
        none of you.

BAROKA: It follows the pattern—a firm refusal
        At the start. Why will she not?

SADIKU: That is the strange part of it. She says you're much
        too old. If you ask me, I think that she is really off her head.
        All this excitement of the books has been too much for her.

BAROKA [*springs to his feet.*]:
        She says . . . That I am old
        That I am much too old? Did a slight
        Unripened girl say this of me?

SADIKU: My lord, I heard the incredible words with my ears,
        and I thought the world was mad.

BAROKA: But is it possible, Sadiku? Is this right?

Did I not, at the festival of Rain,
Defeat the men in the log-tossing match?
Do I not still with the most fearless ones,
Hunt the leopard and the boa at night
And save the farmers' goats from further harm?
And does she say I'm old?
Did I not, to announce the Harmattan,
Climb to the top of the silk-cotton tree,
Break the first pod, and scatter tasselled seeds
To the four winds—and this but yesterday?
Do any of my wives report
A failing in my manliness?
The strongest of them all
Still wearies long before the Lion does!
And so would she, had I the briefest chance
To teach this unfledged birdling
That lacks the wisdom to embrace
The rich mustiness of age . . . if I could once . . .
Come hither, soothe me, Sadiku
For I am wroth at heart.

[*Lies back on the bed, staring up as before. Sadiku takes her place at the foot of the bed and begins to tickle the soles of his feet. Baroka turns to the left suddenly, reaches down the side, and comes up with a copy of the magazine. Opens it and begins to study the pictures. He heaves a long sigh.*]

That is good, Sadiku, very good.

[*He begins to compare some pictures in the book, obviously his own and Sidi's. Flings the book away suddenly and stares at the ceiling for a second or two. Then, unsmiling.*]

Perhaps it is as well, Sadiku.

SADIKU: My lord, what did you say?
BAROKA: Yes, faithful one, I say it is as well.
The scorn, the laughter and the jeers
Would have been bitter
Had she consented and my purpose failed,
I would have sunk with shame.
SADIKU: My lord, I do not understand.
BAROKA: The time has come when I can fool myself
No more. I am no man, Sadiku. My manhood

Ended near a week ago.

SADIKU: The gods forbid.

BAROKA: I wanted Sidi because I still hoped—
A foolish thought I know, but still—I hoped
That, with a virgin young and hot within,
My failing strength would rise and save my pride.
[*Sadiku begins to moan.*]
A waste of hope. I knew it even then.
But it's a human failing never to accept
The worst; and so I pandered to my vanity.
When manhood must, it ends.
The well of living, tapped beyond its depth,
Dries up, and mocks the wastrel in the end.
I am withered and unsapped, the joy
Of ballad-mongers, the aged butt
Of youth's ribaldry.

SADIKU [*tearfully.*]: The gods must have mercy yet.

BAROKA [*as if suddenly aware of her presence, starts up.*]:
I have told this to no one but you,
Who are my eldest, my most faithful wife.
But if you dare parade my shame before the world . . .
[*Sadiku shakes her head in protest and begins to stroke the soles of his feet with renewed tenderness. Baroka sighs and falls back slowly.*]
How irritable I have grown of late
Such doubts to harbour of your loyalty . . .
But this disaster is too much for one
Checked thus as I upon the prime of youth.
That rains that blessed me from my birth
Number a meagre sixty-two;
While my grandfather, that man of teak,
Fathered two sons, late on sixty-five.
But Okiki, my father beat them all
Producing female twins at sixty-seven.
Why then must I, descendant of these lions
Forswear my wives at a youthful sixty-two
My veins of life run dry, my manhood gone!
[*His voice goes drowsy; Sadiku sighs and moans and caresses his feet. His face lights up suddenly with rapture.*]
Sango bear witness! These weary feet

Have felt the loving hands of much design
In women.
My soles have felt the scratch of harsh,
Gravelled hands.
They have borne the heaviness of clumsy,
Gorilla paws.
And I have known the tease of tiny,
Dainty hands,
Toy-like hands that tantalized
My eager senses,
Promised of thrills to come
Remaining
Unfulfilled because the fingers
Were too frail,
The touch too light and faint to pierce
The incredible thickness of my soles.
But thou Sadiku, thy plain unadorned hands
Encase a sweet sensuality which age
Will not destroy. A-ah,
Oyayi! Beyond a doubt Sadiku,
Thou art the queen of them all.
[*Falls asleep.*]

NIGHT

The village centre. Sidi stands by the schoolroom window, admiring her photos as before. Enter Sadiku with a longish bundle. She is very furtive. Unveils the object which turns out to be a carved figure of the Bale, naked and in full detail. She takes a good look at it, bursts suddenly into derisive laughter, sets the figure in front of the tree. Sidi stares in utter amazement.

SADIKU: So we did for you too did we? We did for you in the end. Oh high and mighty lion, have we really scotched you? A—ya-ya-ya . . . we women undid you in the end. I was there when it happened to your father, the great Okiki. I did for him, I, the youngest and freshest of the wives. I killed him with my strength. I called him and he came at me, but no, for him, this was not like other times. I, Sadiku, was I not flame itself and he the flax on old women's spindles? I ate him up! Race of mighty lions, we always consume you, at our pleasure we spin you, at our whim we make you dance; like the foolish top you think the world revolves around you . . . fools! fools! . . . it is you who run giddy while we stand still and watch, and draw your frail thread from you, slowly, till nothing is left but a runty old stick. I scotched Okiki, Sadiku's unopened treasure-house demanded sacrifice, and Okiki came with his rusted key. Like a snake he came at me, like a rag he went back, a limp rag, smeared in shame. . . . [*Her ghoulish laugh re-possesses her.*] Ah, take warning my masters, we'll scotch you in the end . . . [*With a yell she leaps up, begins to dance round the tree, chanting.*] Take warning, my masters
We'll scotch you in the end.
[*Sidi shuts the window gently, comes out, Sadiku, as she comes round again, gasps and is checked in mid-song.*]
SADIKU: Oh it is you my daughter. You should have chosen a better time to scare me to death. The hour of victory is no time for any woman to die.
SIDI: Why? What battle have you won?
SADIKU: Not me alone girl. You too. Every woman. Oh my

daughter, that I have lived to see this day . . . To see him fizzle
with the drabbest puff of a mis-primed 'sakabula'.
[*Resumes her dance.*]
Take warning, my masters
We'll scotch you in the end.

SIDI: Wait Sadiku. I cannot understand.

SADIKU: You will my girl. You will.

Take warning my masters . . .

SIDI: Sadiku, are you well?

SADIKU: Ask no questions my girl. Just join my victory dance.
Oh Sango my lord, who of us possessed your lightning and
ran like fire through that lion's tail . . .

SIDI [*holds her firmly as she is about to go off again.*]:
Stop your loose ranting. You will not
Move from here until you make some sense.

SADIKU: Oh you are troublesome. Do you promise to tell no one?

SIDI: I swear it. Now tell me quickly.
[*As Sadiku whispers, her eyes widen.*]
O-ho-o-o-o-!
But Sadiku, if he knew the truth, why
Did he ask me to . . .
[*Again Sadiku whispers.*]
Ha ha! Some hope indeed. Oh Sadiku
I suddenly am glad to be a woman.
[*Leaps in the air.*]
We won. We won! Hurray for womankind!
[*Falls in behind Sadiku.*]
Take warning, my masters
We'll scotch you in the end. [*Lakunle enters unobserved.*]

LAKUNLE: The full moon is not yet, but
The women cannot wait.
They must go mad without it.
[*The dancing stops. Sadiku frowns.*]

SADIKU: The scarecrow is here. Begone fop! This is the world of
women. At this moment our star sits in the centre of the sky.
We are supreme. What is more, we are about to perform a
ritual. If you remain, we will chop you up, we will make you
the sacrifice.

LAKUNLE: What is the hag gibbering?

SADIKU [*advances menacingly.*]: You less than man, you less than the littlest woman, I say begone!

LAKUNLE [*nettled.*]: I will have you know that I am a man
As you will find out if you dare
To lay a hand on me.

SADIKU [*throws back her head in laughter.*]: You a man? Is Baroka not more of a man than you? And if he is no longer a man, then what are you? [*Lakunle, understanding the meaning, stands rooted, shocked.*] Come on, dear girl, let him look on if he will. After all, only *men* are barred from watching this ceremony. Take warning, my masters
We'll . . .

SIDI: Stop. Sadiku stop. Oh such an idea
Is running in my head. Let me to the palace for
This supper he promised me. Sadiku, what a way
To mock the devil. I shall ask forgiveness
For my hasty words. . . . No need to change
My answers and consent to be his bride—he might
Suspect you've told me. But I shall ask a month
To think on it.

SADIKU [*somewhat doubtful.*]: Baroka is no child you know, he will know I have betrayed him.

SIDI: No, he will not. Oh Sadiku let me go.
I long to see him thwarted, to watch his longing
His twitching hands which this time cannot
Rush to loosen his trouser cords.

SADIKU: You will have to match the fox's cunning. Use your bashful looks and be truly repentant. Goad him my child, torment him until he weeps for shame.

SIDI: Leave it to me. He will never suspect you of deceit.

SADIKU [*with another of her energetic leaps.*]: Yo-rooo o! Yo-rororo o!
Shall I come with you?

SIDI: Will that be wise? You forget
We have not seen each other.

SADIKU: Away then. Away woman. I shall bide here.
Haste back and tell Sadiku how the no-man is.
Away, my lovely child.

LAKUNLE [*he has listened with increasing horror.*]:
No, Sidi, don't. If you care

One little bit for what I feel,
Do not go to torment the man.
Suppose he knows that you have come to jeer—
And he will know, if he is not a fool—
He is a savage thing, degenerate
He would beat a helpless woman if he could. . . .

SIDI [*running off gleefully.*]: Ta-raa school teacher. Wait here for me.

LAKUNLE [*stamps his foot helplessly.*]:
Foolish girl! . . . And this is all your work.
Could you not keep a secret?
Must every word leak out of you
As surely as the final drops
Of mother's milk
Oozed from your flattened breast
Generations ago?

SADIKU: Watch your wagging tongue, unformed creature!

LAKUNLE: If any harm befalls her . . .

SADIKU: Woman though she is, she can take better care of herself than you can of her. Fancy a thing like you actually wanting a girl like that, all to your little self. [*Walks round him and looks him up and down.*] Ah! Oba Ala is an accommodating god. What a poor figure you cut!

LAKUNLE: I wouldn't demean myself to bandy words
With a woman of the bush.

SADIKU: At this moment, your betrothed is supping with the Lion.

LAKUNLE [*pleased at the use of the word 'betrothed'.*]:
Well, we are not really betrothed as yet,
I mean, she is not promised yet.
But it will come in time, I'm sure.

SADIKU [*bursts into her cackling laughter.*]: The bride-price, is that paid?

LAKUNLE: Mind your own business.

SADIKU: Why don't you do what other men have done. Take a farm for a season. One harvest will be enough to pay the price, even for a girl like Sidi. Or will the smell of the wet soil be too much for your delicate nostrils?

LAKUNLE: I said mind your own business.

SADIKU: A—a—ah. It is true what they say then. You are going to

convert the whole village so that no one will ever pay the
bride-price again. Ah, you're a clever man. I must admit that it
is a good way for getting out of it, but don't you think you'd
use more time and energy that way than you would if . . .

LAKUNLE [with conviction.]: Within a year or two, I swear,
This town shall see a transformation
Bride-price will be a thing forgotten
And wives shall take their place by men.
A motor road will pass this spot
And bring the city ways to us.
We'll buy saucepans for all the women
Clay pots are crude and unhygienic
No man shall take more wives than one
That's why they're impotent too soon.
The ruler shall ride cars, not horses
Or a bicycle at the very least.
We'll burn the forest, cut the trees
Then plant a modern park for lovers
We'll print newspapers every day
With pictures of seductive girls.
The world will judge our progress by
The girls that win beauty contests.
While Lagos builds new factories daily
We only play 'ayo' and gossip.
Where is our school of ballroom dancing?
Who here can throw a cocktail party?
We must be modern with the rest
Or live forgotten by the world
We must reject the palm wine habit
And take to tea, with milk and sugar.
[Turns on Sadiku who has been staring at him in terror. She retreats,
and he continues to talk down at her as they go round, then down and
offstage, Lakunle's hectoring voice trailing away in the distance.]
This is my plan, you withered face
And I shall start by teaching you.
From now you shall attend my school
And take your place with twelve-year olds.
For though you're nearly seventy,
Your mind is simple and unformed.

Have you no shame that at your age,
You neither read nor write nor think?
You spend your days as senior wife,
Collecting brides for Baroka.
And now because you've sucked him dry,
You send my Sidi to his shame. . . .

[*The scene changes to Baroka's bedroom. On the left in a one-knee-on-floor posture, two men are engaged in a kind of wrestling, their arms clasped round each other's waist, testing the right moment to heave. One is Baroka, the other a short squat figure of apparent muscular power. The contest is still in the balanced stage. In some distant part of the house, Sidi's voice is heard lifted in the familiar general greeting, addressed to no one in particular.*]

SIDI: A good day to the head and people
Of this house.

[*Baroka lifts his head, frowns as if he is trying to place the voice.*]

A good day to the head and people
Of this house.

[*Baroka now decides to ignore it and to concentrate on the contest. Sidi's voice draws progressively nearer. She enters nearly backwards, as she is still busy admiring the room through which she has just passed. Gasps on turning round to see the two men.*]

BAROKA [*without looking up.*]: Is Sadiku not at home then?

SIDI [*absent-mindedly.*]: Hm?

BAROKA: I asked, is Sadiku not at home?

SIDI [*recollecting herself, she curtseys quickly.*]: I saw no one, Baroka.

BAROKA: No one? Do you mean there was no one
To bar unwanted strangers from my privacy?

SIDI [*retreating.*]: The house . . . seemed . . . empty.

BAROKA: Ah, I forget. This is the price I pay
Once every week, for being progressive.
Prompted by the school teacher, my servants
Were prevailed upon to form something they call
The Palace Workers' Union. And in keeping
With the habits—I am told—of modern towns,
This is their day off.

SIDI [*seeing that Baroka seems to be in a better mood, she becomes somewhat bolder. Moves forward—saucily.*]:
Is this also a day off

For Baroka's wives?

BAROKA [*looks up sharply, relaxes, and speaks with a casual voice.*]:
No, the madness has not gripped them—yet.
Did you not meet with one of them?

SIDI: No, Baroka. There was no one about.

BAROKA: Not even Ailatu, my favourite?
Was she not at her usual place,
Beside my door?

SIDI [*absently. She is deeply engrossed in watching the contest.*]:
Her stool is there. And I saw
The slippers she was embroidering.

BAROKA: Hm. Hm. I think I know
Where she'll be found. In a dark corner
Sulking like a slighted cockroach.
By the way, look and tell me
If she left her shawl behind.
[*So as not to miss any part of the tussle, she moves backwards, darts
a quick look round the door and back again.*]

SIDI: There is a black shawl on the stool.

BAROKA [*a regretful sigh.*]:
Then she'll be back tonight. I had hoped
My words were harsh enough
To free me from her spite for a week or more.

SIDI: Did Ailatu offend her husband?

BAROKA: Offend? My armpit still weeps blood
For the gross abuse I suffered from one
I called my favourite.

SIDI [*in a disappointed voice.*]:
Oh. Is that all?

BAROKA: Is that not enough? Why child?
What more could the woman do?

SIDI: Nothing. Nothing, Baroka. I thought perhaps—
Well—young wives are known to be—
Forward—sometimes—to their husbands.

BAROKA: In an ill-kept household perhaps. But not
Under Baroka's roof. And yet,
Such are the sudden spites of women
That even I cannot foresee them all.
And child—if I lose this little match

Remember that my armpit
Burns and itches turn by turn.
[*Sidi continues watching for some time, then clasps her hand over her
mouth as she remembers what she should have done to begin with.
Doubtful how to proceed, she hesitates for some moments, then comes
to a decision and kneels.*]

SIDI: I have come, Bale, as a repentant child.

BAROKA: What?

SIDI [*very hesitantly, eyes to the floor, but she darts a quick look up when
she thinks the Bale isn't looking.*]
The answer which I sent to the Bale
Was given in a thoughtless moment. . . .

BAROKA: Answer, child? To what?

SIDI: A message brought by . . .

BAROKA [*groans and strains in a muscular effort.*]:
Will you say that again? It is true that for supper
I did require your company. But up till now
Sadiku has brought no reply.

SIDI [*amazed.*]: But the other matter! Did not the Bale
Send . . . did Baroka not send . . . ?

BAROKA [*with sinister encouragement.*]:
What did Baroka not, my child?

SIDI [*cowed, but angry, rises.*]:
It is nothing, Bale. I only hope
That I am here at the Bale's invitation.

BAROKA [*as if trying to understand, he frowns as he looks at her.*]:
A-ah, at last I understand. You think
I took offence because you entered
Unannounced?

SIDI: I remember that the Bale called me
An unwanted stranger.

BAROKA: That could be expected. Is a man's bedroom
To be made naked to any flea
That chances to wander through?
[*Sidi turns away, very hurt.*]
Come, come, my child. You are too quick
To feel aggrieved. Of course you are
More than welcome. But I expected Ailatu
To tell me you were here.

[*Sidi curtseys briefly with her back to Baroka. After a while, she turns round. The mischief returns to her face. Baroka's attitude of denial has been a setback but she is now ready to pursue her mission.*]

SIDI: I hope the Bale will not think me
Forward. But, like everyone, I had thought
The Favourite was a gentle woman.

BAROKA: And so had I.

SIDI [*slyly.*]: One would hardly think that *she*
Would give offence without a cause
Was the Favourite . . . in some way . . .
Dissatisfied . . . with her lord and husband?
[*With a mock curtsey, quickly executed as Baroka begins to look up.*]

BAROKA [*slowly turns towards her.*]:

                              Now that
Is a question which I never thought to hear
Except from a school teacher. Do you think
The Lion has such leisure that he asks
The whys and wherefores of a woman's
Squint?
[*Sidi steps back and curtseys. As before, and throughout this scene, she is easily cowed by Baroka's change of mood, all the more easily as she is, in any case, frightened by her own boldness.*]

SIDI: I meant no disrespect . . .

BAROKA [*gently.*]: I know. [*Breaks off.*] Christians on my
Fathers' shrines, child!
Do you think I took offence? A—aw
Come in and seat yourself. Since you broke in
Unawares, and appear resolved to stay,
Try, if you can, not to make me feel
A humourless old ram. I allow no one
To watch my daily exercise, but as we say,
The woman gets lost in the woods one day
And every wood deity dies the next.
[*Sidi curtseys, watches, and moves forward warily, as if expecting the two men to spring apart too suddenly.*]

SIDI: I think he will win.

BAROKA: Is that a wish, my daughter?

SIDI: No, but—[*Hesitates, but boldness wins.*]
If the tortoise cannot tumble

It does not mean that he can stand.

[*Baroka looks at her, seemingly puzzled. Sidi turns away, humming.*]

BAROKA: When the child is full of riddles, the mother
Has one water-pot the less.

[*Sidi tip-toes to Baroka's back and pulls asses' ears at him.*]

SIDI: I think he will win.

BAROKA: He knows he must. Would it profit me
To pit my strength against a weakling?
Only yesterday, this son of—I suspect—
A python for a mother, and fathered beyond doubt
By a blubber-bottomed baboon,

[*The complimented man grins.*]

Only yesterday, he nearly
Ploughed my tongue with my front teeth
In a friendly wrestling bout.

WRESTLER [*encouraged, makes an effort.*]: Ugh. Ugh.

SIDI [*bent almost over them. Genuinely worried.*]:
Oh! Does it hurt?

BAROKA: Not yet . . . but, as I was saying
I change my wrestlers when I have learnt
To throw them. I also change my wives
When I have learnt to tire them.

SIDI: And is this another . . . changing time
For the Bale?

BAROKA: Who knows? Until the finger nails
Have scraped the dust, no one can tell
Which insect released his bowels.

[*Sidi grimaces in disgust and walks away. Returns as she thinks up a new idea.*]

SIDI: A woman spoke to me this afternoon.

BAROKA: Indeed. And does Sidi find this unusual—
That a woman speak with her in the afternoon?

SIDI [*stamping.*]: No. She had the message of a go-between.

BAROKA: Did she? Then I rejoice with you.

[*Sidi stands biting her lips. Baroka looks at her, this time with deliberate appreciation.*]

And now I think of it, why not?
There must be many men who
Build their loft to fit your height.

SIDI [*unmoving, pointedly.*]: Her message came from one
    With many lofts.
BAROKA: Ah! Such is the greed of men.
SIDI: If Baroka were my father
    [*Aside.*]—which many would take him to be—
    [*Makes a rude sign.*]
    Would he pay my dowry to this man
    And give his blessings?
BAROKA: Well, I must know his character.
    For instance, is the man rich?
SIDI: Rumour has it so.
BAROKA: Is he repulsive?
SIDI: He is old. [*Baroka winces.*]
BAROKA: Is he mean and miserly?
SIDI: To strangers—no. There are tales
    Of his open-handedness, which are never
    Quite without a motive. But his wives report
    —To take one little story—
    How he grew the taste for ground corn
    And pepper—because he would not pay
    The price of snuff!
    [*With a sudden burst of angry energy, Baroka lifts his opponent and
    throws him over his shoulder.*]
BAROKA: A lie! The price of snuff
    Had nothing to do with it.
SIDI [*too excited to listen.*]: You won!
BAROKA: By the years on my beard, I swear
    They slander me!
SIDI [*excitedly.*]: You won. You won!
    [*She breaks into a kind of shoulder dance and sings.*]
    Yokolu Yokolu. Ko ha tan bi
    Iyawo gb'oko san'le
    Oko yo 'ke . . .[1]
    [*She repeats this throughout Baroka's protests. Baroka is pacing
    angrily up and down. The defeated man, nursing a hip, goes to the
    corner of the room and lifts out a low 'ako' bench. He sits on the*

1. 'Yokolu, Yokolu, what say you now?
   The wife knocked down the husband
   And he now sprouts a hunchback . . .'

floor, and soon, Baroka joins him; using only their arms now, they
place their elbows on the bench and grip hands. Baroka takes his off
again, replaces it, takes it off again, and so on during the rest of his
outburst.]

BAROKA: This means nothing to me of course. Nothing!
But I know the ways of women, and I know
Their ruinous tongues.
Suppose that, as a child—only suppose—
Suppose then, that as a child, I—
And remember, I only use myself
To illustrate the plight of many men. . . .
So, once again, suppose that as a child
I grew to love 'tanfiri'—with a good dose of pepper
And growing old, I found that—
Sooner than die away, my passion only
Bred itself upon each mouthful of
Ground corn and pepper I consumed.
Now, think child, would it be seemly
At my age, and the father of children,
To be discovered, in public
Thrusting fistfuls of corn dust and pepper
In my mouth? Is it not wise to indulge
In the little masquerade of a dignified
Snuff box?—But remember, I only make
A pleading for this prey of women's
Malice. I feel his own injustice,
Being myself, a daily fellow-sufferer!
[*Baroka seems to realize for the first time that Sidi has paid no*
attention to his explanation. She is, in fact, still humming and
shaking her shoulders. He stares questioningly at her. Sidi stops,
somewhat confused and embarrassed, points sheepishly to the wrestler.]

SIDI: I think this time he will win.
[*Baroka's grumbling subsides slowly. He is now attentive to the*
present bout.]

BAROKA: Now let us once again take up
The questioning. [*Almost timidly.*] Is this man
Good and kindly.

SIDI: They say he uses well
His dogs and horses.

BAROKA [*desperately.*]:
  Well is he fierce then? Reckless!
  Does the bush cow run to hole
  When he hears his beaters' Hei-ei-wo-rah!

SIDI: There are heads and skins of leopards
  Hung around his council room.
  But the market is also
  Full of them.

BAROKA: Is he not wise? Is he not sagely?
  Do the young and old not seek
  His counsel?

SIDI: The fox is said to be wise
  So cunning that he stalks and dines on
  New-hatched chickens.

BAROKA [*more and more desperate.*]:
  Does he not beget strength on wombs?
  Are his children not tall and stout-limbed?

SIDI: Once upon a time.

BAROKA: Once upon a time?
  What do you mean, girl?

SIDI: Just once upon a time.
  Perhaps his children have of late
  Been plagued with shyness and refuse
  To come into the world. Or else
  He is so tired with the day's affairs
  That at night, he turns his buttocks
  To his wives. But there have been
  No new reeds cut by his servants,
  No new cots woven.
  And his household gods are starved
  For want of child-naming festivities
  Since the last two rains went by.

BAROKA: Perhaps he is a frugal man.
  Mindful of years to come,
  Planning for a final burst of life, he
  Husbands his strength.

SIDI [*giggling. She is actually stopped, half-way, by giggling at the
  cleverness of her remark.*]:
  To husband his wives surely ought to be

A man's first duties—at all times.

BAROKA: My beard tells me you've been a pupil,
A most diligent pupil of Sadiku.
Among all shameless women,
The sharpest tongues grow from that one
Peeling bark—Sadiku, my faithful lizard!
[*Growing steadily warmer during this speech, he again slaps down his opponent's arm as he shouts 'Sadiku'.*]

SIDI [*backing away, aware that she has perhaps gone too far and betrayed knowledge of the 'secret'.*]:
I have learnt nothing of anyone.

BAROKA: No more. No more.
Already I have lost a wrestler
On your account. This town-bred daring
Of little girls, awakes in me
A seven-horned devil of strength.
Let one woman speak a careless word
And I can pin a wriggling—Bah!
[*Lets go the man's arm. He has risen during the last speech but held on to the man's arm, who is forced to rise with him.*]
The tappers should have called by now.
See if we have a fresh gourd by the door.
[*The wrestler goes out. Baroka goes to sit on the bed, Sidi eyeing him, doubtfully.*]
What an ill-tempered man I daily grow
Towards. Soon my voice will be
The sand between two grinding stones.
But I have my scattered kindliness
Though few occasions serve to herald it.
And Sidi, my daughter, you do not know
The thoughts which prompted me
To ask the pleasure that I be your host
This evening. I would not tell Sadiku,
Meaning to give delight
With the surprise of it. Now, tell me, child
Can you guess a little at this thing?

SIDI: Sadiku told me nothing.

BAROKA: You are hasty with denial. For how indeed
Could Sadiku, since I told her

Nothing of my mind? But, my daughter,
Did she not, perhaps . . . invent some tale?
For I know Sadiku loves to be
All-knowing.

SIDI: She said no more, except the Bale
Begged my presence.

BAROKA [*rises quickly to the bait.*]:
Begged? Bale Baroka begged?
[*Wrestler enters with gourd and calabash cups. Baroka relapses.*]
Ah! I see you love to bait your elders.
One way the world remains the same,
The child still thinks she is wiser than
The cotton head of age.
Do you think Baroka deaf or blind
To little signs? But let that pass.
Only, lest you fall victim to the schemes
Of busy women, I will tell you this—
I know Sadiku plays the match-maker
Without the prompting. If I look
On any maid, or call her name
Even in the course of harmless, neighbourly
Well-wishing—How fares your daughter?
—Is your sister now recovered from her
Whooping cough?—How fast your ward
Approaches womanhood! Have the village lads
Begun to gather at your door?—
Or any word at all which shows I am
The thoughtful guardian of the village health,
If it concerns a woman, Sadiku straightway
Flings herself into the role of go-between
And before I even don a cap, I find
Yet another stranger in my bed!

SIDI: It seems a Bale's life
Is full of great unhappiness.

BAROKA: I do not complain. No, my child
I accept the sweet and sour with
A ruler's grace. I lose my patience
Only when I meet with
The new immodesty with women.

Now, my Sidi, you have not caught
This new and strange disease, I hope.

SIDI [*curtseying*.]: The threading of my smock—
Does Baroka not know the marking
Of the village loom?

BAROKA: But will Sidi, the pride of mothers,
Will she always wear it?

SIDI: Will Sidi, the proud daughter of Baroka,
Will she step out naked?
[*A pause. Baroka surveys Sidi in an almost fatherly manner and she bashfully drops her eyes.*]

BAROKA: To think that once I thought,
Sidi is the eye's delight, but
She is vain, and her head
Is feather-light, and always giddy
With a trivial thought. And now
I find her deep and wise beyond her years.
[*Reaches under his pillow, brings out the now familiar magazine, and also an addressed envelope. Retains the former and gives her the envelope.*]
Do you know what this means?
The trim red piece of paper
In the corner?

SIDI: I know it. A stamp. Lakunle receives
Letters from Lagos marked with it.

BAROKA [*obviously disappointed*.]:
Hm. Lakunle. But more about him
Later. Do you know what it means—
This little frippery?

SIDI [*very proudly*.]:
Yes. I know that too. Is it not a tax on
The habit of talking with paper?

BAROKA: Oh. Oh. I see you dip your hand
Into the pockets of the school teacher
And retrieve it bulging with knowledge.
[*Goes to the strange machine, and pulls the lever up and down.*]
Now this, not even the school teacher can tell
What magic this performs. Come nearer,
It will not bite.

SIDI: I have never seen the like.

BAROKA: The work dear child, of the palace blacksmiths
    Built in full secrecy. All is not well with it—
    But I will find the cause and then Ilujinle
    Will boast its own tax on paper, made with
    Stamps like this. For long I dreamt it
    And here it stands, child of my thoughts.

SIDI [wonder-struck.]: You mean . . . this will work some day?

BAROKA: Ogun has said the word. And now my girl
    What think you of that image on the stamp
    This spiderwork of iron, wood, and mortar?

SIDI: Is it not a bridge?

BAROKA: It is a bridge. The longest—so they say
    In the whole country. When not a bridge,
    You'll find a print of groundnuts
    Stacked like pyramids,
    Or palm trees, or cocoa trees, and farmers
    Hacking pods, and workmen
    Felling trees and tying skinned logs
    Into rafts. A thousand thousand letters
    By road, by rail, by air,
    From one end of the world to another,
    And not one human head among them.
    Not one head of beauty on the stamp!

SIDI: But I once saw Lakunle's letter
    With a head of bronze.

BAROKA: A figurehead, my child, a lifeless work
    Of craft, with holes for eyes, and coldness
    For the warmth of life and love
    In youthful cheeks like yours,
    My daughter . . .
    [Pauses to watch the effect on Sidi.]
      . . . Can you see it, Sidi?
    Tens of thousands of these dainty prints
    And each one with this legend of Sidi.
    [Flourishes the magazine, open in the middle.]
    The village goddess, reaching out
    Towards the sun, her lover.
    Can you see it, my daughter!

[*Sidi drowns herself totally in the contemplation, takes the magazine but does not even look at it. Sits on the bed.*]

BAROKA [*very gently.*]:

    I hope you will not think it too great
    A burden, to carry the country's mail
    All on your comeliness.

[*Walks away, an almost business-like tone.*]

                  Our beginnings will
    Of course be modest. We shall begin
    By cutting stamps for our own village alone.
    As the schoolmaster himself would say—
    Charity begins at home.

[*Pause. Faces Sidi from nearly the distance of the room.*]

                  For a long time now,
    The town-dwellers have made up tales
    Of the backwardness of Ilujinle
    Until it hurts Baroka, who holds
    The welfare of his people deep at heart.
    Now, if we do this thing, it will prove more
    Than any single town has done!

[*The wrestler, who has been listening open-mouthed, drops his cup in admiration. Baroka, annoyed, realizing only now in fact that he is still in the room, waves him impatiently out.*]

    I do not hate progress, only its nature
    Which makes all roofs and faces look the same.
    And the wish of one old man is
    That here and there,

[*Goes progressively towards Sidi, until he bends over her, then sits beside her on the bed.*]

    Among the bridges and the murderous roads,
    Below the humming birds which
    Smoke the face of Sango, dispenser of
    The snake-tongue lightning; between this moment
    And the reckless broom that will be wielded
    In these years to come, we must leave
    Virgin plots of lives, rich decay
    And the tang of vapour rising from
    Forgotten heaps of compost, lying
    Undisturbed . . . But the skin of progress

Masks, unknown, the spotted wolf of sameness . . .
Does sameness not revolt your being,
My daughter?
[*Sidi is capable only of a bewildered nod, slowly.*]

BAROKA [*sighs, hands folded piously on his lap.*]:
I find my soul is sensitive, like yours.
Indeed, although there is one—no more think I—
One generation between yours and mine,
Our thoughts fly crisply through the air
And meet, purified, as one.
And our first union
Is the making of this stamp.
The one redeeming grace on any paper tax
Shall be your face. And mine,
The soul behind it all, worshipful
Of Nature for her gift of youth
And beauty to our earth. Does this
Please you, my daughter?

SIDI: I can no longer see the meaning, Baroka.
Now that you speak
Almost like the school teacher, except
Your words fly on a different path,
I find . . .

BAROKA: It is a bad thing, then, to sound
Like your school teacher?

SIDI: No, Bale, but words are like beetles
Boring at my ears, and my head
Becomes a jumping bean. Perhaps after all,
As the school teacher tells me often,
[*Very miserably.*]
I have a simple mind.

BAROKA [*pats her kindly on the head.*]:
No, Sidi, not simple, only straight and truthful
Like a freshwater reed. But I do find
Your school teacher and I are much alike.
The proof of wisdom is the wish to learn
Even from children. And the haste of youth
Must learn its temper from the gloss
Of ancient leather, from a strength

Knit close along the grain. The school teacher
And I, must learn one from the other.
Is this not right?
[*A tearful nod.*]

BAROKA: The old must flow into the new, Sidi,
Not blind itself or stand foolishly
Apart. A girl like you must inherit
Miracles which age alone reveals.
Is this not so?

SIDI: Everything you say, Bale,
Seems wise to me.

BAROKA: Yesterday's wine alone is strong and blooded, child,
And though the Christians' holy book denies
The truth of this, old wine thrives best
Within a new bottle. The coarseness
Is mellowed down, and the rugged wine
Acquires a full and rounded body . . . .
Is this not so—my child?
[*Quite overcome, Sidi nods.*]

BAROKA: Those who know little of Baroka think
His life one pleasure-living course.
But the monkey sweats, my child,
The monkey sweats,
It is only the hair upon his back
Which still deceives the world. . . .
[*Sidi's head falls slowly on the Bale's shoulder. The Bale remains in
his final body-weighed-down-by-burdens-of-State attitude.*

*Even before the scene is completely shut off a crowd of dancers burst in
at the front and dance off at the opposite side without slackening pace.
In their brief appearance it should be apparent that they comprise a
group of female dancers pursuing a masked male. Drumming and
shouts continue quite audibly and shortly afterwards. They enter and
re-cross the stage in the same manner.*

*The shouts fade away and they next appear at the market clearing. It
is now full evening. Lakunle and Sadiku are still waiting for Sidi's
return. The traders are beginning to assemble one by one, ready for
the evening market. Hawkers pass through with oil-lamps beside
their ware. Food sellers enter with cooking-pots and foodstuffs, set up
their 'adogan' or stone hearth and build a fire.*]

All this while, Lakunle is pacing wretchedly, Sadiku looks on placidly.]

LAKUNLE [*he is pacing furiously.*]:
   He's killed her.
   I warned you. You know him,
   And I warned you.
   [*Goes up all the approaches to look.*]
   She's been gone half the day. It will soon
   Be daylight. And still no news.
   Women have disappeared before.
   No trace. Vanished. Now we know how.
   [*Checks, turns round.*]
   And why!
   Mock an old man, will you? So?
   You can laugh? Ha ha! You wait.
   I'll come and see you
   Whipped like a dog. Baroka's head wife
   Driven out of the house for plotting
   With a girl.
   [*Each approaching footstep brings Lakunle to attention, but it is only a
   hawker or a passer-by. The wrestler passes. Sadiku greets him
   familiarly. Then, after he has passed, some significance of this breaks
   on Sadiku and she begins to look a little puzzled.*]

LAKUNLE: I know he has dungeons. Secret holes
   Where a helpless girl will lie
   And rot for ever. But not for nothing
   Was I born a man. I'll find my way
   To rescue her. She little deserves it, but
   I shall risk my life for her.
   [*The mummers can now be heard again, distantly. Sadiku and
   Lakunle become attentive as the noise approaches, Lakunle
   increasingly uneasy. A little, but not too much notice is paid by the
   market people.*]
   What is that?

SADIKU: If my guess is right, it will be mummers.
   [*Adds slyly.*]
   Somebody must have told them the news.

LAKUNLE: What news?
   [*Sadiku chuckles darkly and comprehension breaks on the school
   teacher.*]

Baroka! You dared . . . ?
Woman, is there no mercy in your veins?
He gave you children, and he stood
Faithfully by you and them.
He risked his life that you may boast
A warrior-hunter for your lord . . . But you—
You sell him to the rhyming rabble
Gloating in your disloyalty . . .

SADIKU [*calmly dips her hand in his pocket.*]:
Have you any money?

LAKUNLE [*snatching out her hand.*]:
Why? What? . . . Keep away, witch! Have you
Turned pickpocket in your dotage?

SADIKU: Don't be a miser. Will you let them go without giving
you a special performance?

LAKUNLE: If you think I care for their obscenity . . .

SADIKU [*wheedling.*]: Come on, school teacher. They'll expect it of
you . . . The man of learning . . . the young sprig of foreign
wisdom . . . You must not demean yourself in their eyes . . .
you must give them money to perform for your lordship. . . .
[*Re-enter the mummers, dancing straight through (more centrally this
time) as before. Male dancer enters first, pursued by a number of
young women and other choral idlers. The man dances in tortured
movements. He and about half of his pursuers have already danced
offstage on the opposite side when Sadiku dips her hand briskly in
Lakunle's pocket, this time with greater success. Before Lakunle can
stop her, she has darted to the drummers and pressed a coin apiece on
their foreheads, waving them to possession of the floor. Tilting
their heads backwards, they drum her praises. Sadiku denies the
credit, points to Lakunle as the generous benefactor. They transfer
their attention to him where he stands biting his lips at the trick.
The other dancers have now been brought back and the drummers
resume the beat of the interrupted dance. The treasurer removes the
coins from their foreheads and places them in a pouch. Now begins
the dance of virility which is of course none other than the Baroka
story. Very athletic movements. Even in his prime, 'Baroka' is made
a comic figure, held in a kind of tolerant respect by his women. At his
decline and final downfall, they are most unsparing in their taunts
and tantalizing motions. Sadiku has never stopped bouncing on her*

*toes through the dance, now she is done the honour of being
invited to join at the kill. A dumb show of bashful refusals, then she
joins them, reveals surprising agility for her age, to the wild
enthusiasm of the rest who surround and spur her on.
With 'Baroka' finally scotched, the crowd dances away to their
incoming movement, leaving Sadiku to dance on oblivious of their
departure. The drumming becomes more distant and she unwraps her
eyelids. Sighs, looks around her, and walks contentedly towards
Lakunle. As usual he has enjoyed the spectacle in spite of himself,
showing especial relish where 'Baroka' gets the worst of it from his
women. Sadiku looks at him for a moment while he tries to replace
his obvious enjoyment with disdain. She shouts 'Boo' at him, and
breaks into a dance movement, shakes a sudden leg at Lakunle.]*

SADIKU: Sadiku of the duiker's feet . . . that's what the men used to
    call me. I could twist and untwist my waist with the
    smoothness of a water snake . . .

LAKUNLE: No doubt. And you are still just as slippery.
    I hope Baroka kills you for this.
    When he finds out what your wagging tongue
    Has done to him, I hope he beats you
    Till you choke on your own breath. . . .
    *[Sidi bursts in, she has been running all the way. She throws
    herself on the ground against the tree and sobs violently,
    beating herself on the ground.]*

SADIKU *[on her knees beside her.]*: Why, child. What is the matter?

SIDI *[pushes her off.]*:
    Get away from me. Do not touch me.

LAKUNLE *[with a triumphant smile, he pulls Sadiku away and takes her
    place.]*:
    Oh, Sidi, let me kiss your tears. . . .

SIDI *[pushes him so hard that he sits down abruptly.]*:
    Don't touch me.

LAKUNLE *[dusting himself.]*:
    He must have beaten her.
    Did I not warn you both?
    Baroka is a creature of the wilds,
    Untutored, mannerless, devoid of grace.
    *[Sidi only cries all the more, beats on the ground with clenched fists,
    and stubs her toes in the ground.]*

Chief though he is,
I shall kill him for this . . .
No. Better still, I shall demand
Redress from the central courts.
I shall make him spend
The remainder of his wretched life
In prison—with hard labour.
I'll teach him
To beat defenceless women. . . .

SIDI [*lifting her head.*]:
Fool! You little fools! It was a lie.
The frog. The cunning frog!
He lied to you, Sadiku.

SADIKU: Sango forbid!

SIDI: He told me . . . afterwards, crowing.
It was a trick.
He knew Sadiku would not keep it to herself,
That I, or maybe other maids would hear of it
And go to mock his plight.
And how he laughed!
How his frog-face croaked and croaked
And called me little fool!
Oh how I hate him! How I loathe
And long to kill the man!

LAKUNLE [*retreating.*]: But Sidi, did he . . . ? I mean . . .
Did you escape?
[*Louder sobs from Sidi.*]
Speak, Sidi, this is agony.
Tell me the worst; I'll take it like a man.
Is it the fright which affects you so,
Or did he . . . ? Sidi, I cannot bear the thought.
The words refuse to form.
Do not unman me, Sidi. Speak
Before I burst in tears.

SADIKU [*raises Sidi's chin in her hand.*]:
Sidi, are you a maid or not?
[*Sidi shakes her head violently and bursts afresh in tears.*]

LAKUNLE: The Lord forbid!

SADIKU: Too late for prayers. Cheer up. It happens to the best of us.

LAKUNLE: Oh heavens, strike me dead!
Earth, open up and swallow Lakunle.
For he no longer has the wish to live.
Let the lightning fall and shrivel me
To dust and ashes. . . .
[Recoils.]
No, that wish is cowardly. This trial is my own.
Let Sango and his lightning keep out of this. It
Is my cross, and let it not be spoken that
In the hour of need, Lakunle stood
Upon the scales and was proved wanting.
My love is selfless—the love of spirit
Not of flesh.
[Stands over Sidi.]
Dear Sidi, we shall forget the past.
This great misfortune touches not
The treasury of my love.
But you will agree, it is only fair
That we forget the bride-price totally
Since you no longer can be called a maid.
Here is my hand, if on these terms
You'll be my cherished wife.
We'll take an oath, between us three
That this shall stay
A secret to our dying days . . .
[Takes a look at Sadiku and adds quickly.]
Oh no, a secret even after we're dead and gone.
And if Baroka dares to boast of it,
I'll swear he is a liar—and swear by Sango too!
[Sidi raises herself slowly, staring at Lakunle with unbelieving
eyes. She is unsmiling, her face a puzzle.]
SIDI: You would? You would marry me?
LAKUNLE [puffs out his chest.]: Yes.
[Without a change of expression, Sidi dashes suddenly off the stage.]
SADIKU: What on earth has got into her?
LAKUNLE: I wish I knew
She took off suddenly
Like a hunted buck.
[Looks offstage.]

I think—yes, she is,
She is going home.
Sadiku, will you go?
Find out if you can
What she plans to do.
[*Sadiku nods and goes. Lakunle walks up and down.*]
And now I know I am the biggest fool
That ever walked this earth.
There are women to be found
In every town or village in these parts,
And every one a virgin.
But I obey my books.
[*Distant music. Light drums, flutes, box-guitars, 'sekere'.*]
'Man takes the fallen woman by the hand'
And ever after they live happily.
Moreover, I will admit,
It solves the problem of her bride-price too.
A man must live or fall by his true
Principles. That, I had sworn,
Never to pay.
[*Enter Sadiku.*]

SADIKU: She is packing her things. She is gathering her clothes and
trinkets together, and oiling herself as a bride does before her
wedding.

LAKUNLE: Heaven help us! I am not impatient.
Surely she can wait a day or two at least.
There is the asking to be done,
And then I have to hire a praise-singer,
And such a number of ceremonies
Must firstly be performed.

SADIKU: Just what I said but she only laughed at me and called me
a . . . a . . . what was it now . . . a bra . . . braba . . .
brabararian. It serves you right. It all comes of your teaching. I
said what about the asking and the other ceremonies. And she
looked at me and said, leave all that nonsense to savages and
brabararians.

LAKUNLE: But I must prepare myself.
I cannot be
A single man one day and a married one the next.

It must come gradually.
I will not wed in haste.
A man must have time to prepare,
To learn to like the thought.
I must think of my pupils too:
Would they be pleased if I were married
Not asking their consent . . . ?
[*The singing group is now audible even to him.*]
What is that? The musicians?
Could they have learnt so soon?

SADIKU: The news of a festivity travels fast. You ought to know
that.

LAKUNLE: The goddess of malicious gossip
Herself must have a hand in my undoing.
The very spirits of the partial air
Have all conspired to blow me, willy-nilly
Down the slippery slope of grim matrimony.
What evil have I done . . . ? Ah, here they come!
[*Enter crowd and musicians.*]
Go back. You are not needed yet. Nor ever.
Hence parasites, you've made a big mistake.
There is no one getting wedded; get you home.
[*Sidi now enters. In one hand she holds a bundle, done up in a
richly embroidered cloth: in the other the magazine. She is radiant,
jewelled, lightly clothed, and wears light leather-thong sandals. They
all go suddenly silent except for the long-drawn O-Ohs of admiration.
She goes up to Lakunle and hands him the book.*]

SIDI: A present from Sidi.
I tried to tear it up
But my fingers were too frail.
[*To the crowd.*]
Let us go.
[*To Lakunle.*]
You may come too if you wish,
You are invited.

LAKUNLE [*lost in the miracle of transformation.*]:
Well I should hope so indeed
Since I am to marry you.

SIDI [*turns round in surprise.*]:

Marry who . . . ? You thought . . .
Did you really think that you, and I . . .
Why, did you think that after him,
I could endure the touch of another man?
I who have felt the strength,
The perpetual youthful zest
Of the panther of the trees?
And would I choose a watered-down,
A beardless version of unripened man?

LAKUNLE [bars her way.]:
I shall not let you.
I shall protect you from yourself.

SIDI [gives him a shove that sits him down again, hard against the tree base.]:
Out of my way, book-nourished shrimp.
Do you see what strength he has given me?
That was not bad. For a man of sixty,
It was the secret of God's own draught
A deed for drums and ballads.
But you, at sixty, you'll be ten years dead!
In fact, you'll not survive your honeymoon. . . .
Come to my wedding if you will. If not . . .
[She shrugs her shoulders. Kneels down at Sadiku's feet.]
Mother of brides, your blessing . . .

SADIKU [lays her hand on Sidi's head.]: I invoke the fertile gods. They
will stay with you. May the time come soon when you shall be
as round-bellied as a full moon in a low sky.

SIDI [hands her the bundle.]:
Now bless my worldly goods.
[Turns to the musicians.]
Come, sing to me of seeds
Of children, sired of the lion stock.
[The musicians resume their tune. Sidi sings and dances.]
Mo te'ni. Mo te'ni.
Mo te'ni. Mo te'ni.
Sun mo mi, we mo mi
Sun mo mi, fa mo mi
Yarabi lo m'eyi t'o le d'omo . . .
[Festive air, fully pervasive. Oil lamps from the market multiply as

traders desert their stalls to join them. A young girl flaunts her dancing buttocks at Lakunle and he rises to the bait. Sadiku gets in his way as he gives chase. Tries to make him dance with her. Lakunle last seen, having freed himself of Sadiku, clearing a space in the crowd for the young girl.

The crowd repeat the song after Sidi.]

Tolani Tolani

T'emi ni T'emi ni

Sun mo mi, we mo mi

Sun mo mi, fa mo mi

Yarabi lo m'eyi t'o le d'omo.[1]

---

1. 'My net is spread, my net is spread
   Come close to me, wrap yourself around me
   Only God knows which moment makes the child ...

   'Tolani Tolani
   She belongs to me, belongs to me
   Come close to me, wrap yourself around me
   Only God knows which moment makes the child.'

THE END

KONGI'S HARVEST

Characters

OBA DANLOLA	*a traditional ruler*
SARUMI	*a junior Oba*
DAODU	*son to Sarumi and heir to Danlola's throne*
WURAOLA	*Danlola's favourite wife*
OGBO AWERI	*Head of the Oba's defunct Conclave of Elders*
DENDE	*servant to Danlola*
SEGI	*a courtesan, Kongi's ex-mistress*
KONGI	*President of Isma*
ORGANIZING SECRETARY	
FIRST AWERI	
SECOND AWERI	
THIRD AWERI	*members of the Reformed Aweri Fraternity*
FOURTH AWERI	
FIFTH AWERI	
SIXTH AWERI	
SUPERINTENDENT	
CAPTAIN OF THE CARPENTER'S BRIGADE	
RIGHT AND LEFT EARS OF STATE	

Retinue, Drummers, Praise-singers, the Carpenters' Brigade, Photographer, night club habituées.

The action takes place on the eve and the day of the national celebrations of Isma.

Kongi's Harvest was first performed in August 1965 in Lagos by the 1960 MASKS and ORISUN Theatre.

Translations of the Yoruba songs will be found on pp. 139ff.

HEMLOCK

A roll of drums such as accompanies a national anthem. Presumably the audience will rise. The curtain rises with them. Grouped solemnly behind it are Oba Danlola, Wuraola his favourite wife, his Ogbo Aweri, Dende, and Danlola's retinue of drummers and buglers. They break into the following anthem:

> The pot that will eat fat
> Its bottom must be scorched
> The squirrel that will long crack nuts
> Its footpad must be sore
> The sweetest wine has flowed down
> The tapper's shattered shins
> And there is more, oh-oh
> Who says there isn't more
> Who says there isn't plenty a word
> In a penny newspaper
>
> Ism to ism for ism is ism
> Of isms and isms on absolute-ism
> To demonstrate the tree of life
> Is sprung from broken peat
> And we the rotted bark, spurned
> When the tree swells its pot
> The mucus that is snorted out
> When Kongi's new race blows
> And more, oh there's a harvest of words
> In a penny newspaper
>
> They say, oh how
> They say it all on silent skulls
> But who cares? Who but a lunatic
> Will bandy words with boxes
> With government rediffusion sets
> Which talk and talk and never
> Take a lone word in reply.

> I cannot counter words, oh
> I cannot counter words of
> A rediffusion set
> My ears are sore
> But my mouth is 'agbayun'
> For I do not bandy words
> No I do not bandy words
> With a government loudspeaker.

SUPERINTENDENT [*rushes in, agitated.*]: Kabiyesi, be your age. These antics may look well on a common agitator but really, an elder is an elder, and a king does not become a menial just because he puts down his crown to eat.

DANLOLA [*to the beat of 'gbedu' drum, steps into slow, royal dance.*]:

> E ma gun'yan Oba kere o
> E ma gun'yan Oba kere
> Kaun elepini ko se e gbe mi
> Eweyo noin ni i fi yo'nu
> E ma gun'yan Oba kere

> Don't pound the king's yam
> In a small mortar
> Don't pound the king's yam
> In a small mortar
> Small as the spice is
> It cannot be swallowed whole
> A shilling's vegetable must appease
> A halfpenny spice.

SUPERINTENDENT: It won't work, Kabiyesi, it won't work. Every evening you gather your friends together and desecrate the National Anthem. It has to stop!

SARUMI:

> Oba ni i f'epo inu ebo ra'ri
> Orisa l'oba
> Oba ni i f'epo inu ebo r'awuje
> Orisa l'oba.

> None but the king
> Takes the oil from the crossroads
> And rubs it in his 'awuje'
> The king is a god.

SUPERINTENDENT: I say you desecrate our National Anthem. I
 have to do something about it. And stop that unholy noise.
 [*Seizes the lead drummer by the wrist. Everything stops. Complete
 silence.*]

DANLOLA [*slowly.*]: You stopped the royal drums?

SUPERINTENDENT: I shall speak to the Secretary about this . . .

DANLOLA [*suddenly relaxed.*]: No, it is nothing new. Your betters
 Stopped the drums a long time ago
 And you the slave in khaki and brass buttons
 Now lick your masters' spit and boast,
 We chew the same tobacco.

SUPERINTENDENT [*turning to Sarumi.*]: Look, you better warn
 him . . .

SARUMI: We do not hear the jackal's call
 When the Father speaks.

SUPERINTENDENT: This cannot continue. I shall insist that the
 Secretary put you all in different sections of the camp. This
 cannot go on.

DANLOLA: Good friend, you merely stopped
 My drums. But they were silenced
 On the day when Kongi cast aside
 My props of wisdom, the day he
 Drove the old Aweri from their seats.
 What is a king without a clan
 Of elders? What will Kongi be without . . .
 Sarumi, what name was it again?

SARUMI: The Reformed Aweri Fraternity.

DANLOLA: A big name for little heads.
 And now, he wants to eat
 The first of the New Yam. The mashed
 Weak yams on which the crow
 Weaned our Leader his son still stick
 Between his teeth and prove too tough
 For his adult comfort, but he seeks
 To eat the first of the New Yam.
 [*The retainers burst into derisive laughter and the Superintendent
 becomes incensed.*]

SUPERINTENDENT: You see if I don't do something about that

subversive kind of talk. . . . E-eh!

[*He looks down and sees for the first time what Danlola has used for a wrapper under his 'agbada'. Looks rapidly up at a flagpole in the middle of the yard and back again to Danlola's legs.*]

SUPERINTENDENT: Kabiyesi, is that not our national flag?

DANLOLA: Did you not deprive me of my national trousers?

SUPERINTENDENT: Yes, to keep you from escaping.

DANLOLA: The nude shanks of a king
Is not a sight for children—
It will blind them.
When an Oba stops the procession
And squats on the wayside,
It's on an urgent matter
Which spares neither king nor god.
Wise heads turn away
Until he's wiped his bottom.

SUPERINTENDENT [*wildly.*]: We'll soon see about that. You want to cost me my job do you?

[*He rushes at Danlola and whips off the flag. Danlola first rapidly gathers his 'agbada' round his legs to protect his semi-nudity, then shrugs and tries to assume a dignified indifference.*]

DANLOLA: It was our fathers who said, not I—
A crown is a burden when
The king visits his favourite's
Chambers. When the king's wrapper
Falls off in audience, wise men know
He wants to be left alone. So—

[*Shoos him off with a contemptuous gesture.*]

SUPERINTENDENT [*going.*]: Too much indulgence, that's why. It's all the fault of the Organizing Secretary permitting your wives and all these other creatures to visit you. And you are not even grateful.

DANLOLA [*bursts into laughter.*]: We curse a wretch denying cause
For gratitude deserved, but it is
A mindless clown who dispenses
Thanks as a fowl scatters meal
Not caring where it falls. Thanks?
In return for my long fingers of largesse
Your man knows I love to have my hairs

Ruffled well below the navel.
Denied that, are you or he the man
To stop me breaking out of camp?
And granting my retainers leave
To keep me week-end company—is that also
Reason for the grass to tickle [*slapping his belly.*]
The royal wine-gourd? Well?
What says the camp superintendent?
Shall I . . . ?
[*Makes a motion as if he means to prostrate himself.*]

RETAINERS [*step forward, shouting in alarm.*]: Ewo![1]

DANLOLA: But he says I must. Let me
Prostrate myself to him.
[*Again the gesture. He and his retainers get involved in a mock-struggle.*]

SUPERINTENDENT: I did not make any impious demands of you.
All I asked was for more respect to constituted authority.
I didn't ask for a curse on my head.

DANLOLA: Curse? Who spoke of curses?
To prostrate to a loyal servant
Of Kongi—is that a curse?

SUPERINTENDENT: Only a foolish child lets a father prostrate to
him. I don't ask to become a leper or a lunatic. I have no wish
to live on sour berries.

DANLOLA: All is well. The guard has waived
His rights and privileges. The father
Now prostrates himself in gratitude.

SUPERINTENDENT [*shouting.*]: I waived nothing. I had nothing to
waive, nothing to excuse. I deny any rights and beg you not to
cast subtle damnations on my head.

DANLOLA: Oh but what a most suspicious mould
Olukori must have used for casting man.
Subtle damnations? If I was
Truly capable of that, would I
Now be here, thanking you for little
Acts of kindness flat on my face?
[*Again his act.*]

SUPERINTENDENT [*forestalls him by throwing himself down.*]: I call
you all to witness. Kabiyesi, I am only the fowl droppings that

1. Taboo.

stuck to your slippers when you strolled in the backyard. The
child is nothing; it is only the glory of his forbears that the
world sees and tolerates in him.

SARUMI: Ah, don't be angry with him
Oba Danlola, don't be angry
With your son. If the baobab shakes
Her head in anger, what chance
Has the rodent when
An ear-ring falls
And hits the earth with thunder.

DANLOLA [*swelling, swelling . . .*]:
He paraded me to the world
L'ogolonto[1] I leave this abuse
To the judgement of the. . . .

SUPERINTENDENT: Please—plead with him. Intercede for me.

SARUMI: Kabiyesi, a father employs only a small stick on his child,
he doesn't call in the policeman to take him to gaol. Don't give
voice to the awesome names on an Oba's tongue; when you
feel kinder, they cannot easily be recalled. They must fulfil
what task they were called to do.
[*The retainers intervene, pleading with Danlola. His drummers try to
soothe him and Wura kneels to placate his anger. Gradually he
calms down, slowly, as Sarumi sings.*]

SARUMI: Ah, Danlola, my father,
Even so did I
Wish your frown of thunder away
When the Aweri were driven from
Their ancient conclave. Then you said . . .

DRUMMER: This is the last
That we shall dance together
They say we took too much silk
For the royal canopy
But the dead will witness
We never ate the silkworm.

SARUMI: They complained because
The first of the new yams
Melted first in an Oba's mouth
But the dead will witness
We drew the poison from the root.

1. Stark naked.

[*As the king's men begin a dirge of 'ege', Danlola sits down slowly onto a chair, withdrawing more and more into himself.*]

DRUMMER: I saw a strange sight
    In the market this day
    The day of the feast of Agemo
    The sun was high
    And the king's umbrella
    Beneath it. . . .

SARUMI: We lift the king's umbrella
    Higher than men
    But it never pushes
    The sun in the face.

DRUMMER: I saw a strange sight
    In the market this day
    The sun was high
    But I saw no shade
    From the king's umbrella.

OGBO AWERI: This is the last
    That we shall dance together
    This is the last the hairs
    Will lift on our skin
    And draw together
    When the gbedu rouses
    The dead in oshugbo[1]. . . .

SARUMI: This is the last our feet
    Shall speak to feet of the dead
    And the unborn cling
    To the hem of our robes
    Oh yes, we know they say
    We wore out looms
    With weaving robes for kings
    But I ask, is popoki[2]
    The stuff to let down
    To unformed fingers clutching up
    At life?

OGBO AWERI: Did you not see us
    Lead twins by the hand?
    Did you not see us

1. Shrine of Oro (cult of the dead).   2. Thick coarse, woven cloth.

Shade the albino's eyes
From the hard sun, with a fan
Of parrot feathers?
Even so did the god[1] enjoin
Whose hands of chalk
Have formed the cripple
And the human bat of day.

SARUMI: Don't pound the king's yam
With a small pestle
Let the dandy's wardrobe
Be as lavish as the shop
Of the dealer in brocades
It cannot match an elder's rags.

DANLOLA [*almost to himself.*]: This dance is the last
Our feet shall dance together
The royal python may be good
At hissing, but it seems
The scorpion's tail is fire.

DRUMMER: The king's umbrella
Gives no more shade
But we summon no dirge-master.
The tunnel passes through
The hill's belly
But we cry no defilement.
A new-dug path may lead
To the secret heart of being.
Ogun is still a god
Even without his navel.

OGBO AWERI: Observe, when the monster child
Was born, Opele[2] taught us to
Abandon him beneath the buttress tree
But the mother said, oh no,
A child is still a child
The mother in us said, a child
Is still the handiwork of Olukori.

SARUMI: Soon the head swelled
Too big for pillow
And it swelled too big

1. Obatala, a Yoruba deity.   2. Vehicle for Ifa (divination).

For the mother's back
And soon the mother's head
Was nowhere to be seen
And the child's slight belly
Was strangely distended.

DANLOLA [*comes forward, dancing softly.*]:
This is the last
Our feet shall touch together
We thought the tune
Obeyed us to the soul
But the drums are newly shaped
And stiff arms strain
On stubborn crooks, so
Delve with the left foot
For ill-luck; with the left
Again for ill-luck; once more
With the left alone, for disaster
Is the only certainty we know.

[*The bugles join in royal cadences, the two kings dance slow, mournful steps, accompanied by their retinue. Coming down on the scene, a cage of prison bars separating Danlola from Sarumi and the other visitors who go out backwards herded off by the Superintendent.*]

FIRST PART

The action alternates between two scenes, both of which are present on different parts of the stage and are brought into play in turn, by lights. First, Kongi's retreat in the mountains, the Reformed Aweri Fraternity in session. Kongi is seen dimly in his own cell, above the Aweri. Rising slowly, a chant in honour of Kongi.

FOURTH AWERI: We need an image. Tomorrow being our first appearance in public, it is essential that we find an image.

FIFTH: Why?

THIRD: Why? Is that question necessary?

FIFTH: It is. Why do we need an image?

THIRD: Well, if you don't know that. . . .

FOURTH: He doesn't, so I'll answer the question. Especially as he seems to be staying awake at last.

FIFTH: Don't sneer. I've heard your snores twice at least this session.

FOURTH: Kindly return to the theme of this planning session. The problem of an image for ourselves.

SECOND: Isn't it enough just to go in as Kongi's disciples?

FOURTH: Magi is more dignified. We hold after all the position of the wise ones. From the recognition of us as the Magi, it is one step to his inevitable apotheosis.

FIRST: Which is to create a new oppositional force.

SECOND: Kongi is a great strategist. He will not take on too many opponents at once.

FIFTH: I still have not been told why we need an image.

THIRD: You are being very obstructive.

FIFTH: Why do we need an image?

FIRST: I suggest we pattern ourselves on our predecessors. Oh I do admit they were a little old-fashioned, but they had er . . . a certain style. Yes, I think style is the word I want. Style. Yes, I think we could do worse than model ourselves on the old Aweri.

FIFTH: You mean, speak in proverbs and ponderous tone rhythms?

FOURTH: I'm afraid that is out anyway. Kongi would prefer a clean break from the traditional conclave of the so-called wise ones.

FIRST: They were remote, impersonal—we need these aspects. They breed fear in the common man.

SECOND: The paraphernalia helped too, don't forget that.

SIXTH: I have no intention of making myself look ridiculous in that outfit.

FOURTH: Welcome back to the discussion. I take it you know the subject.

SIXTH: No. Enlighten me.

FOURTH: The subject is an image for the Reformed Aweri Fraternity of which you are a member in your waking moments.

FIFTH: And why do we need an image?

THIRD: Will you for Kongi's sake stop repeating that question?

FIFTH: When will you learn not to speak for Kongi?

FOURTH: Is this yet another effort to divert this discussion?

FIFTH: There is no discussion. Until Kongi makes up his mind just what image his is going to be this time, you can do nothing. I am going back to sleep.

FIRST: The emphasis of our generation is—youth. Our image therefore should be a kind of youthful elders of the state. A conclave of modern patriarchs.

THIRD: Yes, yes. Nice word patriarch, I'm glad you used it. Has a nice reverent tone about it. Very nice indeed, very nice.

SECOND: I agree. Conjures up quite an idyllic scene.

THIRD: Yes, yes, children handing the patriarch his pipe at evening, crouching at his feet to sip raindrops of wisdom.

FIFTH: And dodging hot ashes as age shakes his rheumatic hand and the pipe overturns?

THIRD: You seem to turn a sour tongue on every progress we make in this discussion. Why don't you simply stay asleep?

FIFTH: When the patriarch overturns his pipe, make way. It is no time for piety.

THIRD: Well, now you've let off your crosswinds of advice, I hope your stomach pipes you sweeter to sleep.

FOURTH: We might consider a scientific image. This would be a positive stamp and one very much in tune with our contemporary situation. Our pronouncements should be dominated by a positive scientificism.

THIRD: A brilliant conception. I move we adopt it at once.

SIXTH: What image exactly is positive scientificism?

THIRD: Whatever it is, it is not long-winded proverbs and senile
pronouncements. In fact we could say a step has already been
taken in that direction. If you've read our Leader's last
publication. . .

FIFTH: Ah yes. Nor proverbs nor verse, only ideograms in
algebraic quantums. If the square of XQY(2bc) equals QA into
the square root of X, then the progressive forces must prevail
over the reactionary in the span of ·32 of a single generation.

FOURTH: I trust you understood that as well as you remember it.

FIFTH: No. As well as *you* understand it.

FOURTH: I've had enough of your negative attitude . . . !

*Coloured lights, and the sustained chord of a juju band guitar gone typically
mad brings on the night club scene, a few dancers on, the band itself offstage.
Daodu is dancing with Segi.*
*Enter Secretary flanked by the Right and Left Ear of State. Reactions are
immediate to their entry. A few night-lifers pick up their drinks and go in,
there are one or two aggressive departures, some stay on defiantly, others
obsequiously try to attract attention and say a humble greeting. Daodu and
Segi dance on. The music continues in the background.*

SECRETARY [*approaches the pair*.]: Like a word with you. In private.

SEGI [*very sweetly*.]: You can see I'm occupied Mr. Secretary.

SECRETARY: I don't mean you. Your boy friend.

SEGI: He's busy too.

SECRETARY: Madam, I haven't come to make trouble.

SEGI [*very gently*.]: You couldn't, even if you wanted. Not here.

SECRETARY: I wouldn't be too sure of that.

SEGI: I would.

DAODU: What do you want with me?

SECRETARY: Not here. Let's find somewhere quiet.

[*Daodu leaves Segi at a table and follows the Secretary.*]

SECRETARY [*with abrupt violence*.]: Your uncle is a pain in the neck.

DAODU: Who?

SECRETARY: Your uncle. You are Daodu aren't you? Son of
Sarumi by his wife number six. And Oba Danlola is your
uncle and you the heir-apparent to his throne. And I have
come to tell you that your uncle is a damned stubborn goat, an

obstructive, cantankerous creature and a bloody pain in my neck.

DAODU: I'm sorry to hear that.

SECRETARY: Don't waste my time with apologies. You know who I am of course.

DAODU: I don't believe so.

SECRETARY: Organizing Secretary to the Leader. Those two, the Right and the Left Ears of State. The combination keeps the country non-aligned. Understand?

DAODU: I think so.

SECRETARY: And your guardian and uncle, Danlola, is a pain in my neck. Now tell me, what has he up his sleeves?

DAODU: Up his sleeves?

SECRETARY: Up those voluminous sleeves of his. What is he hiding in there for tomorrow?

DAODU: I thought he's been in detention for nearly a year.

SECRETARY: That doesn't stop him from messing me about. It only gives him an alibi.

DAODU: Hadn't you better turn him loose then?

SECRETARY: I might do that. Yes, I might do that. Hm. [*Looks slowly round.*] Does that woman have to keep looking at me like that?

DAODU: Does she bother you?

SECRETARY: Isn't there anywhere else we can go? I need to concentrate.

DAODU: I can ask her to go in if you like.

SECRETARY: Nonsense. Leave her where she is. I just wish she'd . . . what do they sing about her? What are they saying?

DAODU:
> The being of Segi
> Swirls the night
> In potions round my head
>
> But my complaints
> Will pass.
>
> It is only
> A madman ranting
> When the lady
> Turns her eyes,

Fathomless on those
I summoned as my go-between.

SECRETARY: Elegant. Very elegant. You know, I am very fond of
music. Unfortunately I haven't much time for it. Moreover
one would hardly wish to be found in this sort of place.

DAODU: But you are here now.

SECRETARY: Yes, but only in the line of duty.

DAODU: You should take your duty more seriously and come
more often.

SECRETARY: What? Oh . . . ha . . . ha good idea, good idea.

DAODU: However, what brings you here to see me?

SECRETARY: Ah yes, we must get away from distractions and stick
to business. [*Leans forward suddenly.*] But tell me, is she really as
dangerous as they say? Some men I know have burns to
show for their venture in that direction. The types too you'd
think would know their way around.

DAODU: No. Listen to what they're singing now. *They* know
Segi.

> The wine-hour wind
> That cools us
> Leaves no prints behind
>
> The spring
> Has travelled long
> To soothe our blistered feet
>
> But last year's sands
> Are still at the source
> Unruffled.

SECRETARY: Just the same I wish she'd stop boring into my neck
with her eyes.

DAODU: But she's gone.

SECRETARY [*spins round.*]: When? I didn't see her go.

DAODU: Her presence seemed to disturb you so I asked her to
excuse us.

SECRETARY: You did? When?

DAODU: Just now.

SECRETARY [*narrowly.*]: I didn't see or hear you do anything. Are
you trying to make a fool of me?

DAODU: No.

SECRETARY: Because I warn you, I'm a very dangerous man. I don't care what her reputation is, mine is also something to reckon with.

DAODU:
  Fame, is a flippant lover
  But Segi you made him a slave
  And no poet now can rival
  His devotedness.

  The politician
  Fights for place
  With fat juices
  On the tongue of generations

  The judge
  Is flushed down with wine
  And pissed
  Into the gutter

  But Segi
  You are the stubborn strand
  Of meat, lodged
  Between my teeth

  I picked and picked
  I found it was a silken thread
  Wound deep down my throat
  And makes me sing.

SECRETARY: And makes me thirsty, where is the waiter!

DAODU: Just behind you.

SECRETARY: Where? Oh, get us some beer.

DAODU: It's here.

SECRETARY: I don't remember ordering any.

DAODU: Segi did. She looks after her guests, especially important ones.

[*Secretary changes his mind about replying, digs instead into his pockets.*]
Naturally, it's on the house.

SECRETARY: No thank you. I prefer to pay for my drinks.

DAODU: The waiter won't take it.

SECRETARY: I hope at least I can buy drinks for my assistants. Where are they anyway?

DAODU: Inside, on duty.

SECRETARY: What is that supposed to mean?

DAODU: Keeping their ears open—isn't that what they're paid for? By the way, tell them not to stick their ears out too long or they might get slashed off. People are rather touchy here.

SECRETARY: No need to teach them their job.

DAODU: I thought I'd just mention it. Well, here's to duty.

[*Secretary grunts, drinks with the same pointlessly angry gestures. Lights fade. Kongi's chant. Change of lights into next scene.*]

[*Secretary speaks as he enters.*]

SECRETARY: How goes the planning session?

FIFTH: I am starving.

SECRETARY: That is a normal sensation with people who indulge in fasting.

FIFTH: I do not indulge in fasting. I am fasting under duress.

SECRETARY: I know nothing of that.

FIFTH: Nor do I. But you ask my stomach about it.

THIRD: Damn your greedy stomach.

[*Enter Kongi. They rise quickly.*]

KONGI: Do they have all the facts?

SECRETARY: I was just beginning . . .

KONGI: Do it now. There is little time left.

SECRETARY: The Leader's image for the next Five-Year Development Plan will be that of a benevolent father of the nation. This will be strongly projected at tomorrow's Harvest festival which has been chosen as the official start to the Five-Year Plan. The key-word is Harmony. Total Harmony.

KONGI: I want an immediate disputation on the subject. Then a planning session. [*Goes off.*]

FIFTH: And what, may I ask, does that mean in practical terms? What is the obstructive lump?

SECRETARY: Oba Danlola.

SECOND: What! That man again?

SECRETARY: He still refuses to give up the New Yam?

FIRST: Why is it necessary for him to give it up? He's in detention isn't he?

FIFTH: I could do with a bit of yam right now.

SIXTH: Me too. New or old I couldn't care less.

THIRD: Can't you two shut up your greedy mouths for a change?

FOURTH: If you can, just for a few moments, I would like to set the subject up in neat patterns for a formal disputation. The central problem, I take it, is this reactionary relic of the kingship institution.

SECRETARY: If by that you mean Danlola, yes.

FIRST: The man is in P.D. The state has taken over his functions. What exactly is the problem?

FOURTH: An act of public submission, obviously. Kongi must have his submission in full view of the people. The wayward child admits his errors and begs his father's forgiveness.

FIRST: You'll never do it. I know that stubborn old man, you'll never do it.

FOURTH: Kongi achieves all.

FIRST: Don't read me that catechism of the Carpenters' Brigade man. Be practical.

FOURTH: I am being practical. Now let us see the problem as part of a normal historic pattern. This means in effect that—Kongi must prevail.

FIFTH: Page two, section 3b of the Carpenters' Credo.

FOURTH: Look here. . . .

FIFTH: If you must catechize, at least sing it like the Carpenters. I take it they are the ones waiting from below.

SECOND: It's a horrible noise. I'd like to push a rock down on their heads.

SIXTH: Couldn't you find another choir to serenade the Leader?

SECRETARY: Gentlemen, please. All we want is some way of persuading King Danlola to bring the New Yam to Kongi with his own hands. I have organized the rest—the agricultural show to select the prize-winning yam, the feast, the bazaar, the music, the dance. Only one thing is missing—Oba Danlola. And gentlemen, that problem is yours. Kongi desires that the king perform all his customary spiritual functions, only this time, that he perform them to him, our Leader. Kongi must preside as the Spirit of Harvest, in pursuance of the Five-Year Development Plan.

FOURTH: An inevitable stage in the process of power reversionism.

SECRETARY: Call it what you like. Kongi wants a solution, and fast.

FOURTH: All right. We will hold a formal disputation.

SECRETARY: And the key-word, Kongi insists, must be— Harmony. We need that to counter the effect of the recent bomb-throwing. Which is one of the reasons why the culprits of that outrage will be hanged tomorrow.

[*A nervous silence. They look at one another, stare at their feet.*]

FOURTH: An exercise in scientific exorcism—I approve.

[*Followed by murmurs and head-nodding of agreement by the majority.*

Loud chord on guitar and into the next scene.]

[*Segi's Club.*]

SECRETARY: And what about you sir? What do *you* have in mind?

DAODU: Me?

SECRETARY: Yes you. Tomorrow is State Festival.

DAODU: The Harvest?

SECRETARY: Naturally.

DAODU: I am looking forward to it. We are bound to take the first prize for the New Yam.

SECRETARY: Who are we?

DAODU: We? My farm of course. You know I own a farm.

SECRETARY: Of course I know you own a farm. There is very little I don't know let me tell you. What I don't understand is . . . no, wait a minute, I like to be sure of my facts before I jump. Now, did you say you are going to take the first prize tomorrow?

DAODU: Yes.

SECRETARY: You will compete in the agricultural show?

DAODU: Obviously.

SECRETARY: There is something not quite right somewhere. Or could it be that you are not yet aware that this time it is not your uncle who will eat the New Yam, but our Leader.

DAODU: I know all about that. What is it they say . . . the old order changeth—right?

SECRETARY: Cheers. Wish we had more democratic princes like you. [*He cheers up considerably.*]

When you think of it, I shouldn't be surprised at all. There's a
lot about you which marks you out to be quite exceptional.
Mind you, I won't deny that once or twice you actually had us
worried. Ye-e-es we really thought at one stage we would
have to do something about you.

DAODU: Why?

SECRETARY: Well . . . [looks round him.] I'll be quite honest with
you. We felt you were not quite . . . how should I put it . . .
quite with us, that you were not pulling along with us. I mean
we already had farm co-operatives but you had to start a
farmers' community of your own!

DAODU: But it worked.

SECRETARY: Of course it worked! Damn it man, were you
trying to show us up? [A waiter refills his glass; he downs it.]
It was bad for our morale man, really bad.

DAODU: I am sorry to hear that.

SECRETARY [waves him aside.]: No you're not. I don't know how
you did it but you got results. And your workers—contented
sows the whole bloody lot of them. Oh our people sing too,
but not in tune if you get my meaning. See what I mean?
Very bad for the morale. Listen, I don't mind telling you . . .
we sent in a few spies just to see what you were up to, but
you know what happened?

DAODU [mock ignorance.]: No. Tell me.

SECRETARY: They never came back.

DAODU: Really! I am sorry about that.

SECRETARY: Will you stop saying you're sorry! [Downs the rest of
his beer and calls for more.] Anyway, we couldn't do much about
you. As long as you were contributing to the national
economy . . . you see, my personal motto is Every Ismite
must do his Mite . . . hey, did you hear that?

DAODU [looking round.]: What?

SECRETARY: No, me. Didn't you hear what I said. Came out just
now, just like that, spontaneous. Every Ismite must do his
Mite. How is that for a rallying slogan for tomorrow eh?
Find me a pen quickly before it goes. My memory is like a
basket when I've had a few beers.

DAODU: Let me write it for you.
[Scribbles it on a beer-pad and gives it to him.]

SECRETARY: Let me read it. Every-Ismite-Must-Do-His-Mite!
    Hey, you've added something to it.

DAODU: Don't you like it? I've just thought of it too.

SECRETARY: Ismite-Is-Might! Did you think that up?

DAODU: A moment ago.

SECRETARY: What! You are . . . a prince of slogans. A prince of
    slogans. Waiter! Waiter! bring more beer. You know, this is
    the most profitable night I've had in a long time. You wait
    until I get this to the Leader. [*He rises, flushed and excited.*] End
    of the celebrations. Kongi raises his right fist—his favourite
    gesture have you noticed? raises his right fist and says just the
    one word—Ismite . . .

LAYABOUTS: Is Might!

SECRETARY: Ismite . . .

LAYABOUTS: Is Might.

    [*More people come in from the club and gather round.*]

SECRETARY: Ismite . . .

CROWD [*thunderously.*]: Is Might!

    [*Stops suddenly, then turns to examine his supporters and sinks back
    into his chair, his face wrinkled in disgust.*]

SECRETARY: Does no one come here except prostitutes and
    cut-throats?

    [*In twos, and threes the habituées melt slowly away.*]

[*Kongi's Retreat.*]

FOURTH: Now, a systematic examination of the data. What have
    we got on our plates?

FIFTH: A few crumbs of mouldy bread isn't it?

THIRD: What did you say?

FIFTH: I said a few crumbs of bread. What else do we ever get on
    our plates?

FOURTH: Can't you keep your mind on the subject? I used a
    common figure of speech and you leap straight onto the subject
    of food.

FIFTH: If your mind wasn't licking round the subject all the time
    how come you always pick that kind of expression?

SIXTH: He's right. It was a most unfortunate choice of words—
    what have we got on our plates? After several days of slow
    starvation what other answer do you expect?

THIRD: Can we return to the subject? We need a way to persuade
that old reactionary to . . .

FIFTH: Starve him. Try starving him to death!

FOURTH: That would hardly solve the problem. It needs a live
person to make even a symbolic act of capitulation.

THIRD: Especially when harmony is the ultimate goal. The
ultimate goal.

FOURTH: I think I see something of the Leader's vision of this
harmony. To replace the old superstitious festival by a state
ceremony governed by the principle of Enlightened Ritualism.
It is therefore essential that Oba Danlola, his bitterest opponent,
appear in full antiquated splendour surrounded by his Aweri
Conclave of Elders who, beyond the outward trappings of
pomp and ceremony and a regular supply of snuff, have no
other interest in the running of the state.

SIXTH: Who says?

FOURTH: Kongi says. The period of isolated saws and wisdoms is
over, superseded by a more systematic formulation of
comprehensive philosophies—*our* function, for the benefit of
those who still do not know it.

THIRD: Hear hear.

FOURTH: And Danlola, the retrogressive autocrat, will with his own
hands present the Leader with the New Yam, thereby
acknowledging the supremacy of the State over his former
areas of authority spiritual or secular. From then on, the State
will adopt towards him and to all similar institutions the
policy of glamourized fossilism.

THIRD: Hear hear, very precisely put.

SECOND: You still haven't said how you are going to do it?

FOURTH: I beg your pardon.

SECOND: How will you make the king take part in this—public act
of submission?

FOURTH: Just what is the difficulty? I have outlined the main
considerations haven't I?

SECOND: Outlining the considerations is not exactly a solution.

FOURTH: You all expect me to do all the thinking don't you?

FIFTH: Don't look at me. I've told you I can't think on an empty
stomach.

THIRD: Can't you lay off your filthy stomach?

FIFTH: I can't. Why the hell couldn't Kongi do his fasting alone? I'll tell you why. He loves companions in misery.

FIRST: Look man, enough of you. You didn't have to come.

FIFTH: Yah? I'd like to see any of us refusing that order. And anyway, he said nothing of fasting at the time. Just disputations and planning.

SIXTH: Very true. I knew nothing of the fasting part of it until we were cut off from all contact.

THIRD: Don't you arrogate yourselves to being his companions in misery. You get something to eat. Kongi doesn't eat at all.

FIFTH: All part of his diabolical cleverness. A little bit of dry bread every day just to activate the stomach devils. Much better if we'd gone all out like him.

FIRST: Hey, go easy man. You're asking for P.D. if you go on in that tone.

FIFTH: At least you get fed. And if you have money you can live like a king—ask our dear Organizing Secretary if you don't believe me.

SECRETARY: You are suggesting something nasty Sir?

FIFTH: Don't act innocent with me. If a detainee pays your price you'll see to his comforts. I bet our royal prisoner has put on weight since he came under your charge.

SECRETARY: This is slander.

FIFTH: Sue me.

SECRETARY: I refuse to listen to any more of this.

FIFTH: And a full sex-life too I bet. Are you going to tell me you don't issue week-end permits to his wives?

SECRETARY: You are taking advantage of your privileged position.

FIFTH: I waive it you shameless bribe-collector. Say whatever is on your mind, or take me to court. I waive my philosophic immunity.

SECRETARY: All right. So I take bribes. It only puts me on the same level with you.

THIRD: What!

SECOND: I smell corruption.

SIXTH: Let's hear it. Come on, out with it.

SECRETARY: You've been bought. You've all been bought.

FOURTH [on his feet.]: Withdraw that statement!

THIRD: Immediately.

FIRST: This has me curious. Has anyone been accepting money on my behalf? All I ask is my cut.

FOURTH: It is an unforgivable insult.

FIFTH: Let the man speak. Which of us has been taking money?

SECRETARY: Oh, not money, I know the sight of cash is printed over with INSULT for upright men like you and intellectual minds. Oh no, not cash. But position, yes, position! And the power of being so close to power, 'Well it's difficult but I'll see what I can do'. 'You understand, my private feelings cannot come into this but that's the position. Oh yes, if you think that will help, do mention the fact that I sent you.' And the dark impersonal protocol suits, and the all-purpose face, the give-nothing-away face in conference corridors, star-struck with the power of saying, 'Yes I think I could arrange for you to meet the President.' Of course you've been bought. Bribed with the bribe of an all-powerful signature across a timeless detention order.

[*A brief pause.*]

FIFTH: Hm. What do you think of that, gentlemen?

THIRD: A rotten exposition.

SECRETARY: Well I never did claim to be a theoretician.

SIXTH: I confess I found it very absorbing.

FIFTH: Me too. I quite forgot my hunger for a while.

THIRD: Will you leave your stomach out of it!

SIXTH: Why does that always set you raving?

THIRD: I suffer from ulcers.

SIXTH: Don't we all? Mine are crying out for a decent meal.

THIRD: I tell you it's my ulcers.

SIXTH: I know, I know. You wait until we all break the fast on that New Yam.

FIRST: Which we have not yet secured. Isn't it time we returned to that subject.

FIFTH: You carry on with it. I think I'll have a word with our Organizing Secretary first. We may both find a common ground of understanding. Come this way my friend.

SECRETARY: Kindly resume the disputations. Kongi expects an answer soon.

[*They move to one side.*]

FIFTH: Danlola was in your charge. Kongi rightly expects that you should have broken all his resistance by now. But you haven't, have you?

SECRETARY: He is a stubborn ass.

FIFTH: Well, maybe. Your problem could be quite simple, only it will have to depend on your powers of persuasion.

SECRETARY: What else do you think I've been doing all these months.

FIFTH: Working on that wrong person. Now, before I tell you what to do, we must settle on a fee.

SECRETARY: You . . . want me to pay you?

FIFTH: Naturally. I am a professional theoretician. I must be paid for my services.

SECRETARY: Nothing doing.

FIFTH [turning away.]: In that case I shall contribute my solution to the general pool and let my colleagues take the credit for it.

SECRETARY: Wait.

FIFTH: That's better. You can't pretend that you wouldn't be glad to succeed where he failed.

SECRETARY: But suppose it doesn't work, this mysterious solution of yours.

FIFTH: I can't see why it shouldn't.

SECRETARY: All right, let's hear it.

FIFTH: First, the fee.

SECRETARY: I thought you lot were supposed to be above this sort of thing.

FIFTH: You'll be surprised. Let's get back to business. I know you're making quite a bit out of the Harvest.

SECRETARY: All right, you name your terms.

FIFTH: No, that's not the way it's usually done. You make me an offer. And don't think I'm a novice at this game.

SECRETARY: All right. What about . . . ?
[Casually holds out a closed fist. Fifth Aweri shakes his head.]
No? I've known contracts for a ten-mile road settled for less than. . . .
[Two closed fists.]
You are a hard man. Of course I must admit that the cost of living rises all the time. My contacts in the Ministry of Housing tell me that a modest office block was won by a round figure close to . . .

[*Cups his two hands together, slowly.*]

A juicy, stream-lined shape I think . . .

[*Fifth Aweri turns his back. Secretary speaks hastily.*]

But by no means final. An artist must experiment with shapes.
I would add, by way of attraction, a pair of ears. . . .

[*He sticks out the two thumbs. Obtaining only a wooden response,*
he throws up his hands angrily.]

Well in that case take your solution where you please. Just
how much do you think I will make for myself from organizing
the Harvest anyway. I may as well hand you my entire profits.

FIFTH [*chuckling.*]: Oh I've always longed to see that done by a
professional.

SECRETARY: You would appear to be something of one yourself.

FIFTH: No, to tell you the truth, my interest has been purely
clinical.

SECRETARY: Do you mean you don't want a fee after all?

FIFTH: You bet I do. [*Gives a quick look round, desperately.*]
Food man, food. A bit of the Harvest before the banquet. I've
had enough of this starvation act. Smuggle in some food
tonight.

SECRETARY: Is that all?

FIFTH: But do it carefully. Their noses are so pinched from hunger,
they will smell out any food within a two-mile radius.

SECRETARY: Well, well. Any particular preference?

FIFTH: Yes, food. Just food.

SECRETARY: It's a deal. Now. . .

FIFTH: My solution? Simple. Kongi is the man you have to tackle.

SECRETARY: Please, don't try to make a fool of me.

FIFTH: I am deadly serious. Persuade him to grant some form of
amnesty. Then go to Danlola and tell him that in exchange for
the New Yam, a few of the detainees will be set free.

SECRETARY: And you think that will have the slightest effect on the
old man? He'll say they will be chucked right back again at the
first excuse.

FIFTH: Good. In that case, you will need something more
substantial won't you?

SECRETARY: Like what for heaven's sake?

FIFTH: Think. If Kongi were persuaded to grant a reprieve to the
men condemned to death . . .

SECRETARY: You are out of your mind.

FIFTH: If you are able to assure Danlola that they will be
reprieved . . .

SECRETARY: You are raving. Kongi does not want the New Yam
that badly.

FIFTH: You are good at these things. Rack your brain for some
way of getting him in the right mood.

SECRETARY: You don't know how he hates those men. He wants
them dead—you've no idea how desperately.

FIFTH: I do. But tell him he can kill them later in detention. Have
them shot trying to escape or something. But first, demonstrate
his power over life and death by granting them a last-minute
reprieve. That's it, work on that aspect of it, the drama of a
last-minute reprieve. If I know my Kongi that should appeal
to his flair for gestures.

SECRETARY: It might work.

FIFTH: It will. [*Going.*] And don't come back without my fee. I
can't last much longer.

[*Segi's Club.*]

DAODU: Those are Segi's friends you insulted.

SECRETARY: They are not her type.

DAODU: I assure you they are.

SECRETARY: She belongs in a different class.

DAODU: She won't agree with you.

SECRETARY: What do you come to do here anyway? Are you
Segi's lover?

DAODU: Yes.

SECRETARY: I should have said, current lover.

DAODU: I *am* her current lover.

SECRETARY: There is something I don't understand. This is not the
Segi we hear of. This one seemed to look at you as a woman
should. The Segi we know never does.

DAODU: You keep postponing what you want to say about the
Harvest.

SECRETARY: This place bothers me. I have a sixth sense about
things, that is how I survive in this job. Something is missing.
There should be a pungent odour of fornication about places
like this. Is business slack tonight or something?

DAODU: I'll ask Segi if you like.

SECRETARY: No, no, leave her out of it. She'll confuse me. It was bad enough when I wasn't even drunk.

DAODU: Then what did you come to see me about?

SECRETARY: We closed down these quarters once didn't we?

DAODU: I don't know.

SECRETARY: Yes we did. All the prostitutes were sent off to a rehabilitation camp, and on graduation they became the Women's Auxiliary Corps, a sort of female leg of the Carpenters' Brigade.

DAODU: You must have missed out some.

SECRETARY: Oh no, we were very thorough. Make no mistake about that, we picked the kind of men for the job who would be thorough.

DAODU: Then these came after the er . . . the purge.

SECRETARY: Impossible. It couldn't have flourished so quickly.

DAODU: Why not? Some of the credit is in fact, yours. Do you mean you don't recognize any of them?

SECRETARY: What do you mean? I am not in the habit of consorting with . . .

DAODU: Sit down. Take a look at that one over there . . . don't you know who she is?

SECRETARY [looks intently, gives up.]: She doesn't mean a thing to me.

DAODU: Go inside then. Look in the bar and in the dark corners. See if there is someone you remember.

[As he rises, Segi comes out. He pulls himself right against a wall as if he does not want her to touch him. Segi goes past him without a glance, sits at her former table. Secretary stops suddenly, turns round and stares. Segi keeps her eyes on Daodu who in turn continues to look at the Secretary, in half-mockery. From inside, the music rises.]

DAODU: Don't you like the music any more? They're saying—

> Your eyes were bathed
> In tender waters
> Milk of all mothers
> Flowed through your fingers
> At your hour of birth

And they say of her skin, it is a flash of 'agbadu'[1] through the
sun and into cool shadows. Of her nipples, palm nuts, red
flesh and black shadows, and violent as thorns.

SECRETARY: I can remember her. If I tried hard. But my brain is
all addled.

DAODU: A coiled snake
                     Is beautiful asleep
                     A velvet bolster
                     Laid on flowers

                     If the snake would
                     Welcome me, I do not wish
                     A softer pillow than
                     This lady's breasts

                     But do not fool with one
                     Whose bosom ripples
                     As a python coiled
                     In wait for rabbits.

SECRETARY [*shuts his eyes tightly and holds his head.*]: I know I can
remember. Isn't she the same one of whom they warn
                     Do not stay by the sea
                     At night
                     Mammy Watta frolics by the sea
                     At night
                     Do not play
                     With the Daughter of the sea. . . .
It's picking at my mind but it just will not surface.

DAODU: She is still, but only as
                     The still heart of a storm.
                     Segi, turn on me eyes
                     That were bathed in tender seas
                     And tender springs

[*The Secretary's face becomes clear suddenly, he opens his eyes,
stares hard at Segi.*]

DAODU: Your eyes are
                     Cowrie shells, their cups
                     Have held much brine

1. Black, glistening snake.

It rained
Beads of grace
That hour of your birth

But it fell
From baleful skies.

SECRETARY: I am never wrong. I know now who she is. And the rest of them. Why are they here? Is this another vigil?

DAODU: For the condemned, yes. Not for Kongi.

SECRETARY: I am not really frightened. Yours is a strangely cheerful vigil.

DAODU: We are a cheerful lot. Moreover [looks at his watch.] we are expecting news.

SECRETARY: I came here with a proposal.

DAODU: Which you haven't made.

SECRETARY: If she is who I'm sure now she is, this should interest her.

DAODU: Shall I call her over?

SECRETARY: No. You can tell her afterwards—if you wish.

DAODU: Well? The proposal.

SECRETARY: Five men are awaiting execution.

DAODU: We know that.

SECRETARY: They will be reprieved—if your uncle co-operates. Think about it—I'll be back.

[Flees, looking nervously back.]

[Kongi's Retreat.]
[The Aweri are dozing. Kongi descends from his cell.]

KONGI: I can't hear voices.

SECRETARY: I think they are meditating.

KONGI: Meditating is my province. They are here to hold disputations.

[He looks over the partition.]

That is no meditation. They are fast asleep!

SECRETARY [joins him at the screen.]: You're right. They are sleeping.

KONGI: They are always sleeping. What is the matter with them?

SECRETARY: I heard one or two of them mention hunger.

KONGI: Hunger? They are fed daily aren't they? I see to their food
    myself.

SECRETARY: I think they haven't got used to the diet.

KONGI: Damn their greedy guts. I eat nothing at all.

SECRETARY: Not everyone can be a Kongi.

KONGI: Strike the gong and wake them up.

    [*Secretary strikes the gong, there is no response.*]

SECRETARY: They are practically dead.

KONGI: Dead? How dead? I don't remember condemning any of
    them to death. Or maybe I should?

SECRETARY: You still need them Leader.

KONGI: But they are sleeping.

SECRETARY: Let me try again.

    [*Strikes the gong.*]
    I think they are really out. They've been overworking their
    brains I think.

KONGI: Overwork? Nonsense. They do nothing but quarrel
    among themselves. Every time I set them a subject for
    disputation they quarrel like women and then fall asleep.
    What do they find to quarrel about?

SECRETARY: Philosophy can be a violent subject.

KONGI: You think so? I wonder sometimes. You should have seen
    them during the writing of my last book. I couldn't think for
    the squabbles.

SECRETARY: Oh that must have been plain jealousy.

KONGI: Jealousy? Of whom are they jealous?

SECRETARY: Of one another, my Leader. You shouldn't give your
    books to only one person to write.

KONGI: Really? But he's the best disputant of the lot. I like his
    style. You shall hear the Harvest speech he's prepared for me.
    Four and a half hours—no joke eh?

SECRETARY: Well, it causes dissension. At least let one of the
    others select the title or write the footnotes.

KONGI [*pleased no end.*]: Dear, dear, I had no idea they were so
    jealous. Very disturbing. I like harmony you realize. But I
    never seem to find it. And among my philosophers especially,
    there must be perfect harmony.

SECRETARY: Then write more books. Write enough to go round
    all of them.

KONGI: Oh, would that be wise? It wouldn't do to become too prolific you know. I wouldn't want to be mistaken for a full-time author.

SECRETARY: Your duty to the country, and to the world demands far more works from you than you produce at present. Moreover, it will make your theoreticians happy.

KONGI: Hm. I think I'll trust your judgement. Tell them they can begin work on my next book as soon as the new one is released.

SECRETARY: Who is to write it my Leader?

KONGI: Let them toss for it.

[*Kongi's chant swells louder.*]

SECRETARY: Can you hear them my Leader?

KONGI: What?

SECRETARY: Your Carpenters' Brigade. They have been keeping vigil with you at the foot of the mountain.

KONGI: An inspired creation of mine don't you think?

SECRETARY: They would lay down their lives for you.

KONGI: I trust no one. They will be in attendance tomorrow?

SECRETARY: Need you ask that?

KONGI: They complement my sleepy Aweris here. These ones look after my intellectual needs, the Brigade take care of the occasional physical requirements.

SECRETARY: They will not be needed tomorrow.

KONGI: Just the same, let them stand by. Nothing must disturb the harmony of the occasion . . . ah, I like that song.

SECRETARY: It is an invocation to the Spirit of Harvest to lend you strength.

KONGI [*violently.*]: I *am* the Spirit of Harvest.

[*The Aweri stir.*]

SECRETARY: S-sh. They are waking up.

KONGI [*alarmed, looks round wildly.*]: Who? The people?

[*Recovers slowly, angrily begins to climb the steps leading to his cell. Secretary follows him, appeasing.*]

KONGI: I *am* the Spirit of Harvest.

SECRETARY: Of course my Leader, the matter is not in dispute.

KONGI: I am the SPIRIT of Harvest.

SECRETARY: Of course my Leader.

KONGI: I am the Spirit of HAAR-VEST!

SECRETARY: Of course my Leader. And a benevolent Spirit of Harvest. This year shall be known as the year of Kongi's Harvest. Everything shall date from it.

KONGI [*stops suddenly.*]: Who thought that up?

SECRETARY: It is among the surprise gifts we have planned for our beloved Leader. I shouldn't have let it slip out. . . .

KONGI [*rapt in the idea.*]: You mean, things like 200 K.H.

SECRETARY: A.H. my Leader. After the Harvest. In a thousand years, one thousand A.H. And last year shall be referred to as 1 B.H. There will only be the one Harvest worth remembering.

KONGI: No, K.H. is less ambiguous. The year of Kongi's Harvest. Then for the purpose of back-dating, B.K.H. Before Kongi's Harvest. No reason why we should conform to the habit of two initials only. You lack imagination.

SECRETARY: It shall be as you please my Leader.

KONGI: Now you see why it is all the more important that everything goes forward tomorrow as I wish it? I want the entire nation to subscribe to it. Wake up those hogs!

SECRETARY: It isn't necessary my Leader. I think the little problem of Danlola is nearly solved.

KONGI: Another of your ideas?

SECRETARY: Leave it all to me. I er . . . oh yes, I ought to mention one other matter. I . . . have reason to believe that a press photographer might find his way into your retreat in spite of all our precautions for your privacy.

[*Enter photographer.*]

KONGI: Oh dear, you know I wouldn't like that at all.

[*He strikes a pose of anguish, camera clicks.*]

SECRETARY: In fact we think we know who it is. A foreign journalist, one of the best. He plans to leak it to a chain of foreign newspapers under the caption—Last Day of Meditation; A Leader's Anguish! I have seen some of his work, the work of a genius. He has photographed at least nine heads of state.

KONGI: I wouldn't like it at all.

SECRETARY: If we catch him we shall expel him at once.

KONGI: No, after the Harvest.

SECRETARY: Of course after the Harvest. The Leader's place of meditation should be sancrosanct.

[*Kongi moves to an opening, and poses his best profile.*]

KONGI: Twilight gives the best effect—of course I speak as an amateur.

[*Click.*]

SECRETARY: But you are right. I have noticed its mystical aura in the mountains. I think our man is bound to come at twilight.

KONGI: I don't like being photographed.

SECRETARY: I'll ensure it never happens again.

KONGI: Take care of it and let me hear no more on the subject. Some of these journalists are remarkably enterprising. Nothing you do can stop them.

[*Returns to his table and goes through a series of 'Last Supper' poses—'iyan' (pounded yam) serving variation—while the photographer takes picture after picture.*]

SECRETARY: Yes my Leader.

KONGI: Then go and look after everything. . . . What's the matter? Is there anything else?

SECRETARY: Only the question of amnesty my Leader.

KONGI: Oh, I leave that to you. Release all those who have served their court sentences.

SECRETARY: Too trivial a gesture my Leader. Too trivial for one who holds the power of life and death.

KONGI [*suddenly wary.*]: What do you have in mind exactly?

SECRETARY: The men awaiting execution.

KONGI: I thought so. Who put you up to it.

SECRETARY: Another of my ideas.

KONGI: I like the ones that went before. But not this one.

SECRETARY: It's all part of one and same harmonious idea my Leader. A Leader's Temptation . . . Agony on the Mountains . . . The Loneliness of the Pure . . . The Uneasy Head . . . A Saint at Twilight . . . The Spirit of the Harvest . . . The Face of Benevolence . . . The Giver of Life . . . who knows how many other titles will accompany such pictures round the world. And then my Leader, this is the Year of Kongi's Harvest! The Presiding Spirit as a life-giving spirit—we could project that image into every heart and head, no matter how stubborn.

[*As the Secretary calls each shot, Kongi poses it and the photographer shoots, bows, and departs.*]

KONGI: But those men . . .

SECRETARY: A life-giving Spirit of Harvest, by restoring life, increasing the man-power for the Five-Year Development Plan . . . I could do anything with that image.

KONGI: Hm.

SECRETARY: Such a gesture would even break the back of the opposition. A contemptuous gift of life would prove that their menace is not worth your punishment.

KONGI: Tell you what. You get all the leaders of the dissident groups to appear on the dais with me tomorrow—all of them, and at their head, that wretched king himself and his entire court, bearing the New Yam in his hands. Right? You get him to do that. Him at the head of all the opposing factions. Well? Is there anything else?

SECRETARY: But my Leader, you haven't completed the message.

KONGI: What more do you want? I say I want a total, absolute submission—in full view of the people.

SECRETARY: And of the world press—haven't I promised it my Leader?

KONGI: Then get on with it. There isn't much time left you know.

SECRETARY: But the reprieve. You said nothing of that.

KONGI: Didn't I? Oh, all right. Tell your Danlola I'll reprieve those men if he co-operates fully. Now go.

SECRETARY: Leader, my magnanimous Leader!

KONGI: But look here, we must make it a last-minute reprieve. It will look better that way don't you think? Kongi's act of clemency remains a confidential decision until a quarter of an hour before the hanging—no, five minutes. That's enough of a safety margin isn't it? It had better be!

SECRETARY: It will do my Leader.

KONGI: So keep it under until then. Now go.

[Secretary runs off. Kongi stands for a moment, sunk in a new pose, thoughtful. Seizes the iron bar suddenly and strikes the gong. Strides among the startled Aweri.]

KONGI: Dispute me whether it is politic to grant reprieves to the five men awaiting execution. And DISPUTE you hear! I shall go and meditate upon it.

[Segi's Club.]

SECRETARY: Well?

DAODU: This is a certainty?

SECRETARY: I have Kongi's word. Now I want your uncle's word that he will co-operate with us.

DAODU: I shall obtain it. On those conditions, he cannot refuse me.

SECRETARY: And no one need lose face over it.

[*He is once more expansive, calls for beer.*]

Who really cares for the Festival of New Yam anyway? It is all a matter of face. The struggle began, involved others, and no one dared give ground for the very stink of face. But I have devised a clean solution.

DAODU: The New Yam for the lives of five men. It's a generous bargain.

SECRETARY: Four men. One is dead, hanged himself by the belt. Heard about it on my way here. Publicly, we shall give it out that, as part of the Harvest amnesty, the government has been pleased to release Oba Danlola and a few others, then, as a gesture of reciprocity—the exact words of my official release— as a gesture of reciprocity—the Oba will voluntarily surrender the first yam.

DAODU: The enactment of it alone should appeal to him. Kabiyesi loves to act roles. Like kingship. For him, kingship is a role.

SECRETARY: Now where did I hear that before? Seems I heard it . . . that's right. Now that's funny isn't it? One of the Aweri said exactly the same thing of Kongi. 'A flair for gestures' he said.

DAODU: Maybe that's why they hate each other's guts.

SECRETARY: Professional jealousy eh? Ha, ha, couldn't agree with you more. Well then I'll take Kongi, and you deal with your uncle. I can count on you?

DAODU: As an ally. I shall see him tonight—you will make the arrangements?

SECRETARY: Go and see him now; you'll be admitted. Let him know that the lives of four men hang on his decision.

DAODU: He won't refuse me.

SECRETARY: I must go now. I have to tell Kongi all is well.

DAODU: I thought he was meditating in the mountains.

SECRETARY: I am allowed to go up and see him—on urgent state matters of course.

DAODU: Of course.

[*Secretary goes, looks round, looks off into the club.*]

SECRETARY: Where are those fools gone? [*To a waiter.*] You. Call me those two creatures I came in with.

[*The waiter, a couple of layabouts move as if to cut off his retreat, quietly menacing.*]

DAODU: I think they are gone.

SECRETARY: Gone? Where? I didn't see them leave.

DAODU: They shouldn't have come here.

SECRETARY: As servants of the State they can go anywhere. Anywhere!

DAODU: Too many people remember them. They shouldn't have come here.

SECRETARY [*looks round fearfully.*]: What are you trying to say? I thought we were allies.

DAODU: So we are. I have promised you my uncle's public submission.

SECRETARY: What happened to my Ears of State?

DAODU: You forget. I'm only a farmer. I don't run this place.

SECRETARY: Well who does?

DAODU [*points*]: Over there. Ask her.

[*Secretary stares at her, experiencing fear. Segi rises, comes forward slowly.*]

SECRETARY: You witch! What have you done to them?

DAODU: This is Segi. Once she said to herself, this man's lust, I'll smother it with my beauty.

SECRETARY: Lust?

DAODU: For power.

SEGI: Surely you must know me.

SECRETARY: Kongi's mystery woman. You couldn't be anybody else.

SEGI: Why did you come here?

SECRETARY: A mistake. Just call me the Ears of State and I'll leave.

SEGI: They have already left.

SECRETARY: When? Why?

DAODU: They left with Segi's friends.

SECRETARY [*sits down, dog-tired.*]: Oh! yes, it's all clear now. Your father . . . one of the condemned men.

SEGI: You understand.

SECRETARY: I suppose this means, I am also your prisoner?

DAODU: No, ally.

SECRETARY: In that case . . . I don't wish to remain here.

DAODU: I'll see you out.

[*The layabouts look questioningly at Segi who engages in a silent duel with Daodu. Daodu firmly takes the Secretary by the arm and moves forward. The men make way. Segi is obviously angry, and turns away.*]

SECRETARY: Don't forget my mission.

DAODU: I won't. You understand, your men had to go with others—for safety. Naturally we were suspicious.

SECRETARY: No, no. I've been trying to get those men reprieved.

DAODU: I'll take your message to Oba Danlola.

SECRETARY: My . . . bargaining position is somewhat weaker. . . . When I left Kongi I had five lives. Then they told me one had hanged himself. And now . . . I suppose by now her father has escaped?

DAODU: An hour ago.

SECRETARY: That leaves me only three.

DAODU: It's enough to bargain with, for a New Yam.

SECRETARY: I'm glad you think so. I'll see you at the feast.

[*He slouches off, a heavy pathetic figure. Daodu turns to meet Segi, smiles to break her anger.*]

DAODU: My eyes of rain, Queen of the Harvest night.

SEGI [*slowly relenting, half ashamed.*]: I was so afraid.

DAODU: There is nothing more to fear.

SEGI: I will never be afraid again.

DAODU: Two less for Kongi's grim collection. I am glad the live one is your father.

SEGI: I feel like dancing naked. If I could again believe I would say it was a sign from heaven.

DAODU: Yes, if I were awaiting a sign, this would be it. It may turn me supersitious yet.

SEGI: I want to dance on gbegbe leaves I know now I have not been forgotten.

DAODU: I'll rub your skin in camwood, you'll be flames at the hide of night.

SEGI: Come with me Daodu.

DAODU: Now? There is still much to do before you meet us at the gates.

SEGI: Come through the gates tonight. Now. I want you in me, my Spirit of Harvest.

DAODU: Don't tempt me so hard. I am swollen like prize yam under earth, but all harvest must await its season.

SEGI: There is no season for seeds bursting.

DAODU: My eyes of kernels, I have much preparation to make.

SEGI: I shall help you.

DAODU: Segi, between now and tomorrow's eve, I must somehow obtain some rest.

SEGI: Let me tire you a little more.

DAODU: You cannot know how weary I am. . . . A child could sneeze me off my legs with a little pepper.

SEGI: I must rejoice, and you with me. I am opened tonight. I am soil from the final rains.

DAODU: Promise you won't keep me long. I still have to meet my troublesome king.

SEGI: Only a bit, of your Ismite.

DAODU: Only a bite?

SEGI: Only a mite.

DAODU: Oh Segi! I had thought tonight at least, I would keep my head. [*Enter two women, bearing an unfinished robe.*]

SEGI: Ah, you must try this on before we go. It isn't finished yet but it will be ready for you tomorrow.

DAODU: This!

SEGI: They'll work on it all night if necessary.

DAODU: I didn't mean that, but . . . must I really wear this?

SEGI: Stand still!

[*They drape the robe round him.*]

DAODU: In the name of everything, what am I supposed to be?

SEGI: The Spirit of Harvest.

DAODU: I feel like the prince of orgies, I feel like some decadent deity.

SEGI: Well, that's the idea.

DAODU: Can't something simpler do?

SEGI: No. Now stand still. Be solemn for a moment.

[*She comes round, surveys him. Suddenly she kneels and clings to the hem of his robes. The other women kneel too.*]

My prince . . . my prince . . .

DAODU: Let me preach hatred Segi. If I preached hatred I could match his barren marathon, hour for hour, torrent for torrent . . .

SEGI: Preach life Daodu, only life . . .

DAODU: Imprecations then, curses on all inventors of agonies, on all Messiahs of pain and false burdens . . .

SEGI: Only life is worth preaching my prince.

DAODU [*with mounting passion*]: On all who fashion chains, on farmers of terror, on builders of walls, on all who guard against the night but breed darkness by day, on all whose feet are heavy and yet stand upon the world . . .

SEGI: Life . . . life . . .

DAODU: On all who see, not with the eyes of the dead, but with eyes of Death. . . .

SEGI: Life then. It needs a sermon on life . . . love . . .

DAODU [*with violent anger.*]: Love? Love? You who gave love, how were you requited?

SEGI [*rises.*]: My eyes were open to what I did. Kongi *was* a great man, and I loved him.

DAODU: What will I say then? What can one say on life against the batteries and the microphones and the insistence of one indefatigable madman? What is there strong enough about just living and loving? What!

SEGI: It will be enough that you erect a pulpit against him, even for one moment.

DAODU [*resignedly.*]: I hate to be a mere antithesis to your Messiah of Pain.

[*Segi begins to disrobe him. The women go off with the garment.*]

[*The song in the background comes up more clearly—a dirge.*]

DAODU: Do they all know where they may be tomorrow, by this time?

SEGI: You shouldn't worry about my women. They accepted it long ago.

DAODU: My men also. They have waited a long time for this.

SEGI: This, the last night is mine by right. Ours.

DAODU: Ours. Suddenly I have lost my tiredness. First let me go and speak with my awkward king, then I'll come back to you. [*Going.*]

SEGI: Shall I stop the wake—since there is to be a reprieve?

DAODU: No, let it continue. I find grief sharpens my appetite for living.

SEGI: And loving? Come back quickly Daodu, I'll be waiting.
[*Daodu goes off; the dirge rises. All lights come on for the next scene. There is no break.*]

[*Kongi's retreat.*]
[*Kongi, shaking with anger, the Secretary cowering before him.*]

KONGI: Escaped?

SECRETARY: Not from my camp my Leader. It wasn't from my camp.

KONGI: Escaped? Escaped?

SECRETARY: Only one sir. The other hanged himself.

KONGI: I want him back. I want him back you hear?

SECRETARY: He shall be caught my Leader.

KONGI: I want him back—alive if possible. If not, ANY OTHER WAY! But I want him back!

SECRETARY: It shall be done at once my Leader.

KONGI: Get out! GO AND BRING HIM BACK!
[*Secretary turns to escape.*]
And hear this! The amnesty is OFF! The reprieve is OFF! The others hang tomorrow.

SECRETARY: My Leader, your promise!

KONGI: No Amnesty! No Reprieve! Hang every one of them! Hang them!

SECRETARY: Your promise my Leader. The word of Kongi!

KONGI: And find me the other one for hanging—GET OUT! GET OUT! GET . . . AH . . . AH . . . AH . . .
[*His mouth hanging open, from gasps into spasms and violent convulsions, Kongi goes into an epileptic fit. Over his struggle for breath rises Kongi's chant.*]

SECOND PART

Oba Danlola's palace. Plenty of bustle and activity as if a great preparation were in progress. Danlola is trying out one thing, rejecting it and trying on another.

DANLOLA: Oh, what a home-coming this is!
    I obtained much better service
    In the detention camp.
DENDE: But you did order a sceptre Kabiyesi.
DANLOLA: Do you dare call this a sceptre?
    This dung-stained goat prod, this
    Makeshift sign at crossroads, this
    Thighbone of the crow that died
    Of rickets? Or did you merely
    Steal the warped backscratcher
    Of your hunchback uncle?
DENDE: I got no co-operation at all
    From the blacksmith. It was the best
    I found in the blacksmith's foundry.
DANLOLA: Some soup-pot foundry. Find me
    Such another ladle and I'll
    Shove it up your mother's fundaments.
DAODU [*storms in. Stops short as he sees signs of activity.*]: I was told
    you would not take part in today's procession.
DANLOLA: The ostrich also sports plumes but
    I've yet to see that wise bird
    Leave the ground.
DAODU: But all this preparation . . .
DANLOLA: When the dog hides a bone does he not
    Throw up sand? A little dust in the eye
    Of His Immortality will not deceive
    His clever Organizing Secretary. We need to
    Bury him in shovelfuls.
    [*Re-enter Dende.*]
    You horse manure! Is this a trip

To gather mangoes for the hawker's tray?
Tell me, did I ask for a basket fit
To support your father's goitre? I thought
I specially designed a copper salver.

DENDE: The smith had done nothing at all
About it.

DANLOLA: The smith! The smith! All I hear
Is of some furnace blower called
The smith!

DAODU [*sharply, to Dende.*]: Send for the smith.

DANLOLA: I have more important preparations
Than to break wind with the smith.
Take that thing right back to where
It was aborted from, and tell him
I want my copper salver.

DENDE: Copper, Kabiyesi?

DANLOLA: Copper yes. Copper the colour of earth
In harvest. Do you think I'll serve the first
Of our New Yam in anything but copper?

DAODU: Since you don't intend to be present anyway, why all
this energy?

DANLOLA: The Big Ear of the Man Himself
Has knocked twice on my palace gates—
Twice in one morning—and his spies
Have sneaked in through the broken wall
Of my backyard, where women throw their piss
As many times today.

DAODU: And why does he suspect you?

DANLOLA: I have, dear son, a reputation for
Falling ill on these state occasions.
And, to tell the truth, they make me
Ill. So my friends the Eyes and Ears
Of State set prying fingers to sieve
My chamber pot, diagnose my health,
And analyse every gesture.

DAODU: Isn't it much simpler to go? After all you did promise . . .

DANLOLA: I promised nothing that I will not
Fulfil.

DAODU: You gave your word.

DANLOLA: Indeed I gave my word and if you like
 I swear again to exhaust your eyes and ears
 With that word undergoing fulfilment.
DAODU: You should go. It's a small thing to sacrifice—
 I thought we agreed on that and you gave your word.
DANLOLA: You should, my son, when you deal in politics
 Pay sharp attention to the word. I agreed
 Only that I would prepare myself
 For the grand ceremony, not
 That I would go. Hence this bee hum fit
 For the world's ruling heads jammed
 In annual congress. When my servants
 Are later questioned, they'll bear witness
 How I set the royal craftsmen slaving
 At such short notice to make me ready
 To present the New Yam to my Leader.
DAODU: How do you expect him—them—to take your absence?
DANLOLA: As an act of God. Perhaps I'll be
 Smitten with a heart attack from
 My loyal efforts. Or it could be
 The Oracle forbade me budging from
 My chamber walls today. As the Man
 Himself has often screamed, we are
 A backward superstitious lot, immune
 To Kongi's adult education schemes.
DAODU: I should have believed it. I was warned you might go
 back on your word.
DANLOLA: Now where could you have picked that up?
 In those dives of 'tombo' where you pass
 The hours of sleep?
DAODU: I see it's not Kongi's men alone who have an efficient spy
 system.
DANLOLA: For us, even the dead lend their eyes
 And ears, as do also the unborn.
DAODU: But you find something wrong with the eyes of the
 living?
DANLOLA: They are the eyes of fear. But tell me,
 How is the woman?
DAODU: Who?

DANLOLA: Who? Are you playing lawyer to
    Oba Danlola, the Ears of wind on dry
    Maize leaves? I asked, how fares
    The woman whose eyes unblinking as
    The eyes of the dead have made you drunk?

DAODU: I don't know what woman you mean.

DANLOLA [*bursts suddenly into laughter.*]:
    They say you can always tell the top
    By the way it dances. If anyone had doubts
    Whose son you are, you've proved you are
    No bastard. A-ah, you have picked yourself
    A right cannibal of the female species.

DAODU: I think I'll go on to watch the procession. . . .

DANLOLA: Stay where you are! Tell me, do you
    Know that woman's history? I have myself
    Wandered round some dens of Esu, once,
    And clambered over sweet hillocks
    In the dark, and not missed my way. But
    Daodu, that woman of yours, she scares
    The pepper right up the nostrils
    Of your old man here. She has left victims
    On her path like sugar cane pulp
    Squeezed dry.

DAODU: Men know nothing of Segi. They only sing songs about
    her.

DANLOLA: Much better not to know, believe your father.
    Oh you have chosen to be swallowed whole
    Down the oyster throat of the witch
    Of night clubs. Segi! Son, she'll shave
    Your skull and lubricate it in oil.
    [*Enter Dende.*]

DENDE: Kabiyesi . . . about the er—your royal canopy.

DANLOLA: Well—is it ready at last?

DENDE: No sir. Er—it seems
    The snake-skins have all been used up.

DANLOLA: Then use the one you moulted
    Yesterday, you single-gut
    Hunter of toads!
    [*Enter Secretary.*]

Ah, you were surely
Summoned by my head. You see yourself
How the courtesan is one hour escalating
Her brocade head-tie, and the devil-wind
Whisks it out of sight just when the sun
Has joined to make it dazzle men.

SECRETARY: Kabiyesi, what is the matter?

DANLOLA: The matter? The things they bring me
Anyone would think I was headed
For a pauper's funeral.

SECRETARY: But you will be late. The things you have on you
will do just as well.

DANLOLA: What! These trimmings may serve
A wayward lunatic, but my friend,
We must meet the Leader as
A conquering hero, not welcome him
Like some corner-corner son-in-law.

DENDE [enters.]: Perhaps you would prefer this Kabiyesi.
It belonged to my great
Grandfather on my mother's side. . . .

DANLOLA: Oh, what a joy you must have been
To your great progenitors until
They died of overjoy! The Leader
Visits us today—is that not enough?
Must I ask him also to make a sword
Of state, fit to grace his presence?

SECRETARY: All this is quite unnecessary Kabiyesi. We appreciate
your zeal and I assure you it will not go unmentioned. But it is
your presence our Leader requires. . . .

DANLOLA: You wish to make me a laughing-stock?

SECRETARY: You know how we deal with those who dare make
fun of the Leader's favoured men.

DANLOLA: Then, my dear son-in-politics, this being
The only way in which our dignity
May be retained without the risk
Of conflict with the new authority,
Let us be seen in public only as
Befits our state. Not to add the fact
That this is Harvest. An Oba must emerge

In sun colours as a laden altar.

SECRETARY: Kabiyesi, I don't suggest for a moment that . . .

DANLOLA: I know we are the masquerade without
Flesh or spirit substance, but we can
Afford the best silk on our government
Pension. Now you! Tell the smith he must
Produce the sword I ordered specially.

DENDE: He says that would require at least . . .

DANLOLA: Enough, enough, I'll use this as it is.
Get a new cover on it, some tit-bit
Of leather—and don't tell me you have
No left-over scraps enough to hide
A rusty scabbard. I know your pumice
Stomach can digest it. Move!
A-ah, my good Organizing Secretary of
His Immortality our Kongi, you see
What agonies these simple ceremonies
Demand of us?

SECRETARY: You really haven't that much time you know. It
would be simpler . . .

DANLOLA: You haven't met my heir have you?
Lately returned from everywhere and still
Trying to find his feet. Not surprisingly.
It must be hard to find one's feet in such
Thin arrowheads. Daodu, before you
Flaps the Big Ear of his Immortality.
Make friends with him. Your decaying
Father is most deeply in his debt.
In these trying times, it is good to know
The Big Ear of his government.

SECRETARY Your uncle is a most difficult man.

DANLOLA: Difficult? Me difficult? Why should
A father be difficult and obstruct
His children's progress? No, I have told you
Listen less to those who carry tales
From sheer envy.

SECRETARY: [to Daodu.]: What is he up to?
[Danlola pricks up his ears.]

DAODU: I'm not sure. I am still feeling the ground.

DANLOLA: You'll feel the ground until
    It gives way under you. What
    I ask you, is there to feel?
    Oh, never mind, I suppose it gives
    You children pleasure to pretend
    There are new cunnings left for
    The world to discover . . . Dende!

DENDE [runs in.]: Kabiyesi.

DANLOLA: Dende, do you realize you keep
    A whole nation waiting?

DENDE: Kabiyesi, you asked me to stuff
    The crown with cotton.

DANLOLA: Ah, so I did. Age has shrunk
    The tortoise and the shell is full
    Of air pockets. My head
    Now dances in my crown like a cola-nut
    In the pouch of an ikori cap.
    Well, why do you stand there? Waiting
    Still for the cotton fall of the next
    Harmattan?
    [Dende runs off.]

SECRETARY: Couldn't you manage it at all? We are really
    short of time.

DANLOLA: Manage it? Will there not be six times
    At the least when we must up and bow
    To Kongi? These are no bones
    To rush an old man after a crown
    That falls off his head and rolls
    Into a gutter.
    [Royal drums heard in distance.]

SECRETARY: I will have to leave you. The other Obas are already
    arriving. Someone has to be there to group each entourage in
    their place.

DANLOLA: You must hurry or the confusion
    Will be worse than shoes before the
    Praying-ground at Greater Beiram.

SECRETARY: Kabiyesi, please follow quickly. It will make my
    task easier if I can get all the Obas settled before our Leader
    arrives.

[*Enter Dende.*]

DANLOLA: No, not that one! Is that a crown
    To wear on such a day?

DENDE: But I took it from . . .

DANLOLA: The same dunghill you use for pillow!

DENDE: But Kabiyesi, this is your favourite
    Crown. It belonged to Kadiri, the great
    Ancestor warrior of your lineage.

DANLOLA: Who rests in peace we pray. And now
    My pious wish is—burn it! Burn it
    With firewood from the dessicated trunk
    Of your family tree.

SECRETARY [*stares, speechless and turns in desperation to Daodu.*]:
    Are you coming to the square?

DAODU: Oh I don't really know.

DANLOLA: He never really knows, that thoughtful
    Son of mine. Go with the man. If anyone
    Can conjure you a seat close to the Great
    Visitor himself, he can.

SECRETARY: Yes, I was going to suggest that. Why don't you
    come now? I'm sure I can squeeze you in somewhere.

DAODU: In a minute.

SECRETARY: Good. Kabiyesi, we shall expect you.
    [*He goes.*]

DANLOLA: And I, you. But here, within
    My audience chambers. I have done enough
    Of this play-acting.
    [*Begins leisurely to remove his trappings. Drums, bugles, etc.
    announce the approach of Oba Sarumi and retinue. Dende rushes in.*]

DENDE: Kabiyesi, Oba Sarumi is at the palace gates.

DANLOLA: Let him enter. I suppose he wants
    Our four feet to dance together
    To the meeting-place.

PRAISE-SINGER [*leads in, singing.*]:
            E ma gun' yan Oba kere o
            E ma gun' yan Oba kere
    [*Enter Sarumi, prostrates himself.*]

DANLOLA: Get up, get up man. An Oba Grade I
    By the grace of Chieftancy Succession

Legislation Section II, nineteen-twenty-one
Demands of you, not this lizard posture
But a mere governmental bow—from
The waist, if you still have one.

SARUMI [*joining the singer.*]:
              E ma gun'yan Oba kere o
              E ma gun'yan Oba kere
              Kaun elepini o se e gbe mi
              Eweyo noin ni i fi yo'nu
              Ema gun'yan Oba kere

DANLOLA: Go and tell that to the Leader's men.
    Their yam is pounded, not with the pestle
    But with stamp and a pad of violet ink
    And their arms make omelet of
    Stubborn heads, via police truncheons.

SARUMI: Oba ni f'itan ebo ha'yin
              Orisa l'oba

DANLOLA: At least get up from that position
    Sit down and go easy on my eyes.
    I can't look down without my glasses.

SARUMI [*rises, still singing.*]:
              Oba ni f'epo inu ebo r'awuje
              Orisa l'oba.

DANLOLA: Orisa l'oba? Hadn't you better see
    The new 'orisa' in the market square
    Before you earn yourself a lock-up
    For reactionary statements.

SARUMI: Kabiyesi, your voice was the dawn pigeon
    Which summoned us from drowsy mats
    We do not know the jackal's call
    We do not hear the bonded overseer
    When the father speaks.

DANLOLA: Wise birdlings learn to separate
    The pigeon's cooing from the shrill alarm
    When Ogun stalks the forests.

SARUMI: The boldest hunter knows when
    The gun must be unspiked. When a squirrel
    Seeks sanctuary up the iroko tree
    The hunter's chase is ended. . . .

In Oba Danlola's place his sons
Speak out their minds. [*Dances.*]

PRAISE-SINGER: Ogun o l'oun o j'oba
                 Ogun o l'oun o j'oba
                 Jeje l'Ogun se jeje
                 T'ijoye gb'ade Ire wa ba baba ode o
                 Ogun o l'oun o j'oba

DANLOLA: You'll be more at home performing
At the Festival of Traditional Arts.

SARUMI: Ma binu si mi Oba. . . .

DANLOLA: Look, if you want to please me, dip
in your regal pouch and find me
Some cola-nut. Playing a clown's part
For the Eye and Ear of His Immortality
Has turned my blood to water. I need
The stain of cola to revive
Its royal stain.

SARUMI [*gives him cola.*]:
                 Orogbo ebo, awuje Oba. . . .

DANLOLA: Don't tell me this is cola-nut
From a wayside bowl! Dende!

DENDE [*rushes in.*]: Kabiyesi.

DANLOLA: Bring the schnapps. Esu alone knows
Where this cola-nut was picked. Not that
It matters. The schnapps should take
Good care of sacrificial germs. I suppose
After all your exercise, some schnapps
Would come in handy too.
[*Sarumi's dance grows positively ecstatic, Daodu remains
intensely frustrated but undecided.*]

SARUMI: Ma ma binu si mi Oba
                 B'esumare se binu si'takun
                 To ta kete, to ta kete
                 To ran'ri s'agbede meji orun

                 Ma binu si mi Oba
                 Bi Sango se binu s'araiye.
                 To di pe manamana ni fi i
                 Mba omo enia soro

Ma binu si mi Oba
B'iwin ope se binu s'elemu
To re alangba lu'le
Bi eni ha kuruna l'ori

[*Danlola begins slowly to glow, to expand, to be visibly affected by the praise-singing.*]

Oba o se e te
Bi eni te r'awe
B'ajanaku o rora rin
A t'egun mole
A d'atiro tiro tiro
Oba o se e gbon
Bi eni gbon t'akun
Igbon oba, awon eru
Ogbon oba, iwon eru
Esin to r'ebo ti o sare
Tin nta felefele
Enu alantakun ni o bo.

[*Danlola, totally swelled, steps down from his throne and falls in step with Sarumi. The two Obas cavort round the chamber in sedate, regal steps and the bugles blast a steady refrain. Danlola's wives emerge and join in; the atmosphere is full of the ecstasy of the dance. At its height Daodu moves with sudden decision, pulls out the ceremonial whisk of Danlola and hits the lead drum with the heavy handle. It bursts. There is a dead silence. Danlola and Daodu face each other in a long, terrible silence.*]

SARUMI [*in a horrified whisper*]: Efun!

DANLOLA [*shakes his head slowly*]:
No. Your son has his senses
Intact. He must know what he is doing.

SARUMI: Efun! Efun! Someone has done this to him. Some
enemy has put a curse on my first-born.

DANLOLA [*climbing back to his throne, wearily.*]:
Life gets more final every day. That prison
Superintendent merely lay his hands
On my lead drummer, and stopped
The singing, but you our son and heir
You've seen to the song itself.

DAODU: Kabiyesi . . .

DANLOLA: It is a long long time my limbs
 Rejoiced that way. I swear a snake
 Ran wildly through my veins and left
 Its moulting in my train. . . . A-ah
 Matters will go hard upon
 A royal favourite tonight. I feel
 Life resurrected within me and I
 Shall resurrect my dance on softer springing
 Than this dung-baked floor. In fact
 To confess the truth, I doubt
 If matters can await the dark.
 Call me that Dende.

DAODU: I only want a few words. . . .

DANLOLA: I know the drums were silenced long
 Before you, but you have split
 The gut of our make-believe. Suddenly
 The world has run amok and left you
 Alone and sane behind.

DAODU: In that case, you know I have a reason.

DANLOLA: And I do not choose to hear it.
 When the next-in-line claps his hand
 Over a monarch's mouth, it is time
 For him to take to the final sleep
 Or take to drink and women.

DAODU: It is vital that you hand the Leader what he wants. I
 cannot explain it now. Time is short and we have much to do.
 But I must have your word that you will play your part.

DANLOLA: Make my excuses to him—my son-in-politics
 Will help you. Tell His Immortality
 I sprained my back rehearsing dances
 In honour of his visit. He loves to see
 His Obas prancing to amuse him after all
 And excess zeal should be a credit.

DAODU: I have no thoughts of Kongi. This matter concerns us,
 your children. Don't ask me to say more—I cannot now. I
 dare not. Kabiyesi, this is no time for trivialities. We shall
 all have our dance tonight, when it matters, and I promise you
 the event will make its own amends.

DANLOLA: I wish you luck. Dende!

Where on earth is that fool!
I am not young like you, and these
Sudden surges must be canalized.
Who knows? There may be another son
From this, if so, rest assured
I'll name him after you—to mark
This morning's work.

DAODU: You swore to me. Early this morning you swore to me.

DANLOLA [*with sudden unexpected anger*.]:
And so, you child, did Kongi.
Did he not promise a reprieve
For the condemned men, in return
For the final act of my humiliation?
Well, did he not?

DAODU: Yes, and I know our man will remind him of it.

DANLOLA: Then perhaps you have not heard
What the wooden box announced
As I returned to palace. Such a welcoming
I've never known. Did not one
Of the dying enemies of Kongi
Seize suddenly on life by jumping
Through the prison walls?

DAODU: I heard about it.

DANLOLA: And the radio has put out a price
Upon his head. A life pension
For his body, dead or alive. That
Dear child, is a new way to grant
Reprieves. Alive, the radio blared,
If possible; and if not—DEAD!
I didn't say it, the radio did
In my primitive youth, that would be called
A plain incitement to murder.

DAODU: It means nothing. Nothing can alter what today will
bring. And your compliance is a vital part of it.

DANLOLA: My vital part shall exhaust itself
In my favourite's bed. Call me Wuraola.
Go hand Kongi the New Yam yourself
But count me out.

SARUMI: Kabiyesi, age is nectar

    May the royal household ever
    Savour its blessings.

DANLOLA: Take your son with you,
    Prepare him for my crown and beads
    This king is done.

SARUMI: Kabiyesi, live long, reign long and peaceful. Our line
    does not seek this kind of succession which bears a silent curse.
    I know my son has something for old ears like ours. You have
    to listen.

DANLOLA: Out of my way.

DAODU [*desperately*.]: The woman you warned me about, Segi, the
    witch of night clubs as you labelled her, is the daughter of this
    man who has escaped. And she wants the Harvest to go on as
    we all planned, as much as I.
    [*Danlola turns slowly round.*]

DANLOLA: Is this the truth about that woman?

DAODU: The truth.

DANLOLA [*hesitates and a far-seeing look comes into his eyes.*]:
    There was always something more, I knew,
    To that strange woman beyond
    Her power to turn grown men to infants.
    [*He looks long and kindly at Daodu, then incredulous.*]
    And this woman, you say
    Her father is already free, and yet
    She wants the Harvest to be held
    As . . . planned?

DAODU: She does.

DANLOLA: And what harvest do you children
    Mean to give the world?

DAODU: Kabiyesi, is it not you elders who say . . . ?

DANLOLA: The eyes of divination never close
    But whoever boasts Ifa greeted him
    With open lips . . . well, so be it. Sarumi,
    It seems our son will make us mere
    Spectators at our own feast. But
    Who are we to complain? Dada knows
    He cannot wrestle, will he then preach restraint
    To his eager brother?

SARUMI: Kabiyesi!

DANLOLA: Well, I will not bear the offering
    Past the entrance to the mosque
    Only a phoney drapes himself in deeper indigo
    Than the son of the deceased.
SARUMI [*with gratitude.*]: Kabiyesi!
DANLOLA: Dende!

    [*He sweeps out, the others hurrying after him.*]
    [*Immediately the big parade drum is heard with its One-Two,
    One-Two-Three, penny whistles blow to the tune of the Carpenters'
    Song and the Carpenters' Brigade march in, uniformed, heavy
    mallets swinging from their waists. They clear the stage and reset it
    for the harvest scene—decorated dais, buntings, flags, etc. On a huge
    cyclorama which completely dominates the stage, pictures are
    projected of various buildings, factories, dams, etc., all clearly titled
    Kongi Terminus, Kongi University, Kongi Dam, Kongi Refineries,
    Kongi Airport, etc. Finally, of course, a monster photo of the great
    man himself. They sing their anthem as they work, and form and
    execute a couple of parade movements to the last verse or two.*]

        We are the nation's carpenters
        We build for Isma land
        From the forests of Kuramba
        They bring the timber wild
        And we saw and plane and tame the wood
        To bring the grains to light
        Converting raw material
        To 'Made in Ismaland'.

        Men of peace and honour
        Are the Carpenters' Brigade
        But primed for fight or action
        To defend our motherland
        We spread the creed of Kongism
        To every son and daughter
        And heads too slow to learn it
        Will feel our mallets' weight.

        Though rough and ready workers
        Our hearts are solid gold
        To beat last year's production

Is our target every year
We're total teetotallers
Except on local brew
For it's guts of toughened leather
That survive on Isma gin.

Our hands are like sandpaper
Our fingernails are chipped
Our lungs are filled with sawdust
But our anthem still we sing
We sweat in honest labour
From sunrise unto dawn
For the dignity of labour
And the progress of our land.

For Kongi is our father
And Kongi is our man
Kongi is our mother
Kongi is our man
And Kongi is our Saviour
Redeemer, prince of power
For Isma and for Kongi
We're proud to live or die!

[*The carpenters end with a march downstage with stiff mallet-wielding arms pistoning up in the Nazi salute. Dende, also in uniform, is seen among them trying gamely to keep in step. Enter the Secretary declaiming as he enters.*]

SECRETARY: Kongi comes! And with his carpenters
Spitting fire on his enemies.
Comrades, our not-so-comrade comrades
Have their bottoms ready greased
For singeing, and do not know it. . . .
Hey . . . that is one new face, a very
Mouse among wildcats. Come here.
You seem at once familiar and yet
Completely out of place.

CAPTAIN: A new recruit. Newly defected
From the reactionary camp. You there!
Fall out!

SECRETARY: We must beware of spies.

CAPTAIN: I've put him through the standard tests.
    He's no fifth columnist.

SECRETARY: Your name?

DENDE: Dende.

SECRETARY: The name is even more familiar.
    Who was your last employer?

CAPTAIN: The king himself. Our mortal enemy.

SECRETARY: What!

CAPTAIN: A triumph for the cause sir.
    It should be good for seven weeks
    Of propaganda.

SECRETARY: Hm. That, I'll admit, is one way
    Of viewing the matter. But look here
    A joke is a joke; is he combat worthy?

CAPTAIN: Not as a fighter sir. But, as we are
    Somewhat short on the muscle side—
    The celebrations started a little early
    For some carpenters, and that vigil
    Beneath Kongi's hill of meditation proved
    A disaster, a most debilitating
    Orgy. Even these must nibble cola-nuts
    To keep awake. So I thought, maybe
    We could use him for odd jobs
    And errands. I admit he is
    A sorry looking crow, but at least
    He swells the ranks.

SECRETARY: Well, I shall be on hand to assume
    Full command, if it proves necessary.
    I warn you, this is Kongi's day.
    I've organized towards it for the past
    Twelve months. If anything goes wrong
    He'll have my head, but first I'll scrape
    Your heads clean with your chisels
    Without using lather.

CAPTAIN: I will die for Kongi!

SECRETARY: Let us hope that will not
    Prove necessary. I'd better take this runt
    With me. If any need arises, he will rush

My orders back and forth. Now once again
Bear it in mind—this is my last
Organizing job before retirement
And I wish to retire to my village
Not to a detention camp. Is that clear?

CAPTAIN: We will die for Kongi!

SECRETARY: After my retirement. Now listen
All of you. Far be it from me to sun
My emblems in the square, but merit . . .

DENDE: Is like pregnancy, never seen
But makes its proclamation.

SECRETARY: Well, well, well, the wonder actually
Boasts a voice. Tell me, why did you
Desert the palace? Were you bored
With swapping saws with that disgusting
Lecher?

CAPTAIN: We went parading past the palace—
Just to show the flag you know—
Suddenly there he was doggedly
Marching behind the ranks.
I shooed him off but he swore
He was resolved to be a carpenter.
[*They all burst out laughing.*]

CAPTAIN: Silence! 'Tention! As you were!

DENDE: I like the uniform, I asked Kabiyesi
To make me a uniform but he refused.
[*Again they fall to laughing.*]

CAPTAIN: Silence! 'Tention! The representative
Of our commander-in-chief, the Organizing
Secretary, the Right Hand of Kongi
Our beloved Leader, will now address
The Carpenters' Brigade.

SECRETARY: Comrades, as I began to say, far be it
For me to sun my emblems but I am not
Without experience in the planning
Of moves and strategies on occasions
Such as this. And while it is true
That certain rules of strategy exist
In the manual of the Carpenters' Brigade

Yet is it the mark of genius when
A Field Marshal makes his own. The simplest
Part, you'll be surprised, is
The strategic disposition of your men
As laid down in your book of fundamentals
A man is either born to such basic
Know-how, or he should change his trade.
Even this warrior's progeny here
Can juggle men—what say you sir?

DENDE: Politicians, Kabiyesi used to say,
Are as the seeds in a game of 'ayo'
When it comes to juggling.

SECRETARY: The boy approaches genius.

DENDE: Wise partymen must learn the cunning
To crab and feint, to regroup and then
Disband like hornets.

SECRETARY: I should have come to the same
Training school as you. Now tell me,
What are the realities of conflict
As propounded by your royal sage?

DENDE: First, always outnumber the enemy.

SECRETARY: The man is a profound realist.

DENDE: And when outnumbered, run!

CAPTAIN: A fifth columnist, I knew it!
He's here to demoralize the carpenters.

SECRETARY: Nonsense. Athletics is a noble
Exercise. No need to be ashamed
Or coy about it.

CAPTAIN: This is disgraceful.

SECRETARY: Nothing of the sort. You are privileged
To learn today the ultimate realities
Of war. As your Strategist and Field Marshal
For this occasion, it shall be my duty
To instruct you when events demand
Its application. Come, you lion of Isma.
[*They cross to the other side. He speaks to a group offstage.*]
It's safe to enter now. The stalwarts
Have taken up position.
[*Enter the Aweri. They take their places on the dais. Secretary goes off.*]

THIRD: Your speech is too short.

FOURTH: What are you talking about? It runs to four hours and a half.

THIRD: Then you didn't listen to the news. The President over the border has just spoken for seven. And you know he fancies himself something of a rival to Kongi.

FOURTH: Disaster!

THIRD: Kongi won't like it at all. Can't you scribble something?

FOURTH: Impossible.

THIRD: He won't like it at all.

FOURTH: All right, all right. Don't keep on about it.

THIRD: But what are you going to do?

FOURTH: I'm dry. My brain is shrunk from hunger. I can't think.

THIRD: Add a diatribe on the condemned men.

FOURTH: It's down already. And I've run out of names to call them.

THIRD: Include an exposition on Kongi's reasons for withdrawing the reprieve.

FOURTH: It's all down in the President's prerogatives.

THIRD: Then you've really had it.

FOURTH: Unless . . . you say you listened to the news . . . anything about the one who escaped?

THIRD: He is still at large.

FOURTH: Then there is nothing I can add.

THIRD: I'm afraid not. [*With quiet malice.*] I'm afraid you've really had it.

[*Re-enter Secretary with Dende.*]

SECRETARY: Something is not quite right.
My Number Seven sense refuses
To be silenced. Look here batman
Runner, aide-de-camp, or whatever
You call yourself, go and find me
A vantage point for observation
And remember friend, I have to keep
The entire square under observation
So, select some point quite distant
And reasonably protected. I hope
Your legs are in good training,
My instructions may likely be

Fast and furious. Well, get going man
And remember, not too near. My hearing
And eyesight are in top condition
And anyway, there are enough loudspeakers
To deafen the dead . . . damn! another one
Of these brigades and organizations.
Where on earth do I fit them?
[*Approaching, a male group singing to the rhythm of cutlasses
scraping on hoes.*]
Which reminds me, where are the
Women's Auxiliary Corps? The job
Of cooking the New Yam is theirs.
Lateness means trouble. Captain! Captain!
Where is your women's wing? Have I
Gone blind or are there really no signs
Of cooking preparations?

CAPTAIN: They should have been here to cheer in
My men. We intend to lodge a vigorous
Complaint.

SECRETARY: To hell with that part of it.
I've warned you, if anything goes wrong . . .

CAPTAIN: I had no time to check on them.
I was busy reviving what remained
Of the carpenters.

SECRETARY [*his fingers desperately stuck in his ears.*]:
And who are those metallic lunatics?

DENDE: It sounds like men from Prince Daodu's
Farming settlement.

CAPTAIN: Show-offs, that's all they are
Bloody show-offs.

SECRETARY: That noise, just because they won
The New Yam competition. God, and that
Is one more black mark against
My performance today. I did my best
To rig the results in favour of
The state co-operatives, but that man
Anticipated every move. And then his yam!
Like a giant wrestler with legs
And forearms missing. If only I had

Thought of it in time, I would have
Disqualified him on the grounds
Of it being a most abnormal specimen.

CAPTAIN: Perhaps our women's wing have stayed away
In protest.

SECRETARY: Make one more suggestion like that
And I'll dress you and your carpenters
In women's clothes, and make you do
The cooking.

CAPTAIN: No, no, please . . . they are sure to come.
I could send someone to hurry them
If you . . .

SECRETARY: Don't get nervous. I'd have a harder time
Explaining why your carpenters
Were not on hand. You stick to your job.
Remember, your job is to guard the yam
Every bit of the way. We don't want
Some fatal spice slipped into it do we?

CAPTAIN: We will die for Kongi.

SECRETARY: Good. You have just volunteered
To act as taster. I shall come personally
And supervise the tasting—after the yam
Is cooked, and after it is pounded.
[*The Captain's jaw drops.*]
Cheer up. Nothing is likely
To be tried. But it is just the idea
Of revenge which might occur
To our good friends the old Aweri.
So, keep good watch. You, run and stop
Daodu's yokels at the gate. I cannot
Let them in here—security reasons.
Only state approved institutions
May enter Kongi Square. Mind you
They may appoint a delegate, someone
To bring in the winning yam—only one!
[*Dende runs off.*]
I hope Daodu comes himself, at least
He can act civilized.
[*Royal drums and bugles. Enter Danlola, Sarumi, the old Aweri, and*

retinue. Secretary rushes to group them.]
Kabiyesi! I had begun to rack my brain
For some excuse I hadn't used before
To explain your absence.

DANLOLA: I have only come to see our son dance.

SECRETARY: Dance? Daodu? Does that one dance?
I know he shuffles about in that club
Of Segi's, but don't tell me he will
Actually perform in honour of Kongi.

DANLOLA: I do not know in whose honour
Daodu intends to dance or make others dance
But he bade us to the feast saying
Come see a new Harvest jig, so,
Here we are.

SARUMI: Our sons tell us we've grown too old
To dance to Kongi's tunes. We've come
To see them do better.

SECRETARY: I know his farm won the competition,
But as for dancing. . . . I mean, his men
Are not even permitted here. So how . . . ?

DANLOLA: The bridegroom does not strain his neck
To see a bride bound anyway for his
Bedchamber. So let you and I wait
Like the patient bridegroom.

SECRETARY: Well, well, wonders will never end.
Winning that prize has really turned
Your prince's head . . . oh, I trust . . . I mean
About the other matter, our agreement
Still stands? You will present the yam?

DANLOLA: If the young sapling bends, the old twig
If it resists the wind, can only break.

SECRETARY: You are not angry that the amnesty
Has been revoked? My ancestors will
Bear witness—I did my best.

DANLOLA: It's a foolish elder who becomes
A creditor, since he must wait until
The other world, or outlive his debtors.

SECRETARY: Live long Kabiyesi, we only await
Our women, and then the ceremony

Can begin at last.

[*Enter the women, singing, led by Segi who carries Daodu's cloak.
They dance onto the stage bearing mortar and pestle, cooking
utensils, a cloth-beating unit, etc. They throw up their arms in
derision and mock appeal to the world in general singing—*]

                    Won ma tun gb'omiran de o
                    Kongi ni o je'yan oba.

[*They curtsey to the seated Obas, perform a brief insulting gesture as
they dance past the Reformed Aweri. The Secretary has stood
speechless at the sight of Segi, now recovers himself sufficiently to
approach her. Segi signals to the women to stop.*]

SECRETARY: What do you want here? You should not even
     Dream of coming here.

SEGI: But I belong to the Women's Corps.

SECRETARY [*frantic.*]: Since when? I do not remember you
     Being remotely rehabilitated.

SEGI [*waving at the women.*]: Are all these approved people?

SECRETARY: Yes. They are all in the Women's Corps.

SEGI: They appointed me their leader. By a normal
     Democratic process.

SECRETARY: Captain! Get your men to veto
     The appointment.

SEGI: They also voted to ally with Daodu's Farm Settlement.
     We have deserted the carpenters.

SECRETARY: Aha. There you have overreached
     Yourself. You cannot do that unless
     By express dispensation of Kongi.

SEGI: Yes, but nothing can be done about that until after the
     Harvest, is there? We can seek approval—later—if it is still
     necessary.

SECRETARY [*goes near, near-pleading.*]: Woman what are you
     planning to do?

SEGI: Nothing. We heard Daodu and his men would dance for
     Kongi and we came to second his steps.

SECRETARY: Will you all stop saying that!
     What of a sudden is all this concern
     With Daodu's jitterbug. For one thing
     It is not on the official programme.

SEGI: His New Yam won . . .

SECRETARY: The competition—yes! yes! We all know it.
    But so what? Is that enough excuse
    To turn my pageant into a Farmers' Cabaret?
SEGI: Have the farmers come?
SECRETARY: Yes, but I stopped them at the gate
    Which is exactly where they will
    Be left until the very end.
SEGI: I know. At the gate is where we promised
    We would welcome them.
    [*To the women.*] Let's go.
    Daodu may come in of course? He won . . .
SECRETARY: Yes, he won, he won! Segi, I beg of you
    Don't ruin twelve months of preparation. . . .
    [*The women resume their song, dance out, leaving behind a handful
    of them to attend to cooking preparations. Two women begin a steady
    rhythm with the cloth-beaters, giving Daodu's cloak a final sheen for
    the big occasion.*]
    What can I do? He is entitled
    To make a speech, and if like the Obas
    He chooses to dance for Kongi
    What is wrong in that? I only hope
    It doesn't get out of hand, what with Segi's
    Wild women abetting him.
CAPTAIN: Let him make a fool of himself.
SECRETARY [*slumping down wearily.*]:
    Oh I don't know, I don't know at all.
    Daodu is a cultured man. I had half-hoped
    For some illiterate farm clod who would
    Mumble the usual slogans and take
    His farm stench off as fast as I chose
    To cry 'Shoo'. But these new educated
    Rascals! He's bound to show off and annoy
    Somebody, or else make some ideological
    Blunder, and then I get the blame.
    [*Re-enter the women singing the same song and bearing Daodu aloft.
    Others carry the farming implements which they have taken from
    Daodu's men and use them to supply a noisy rhythm. Daodu carries
    the winning yam above the triumphal entry. They set him down, Segi
    takes the cloak from the women and fits it around his shoulders.*]

SEGI: It is my turn to ask—you are not afraid?

DAODU: No. After all, only a little speech. Nothing need come of it.

SEGI: It seems suddenly futile, putting one's head into the lion's jaws.

DAODU: Nothing may come of it.

SEGI: Nothing may come of it and then you will do something else, and that will be more final.

DAODU: Then pray that something does come of it.

SEGI: It is wrong to feel so selfish, but now that my father has escaped, I wish this plan was never made.

DAODU: I did not work for this merely for your father, Segi. At least, so I tell myself.

SEGI: I know. Forgive me.

DAODU: All I fear is that I won't be allowed to finish what I have to say.

SEGI: You will have enough time. They all have husbands, sons and brothers rotting in forgotten places. When they form a tight ring about you, only death will break it.

SECRETARY [coming forward.]:
I might have known it. I never saw
A man make christmas over such a trifle
As the prize for a monster yam.

DAODU: It is a monster yam, it grew from Kongi's soil.

SECRETARY: Make your speech snappy, that's all
I ask of you. Five minutes at the most
Just be happy and honoured and all that
Stuff, and remember to feel proud to be
A son of Isma. If you exceed five minutes
It will be my duty to cut you off.
Captain stand by, here comes our Leader!

SECRETARY: Now! Ismite . . .

BRIGADE: Is Might!

SECRETARY: Ismite . . .

BRIGADE: Is Might!

SECRETARY: Ismite . . .

BRIGADE: Is Might . . .

SECRETARY: Now—One—Two—Three.

[An orchestra strikes up the national anthem. They all rise. Enter
Kongi, he stands under the flag until the end of the tune and is then

fussily led to his seat by the Secretary. Kongi selects his pose and remains fixed in it throughout.]

[*The Secretary signals frantically to Daodu to begin his presentation speech and to make it snappy. Daodu fastidiously adjusts his robe, takes out a small piece of paper.*]

SECRETARY: Well, it looks like a short speech anyway, so that's not the danger. [*Looks round nervously, sweating profusely.*] So where is it? Something is bound to go wrong. Something always goes wrong.

[*The women form a ring around Daodu with their pestles. Secretary stares in disbelief, especially at their hard, determined faces.*]

I don't think I'll bother to find out. Dende, take me to that observation post. Something tells me this is the moment to start supervising from a distance.

[*Half-runs off, dragging Dende along.*]

DAODU [*looking straight at Kongi.*]:

An impotent man will swear he feels the pangs of labour; when the maniac finally looks over the wall, he finds that there, agony is the raw commodity which he has spent lives to invent. [*Stretches out his arms suddenly, full length.*] Where I have chosen to return in joy, only fools still insist that my fate must be to suffer.

[*The tightness with which he has spoken thus far breaks into laughter; his arms come down.*]

This trip, I have elected to sample the joys of life, not its sorrows, to feast on the pounded yam, not on the rind of yam, to drink the wine myself, not leave it to my ministers for frugal sacraments, to love the women, not merely wash their feet at the well. In pursuit of which, let this yam, upon which I spent a fortune in fertilizers and in experiments with a multitude of strains, let it be taken out, peeled, cooked, and pounded, let bitter-leaf soup simmer in the women's pots and smoked fish release the goodness of the seas; that the Reformed Aweri Fraternity may belch soundly instead of merely salivating, that we may hereby repudiate all Prophets of Agony, unless it be recognized that pain may be endured only in the pursuit of ending pain and fighting terror.

[*Handing over the yam to Danlola.*]

DAODU: So let him, the Jesus of Isma, let him, who has assumed
the mantle of a Messiah, accept from my farming settlement
this gift of soil and remember that a human life once buried
cannot, like this yam, sprout anew. Let him take from the
palm only its wine and not crucify lives upon it.

[*Kongi has remained rapt in his pose.*]

DANLOLA: I don't think he heard a thing.

DAODU: Don't let that worry you. In a few more moments he will
be woken up. And then it will be too late.

DANLOLA [*Looks up sharply, apprehensive, turns slowly round to look
at Kongi, shrugs.*]:

As you wish.

[*Followed by the old Aweri, Danlola bears the New Yam to Kongi.
Kongi places his hands over it in benediction and in that moment
there is a burst of gun-fire which paralyses everyone. Kongi looks
wildly round for some means of protection. The Secretary rushes in a
moment later, obviously shaken. Hesitates, looking at Segi especially
but drawn dutifully to Kongi. He goes up to him and whispers in his
ear. Kongi relaxes gradually, swells with triumph. He begins to
chuckle, from a low key his laughter mounts, louder and more
maniacal. His eye fixed on Segi as a confident spider at a fly, he
breaks off suddenly, snaps an urgent instruction to the Secretary.
The man hesitates but Kongi insists, never taking his eye off Segi.
The Secretary slowly approaches her.*]

SECRETARY: I wish you'd kept out of sight. Why did you have to
let Kongi see you?

SEGI: I wanted him to. Anyway what is it?

SECRETARY: I would have waited but he says I'm to tell you at
once. Your father . . . oh Segi what were you people
planning for God's sake. What was he doing here?

SEGI: Go on. Have they caught him?

SECRETARY: Didn't you hear the shots?

DAODU: Oh God!

SEGI: He's dead?

SECRETARY [*nods.*]: What was he trying? Why was he here?
Doesn't anyone know it's never any use.

SEGI: Go away.

SECRETARY: But why did he have to come back? Why didn't he
just keep running, why?

DAODU: He's watching. He's watching.

SEGI: Let him watch. He shan't see me break.

DAODU: You mean to continue?

SEGI: Yes, let it all end tonight. I am tired of being the mouse in his cat-and-mouse game.

SECRETARY: I'm done for, I know it. I'm heading for the border while there is time. Oh there is going to be such a clamp-down after this. . . .

SEGI: Where have they taken him?

SECRETARY: In a schoolroom just across the square.

SEGI: I'll be back directly. Daodu. Let everything go on as planned.

DAODU: Such as what? After what has happened, what?

SEGI: So he came back? Why didn't you tell me?

DAODU: I could do nothing to stop him. When he heard that the reprieve had been withdrawn . . . there was simply nothing I could do. He said he had to do it and no one else.

SEGI: It doesn't matter.

DAODU: We've failed again Segi.

SEGI: No, not altogether.

DAODU: What else can one do now?

SEGI: The season is Harvest, so let there be plenty of everything. The best and the richest. Let us see only what earth has fattened, not what has withered within it.

DAODU: What are you talking about? What do I do now?

SEGI: Sing, damn him, sing! Let none of our people know what has happened. Is it not time for Kongi's speech?

SECRETARY: Yes, he'll begin any moment. He's very much awake now.

DAODU: There should have been no speech. We failed again.

SEGI: Then forget he is there. Let the yam be pounded. I shall return soon with a season's gift for the Leader.

[*The women relieve Oba Danlola of the yam, take it away as Kongi rises slowly, triumphant.*]

KONGI: The Spirit of Harvest has smitten the enemies of Kongi. The justice of earth has prevailed over traitors and conspirators. There is divine blessing on the second Five-Year Development Plan. The spirit of resurgence is cleansed in the blood of the nation's enemies, my enemies, the enemies of our collective spirit, the Spirit of Planting, the Spirit of Harvest, the

Spirit of Inevitable History and Victory, all of which I am.
Kongi is every Ismite, and Ismite . . . [*shoots out a clenched fist.*]
BRIGADE: Is Might. . . .
[*They beat on their drums and clash cymbals deafeningly.*]
KONGI: Ismite . . .
BRIGADE: Is Might. . . .
SEGI: Now.
[*It is the signal for the feast to begin. A real feast, a genuine Harvest orgy of food and drink that permits no spectators, only celebrants. The dancing, the singing are only part of it, the centre is the heart and stomach of a good feast.*]

> Ijo mo ko w'aiye o
> Ipasan ni.
> Ijo mo ko w'aiye o
> Ipasan ni
> Igi lehin were o
> Kunmo lehin were o
> Aiye akowa
> Ade egun ni o
> Aiye akowa
> Ade egun ni o
> Iso lo g'aka m'ogi
> Iso lo g'aka m'ogi
>
> Mo ti d'ade egun
> Pere gungun maja gungun pere
> Mo ti d'ade egun
> Pere gungun maja gungun pere
> Omije osa
> Pere gungun maja gungun pere
> Won tu'to pami
> Pere gungun maja gungun pere
> Kelebe adete
> Pere gungun maja gungun pere
> Mo gbe'gi k'ari
> Pere gungun maja gungun pere
> Mo g'oke abuke
> Pere gungun maja gungun pere
> Isu o won n'ile o

Isu o won n'ile o
Won gb'ori akobi le le
Won fi gun'yan
Igi o won n'ile e
Igi o won n'ile e
Egun itan akobi o
No won fi da'na

Adeyin wa o
Igba ikore ni
Aiye erinkeji
Iyan ni mo wa je
Aiye ti mo tun wa
Iyan ni mo waje
Iyan yi kari
　Ire a kari
Iyan yi kari
　Ayo a b'ori
Etu l'ara mi
　Ire akari
Aiya ni mo wa fe
　Ayo a b'ori
Aiye erin ni mo wa
　Ayo a b'ori
Emu ni mo wa mu
　Ire a kari
Ata ni mo wa ya
　Ayo a bori
Aiye eso eso
　Eso ni baba
　Eso ni baba

[*The rhythm of pounding emerges triumphant, the dance grows frenzied. Above it all on the dais, Kongi, getting progressively inspired harangues his audience in words drowned in the bacchanal. He exhorts, declaims, reviles, cajoles, damns, curses, vilifies, excommunicates, execrates until he is a demonic mass of sweat and foam at the lips.*

Segi returns, disappears into the area of pestles. A copper salver is raised suddenly high; it passes from hands to hands above the

*women's heads; they dance with it on their heads; it is thrown
from one to the other until at last it reaches Kongi's table and
Segi throws open the lid.*

In it, the head of an old man.

*In the ensuing scramble, no one is left but Kongi and the head,
Kongi's mouth wide open in speechless terror.*

A sudden blackout on both.]

HANGOVER

Again Kongi Square. It is near dawn. The square is littered with the debris and the panic of last night's feast. Enter Secretary, a bundle over his shoulder, dragging his tired body by the feet. Sitting seemingly lost beside the road, Dende; the Secretary does not immediately recognize him.

SECRETARY: Good friend, how far is it
    To the border? What! Well, well,
    If it isn't my bold lion of Isma.
    And what, may I ask, happened to
    The Carpenters' Brigade? Did they
    Receive my last instructions?
    Not that there was anything of a genuine
    Battle, if you get my meaning; nonetheless
    It was time to apply
    The ultimate reality of war—
    For their own sakes mind you—
    I hope you made that very plain
    To them. I know the ropes.
    To be there at all at that disgraceful
    Exhibition is to be guilty of treasonable
    Conspiracy et cetera, et cetera.
DENDE: There was no one to take my message
    They had all anticipated
    Your instructions.
SECRETARY: They lack discipline. A good soldier
    Awaits starter's orders. And you?
    What's happened to your Boy Scout movement
    I thought I ordered you to remove
    Your carcass far from the scene of crime.
DENDE: I don't know where to go.
SECRETARY: If you don't find somewhere soon
    There are those who might assist you.
    And their hospitality believe me,
    Is not to be recommended. I say,

Is your problem by any chance
Shortage of funds?

DENDE: Oh no, I spend nothing on myself and
I carry all my savings with me
Everywhere—as a precaution.
As Kabiyesi himself would say. . . .

SECRETARY: Oh? A quiet millionaire are you?
Turn out your pockets.

DENDE: My pockets? What for?

SECRETARY: Don't blow your lungs boy. When a man
Cannot even call briefly home to say
Good-bye to his native land, then hope
Remains his last luxury. Turn out
Your pockets. As your late commander
It is my duty to play censor
To your battle-kit. Come on, come on,
Let's see what keepsakes and
Protection charms you wear to war. . . .
Aha, what's this? You haven't been
Despoiling fallen warriors have you now?

DENDE: Those are rejected bits and pieces
From the things we made for the king
To take to harvest.

SECRETARY: I see . . . a kick-back artist eh?
And starting out so young. Hm,
You carry quite a few trinkets around
With you. Saving up for a bride-price
I bet. Well, well, myself I am partial
To silver, but I'll keep the copper bangle
Till your situation improves. Really,
You astonish me. A runner travels
Light, you are lucky you arrived
Unlooted from the battle front,
It seems there is one lesson of war
Your rogue king failed to teach you—Never
Carry your own ransom on your person—
Never!

[*Enter Danlola, furtively. He is also bundled with his emergency possessions.*]

DANLOLA: Ah my son-in-politics, is the Big Ear
    Of His Immortality still flapping high
    In Kongi's breath?
    [*Secretary quickly releases Dende, recovers from his astonishment at
    seeing Danlola.*]

SECRETARY: Kabiyesi, don't mock a ruined man.

DANLOLA: If you are headed in that direction,
    Then that way leads to the border.

SECRETARY: Do you suggest I am running away?

DANLOLA: Not I. Just the same, I'll be glad
    To keep you company. If any man exists
    Who wisely has prepared for such a day
    It would be you. . . . Oh ho, is that not my Dende?

SECRETARY: Hold nothing against him. Few half-wits
    Can resist a uniform.

DANLOLA: I hope he proved useful.

SECRETARY: The man is a philosopher. We have
    Exchanged many areas of wisdom. Right now
    He is my travelling companion.

DANLOLA: I don't see that you have anything
    To fear. After all, no one could
    Predict that surprise gift. The show
    Was well organized, I mean, until that
    Sudden business, all went well.

SECRETARY: I hope I shall live long enough
    To make good use of your testimonial.
    Went well! That is quite a mouthful!

DANLOLA: But it did go well. Well, as a hurricane
    Blows well. As a bush-fire on dry
    Corn stalks burns well, and with a fine
    Crackle of northern wind behind it.
    As a mat dances well when the man
    Is full of peppers and, with the last
    Guest departed, leaps upon
    The trembling bride. As I ran well
    When I took a final look at Kongi
    And began a rapid dialogue with my legs.

SECRETARY: And me. I never thought I had so much
    Motion between my legs.

DANLOLA: The others? What did the others do?

SECRETARY: I was by then too far away. Kabiyesi,
    It was no time to take notes for posterity.

DANLOLA: What happens now? The hornets' nest
    Is truly stirred. What happens to
    The sleeping world?

SECRETARY [*sinking down*]: Oh I wish I was the mindless smile
    On the face of a contented sow. Of a fat
    Contented sow. Fat I am, and uncharitable
    Tongues have labelled me a sow. But
    Contented? That is one uneasy crown
    Which still eludes my willing head.
    [*Leaps up suddenly.*]
    What are we doing still sitting here?

DANLOLA: For now this is the safest spot to wait
    And Sarumi should join me soon—
    I hope. He's gone with some twelve toughs—
    All volunteers—from among
    Daodu's own farmers. If he's not already
    In Kongi's hands, they'll abduct him
    Forcibly and parcel him across the border.
    And that woman of his.

SECRETARY: He is mad. And that woman, they're both
    Roadside lunatics. Even away from here—
    Take my advice, have them restrained.

DANLOLA: The strange thing is, I think
    Myself I drank from the stream of madness
    For a little while.

SECRETARY [*looks up anxiously.*]:
    It's getting light.

DANLOLA: I'll go and hurry them. You will . . . wait?
    Don't leave us behind I beg of you.
    When Providence guides my feet to a man
    Of your resourcefulness, I know
    Our safety is assured.

SECRETARY: Not Providence, Kabiyesi, but provisions.
    I only paused to glean a few emergency
    Rations from our young philosopher.
    But you are wrong—this idea you have

Of travelling together, most imprudent.
An entourage like that would be suicidally
Conspicuous. Split, then meet once across
The border—that would be my strategy.

DANLOLA: Of course, of course. You see, never would I
Have thought of that.

SECRETARY: You'll learn Kabiyesi, you'll learn.
Survival turns the least adaptable of us
To night chameleons.

DANLOLA: Very true son. Well, I shall delay you
No further. I hope Sarumi has been delayed
By no worse than Daodu's stubbornness.

SECRETARY: Good luck sir. I shall precede you
On active service, non-stop until
I am safe beyond the frontier. Oh,
What of this failed carpenter? Shall I
Take him with me—that is, if you don't mind?

DANLOLA: Oh, let him be. He's bound to do much
As the wind directs him, and anyway,
He is in no danger. He may even join
Our Royal Household Cavalry—in exile—
If we can find him a uniform.

SECRETARY [undecided.]:
Oh, well . . . I was only thinking . . . I mean
I could use a . . . yes, he could sort of
Earn his keep carrying this load for me. . . .
No, he'd only be a nuisance. I'm off.
Better hurry yourself, obstreperous old lecher,
I would wish you a speedy restoration
And a long and happy reign, but it would sound
Like mockery. See you at the border.
[As he leaves, Danlola shakes his head in sad amusement.]

DANLOLA: Safe journey. If I know you
The frontier fence will lose its barbs
At one touch of your purse;
There is already less corruption
In the air, even though your rear
Is turned.
[He starts briskly back in the opposite direction. A mixture of the

royal music and the anthem rises loudly, plays for a short while, comes to an abrupt halt as the iron grating descends and hits the ground with a loud, final clang.]

BLACKOUT

THE END

109.

Don't pound the king's yam
In a small mortar
Small as the spice is
It cannot be swallowed whole
A shilling's vegetable must appease
A halfpenny spice.

The king is
He who chews on the haunch from an offering
The king is a god.

The king is
He who anoints the head's pulse centre
With the oil of sacrifice
The king is a god.

110.

Ogun did not seek the throne
Ogun did not seek the throne
Quietly retired, minding his own business
The nobles brought the crown of Ire
To the ancestor of all hunters
Ogun did not seek the throne

White nut from the offering
Pulse of the Oba's head

Be not angry my king with me
As the rainbow, full of wrath at the root
Drew away, pulled apart
And settled half-way to heaven

Be not angry my king with me

As Sango was angered by the people of earth
Till only with the language of lightning
Does he now hold converse with man

III.

Be not angry with me my king
As the palm ghommid, in anger at the wine-tapper
Plucked the lizard down to earth
As a man scratches scabs from his head.

The king is not for treading on
As a man steps on dried leaves
If the elephant does not warily step
He will tread on a thorn
And hobble like a pair of stilts

The king is not to be shaken off
As a man may brush off cobwebs
A king's beard is an awesome net
A king's wisdom is awesome measure
Whatever fly cuts a careless caper
Around the scent of sacrifice
Will worship down the spider's throat.

130—1.

At my first coming
Scourges all the way
At my first coming
Whips to my skin
Cudgels on the madman's back.

At my first coming
A crown of thorns
At my first coming
A crown of thorns
The foolhardy hedgehog
Was spreadeagled on nails.

I have borne the thorned crown
Shed tears as the sea
I was spat upon
A leper's spittle

A burden of logs
Climbed the hunchback hill
There was no dearth of yam
But the head of the firstborn
Was pounded for yam
There was no dearth of wood
Yet the thigh of the firstborn
Lost its bone for fuel.

Now this second coming
Is time for harvest
This second coming
Is for pounding of yams
The mortar spills over
Goodness abundant
My body is balm
I have come wife-seeking
I am borne on laughter
I have come palm wine thirsting
My rheum is from sweet peppers
Contentment is earth's
Ease for her portion
Peace is triumphant.

THE TRIALS
OF BROTHER JERO

Characters

JEROBOAM a Beach Divine
OLD PROPHET his mentor
CHUME assistant to Jeroboam
AMOPE his wife
A TRADER
MEMBER OF PARLIAMENT

PENITENT
NEIGHBOURS
WORSHIPPERS
A TOUGH MAMMA
A YOUNG GIRL

SCENE I

The stage is completely dark. A spotlight reveals the Prophet, a heavily but neatly bearded man; his hair is thick and high, but well-combed, unlike that of most prophets. Suave is the word for him. He carries a canvas pouch and a divine rod.[1] He speaks directly and with his accustomed loftiness to the audience.

JEROBOAM: I am a Prophet. A prophet by birth and by inclination. You have probably seen many of us on the streets, many with their own churches, many inland, many on the coast, many leading processions, many looking for processions to lead, many curing the deaf, many raising the dead. In fact, there are eggs and there are eggs. Same thing with prophets. I was born a Prophet. I think my parents found that I was born with rather thick and long hair. It was said to come right down to my eyes and down to my neck. For them, this was a certain sign that I was born a natural prophet.
And I grew to love the trade. It used to be a very respectable one in those days and competition was dignified. But in the last few years, the beach has become fashionable, and the struggle for land has turned the profession into a thing of ridicule. Some prophets I could name gained their present beaches by getting women penitents to shake their bosoms in spiritual ecstasy. This prejudiced the councillors who came to divide the beach among us.
Yes, it did come to the point where it became necessary for the Town Council to come to the beach and settle the Prophets' territorial warfare once and for all. My Master, the same one who brought me up in prophetic ways staked his claim and won a grant of land. . . . I helped him, with a campaign led by six dancing girls from the French territory, all dressed as Jehovah's Witnesses. What my old Master did not realize was that I was really helping myself.

1. A metal rod about eighteen inches long, tapered, bent into a ring at the thick end.

Mind you, the beach is hardly worth having these days. The worshippers have dwindled to a mere trickle and we really have to fight for every new convert. They all prefer High Life to the rhythm of celestial hymns. And television too is keeping our wealthier patrons at home. They used to come in the evening when they would not easily be recognized. Now they stay at home and watch television. However, my whole purpose in coming here is to show you one rather eventful day in my life, a day when I thought for a moment that the curse of my old Master was about to be fulfilled. It shook me quite a bit, but . . . the Lord protects his own . . .

[Enter Old Prophet shaking his fist.]

OLD PROPHET: Ungrateful wretch! Is this how you repay the long years of training I have given you? To drive me, your old Tutor, off my piece of land . . . telling me I have lived beyond my time. Ha! May you be rewarded in the same manner. May the Wheel come right round and find you just as helpless as you make me now. . . .

[He continues to mouth curses, but inaudibly.]

JEROBOAM [ignoring him.]: He didn't move me one bit. The old dodderer had been foolish enough to imagine that when I organized the campaign to acquire his land in competition with [ticking them off on his fingers]—The Brotherhood of Jehu, the Cherubims and Seraphims, the Sisters of Judgement Day, the Heavenly Cowboys, not to mention the Jehovah's Witnesses whom the French girls impersonated—well, he must have been pretty conceited to think that I did it all for him.

OLD PROPHET: Ingrate! Monster! I curse you with the curse of the Daughters of Discord. May they be your downfall. May the Daughters of Eve bring ruin down on your head!

[Old Prophet goes off, shaking his fist.]

JEROBOAM: Actually that was a very cheap curse. He knew very well that I had one weakness—women. Not my fault, mind you. You must admit that I am rather good-looking . . . no, don't be misled, I am not at all vain. Nevertheless, I decided to be on my guard. The call of Prophecy is in my blood and I would not risk my calling with the fickleness of women. So I kept away from them. I am still single and since that day when I came into my own, no scandal has ever touched my name. And it was a sad day indeed when I woke up one morning and the first thing to meet my eyes was a Daughter of Eve. You may compare that feeling with waking up and finding a vulture crouched on your bedpost.

BLACKOUT

SCENE II

Early morning.

A few poles with nets and other litter denote a fishing village. Downstage right is the corner of a hut, window on one side, door on the other.

A cycle bell is heard ringing. Seconds after, a cycle is ridden on stage towards the hut. The rider is a shortish man; his feet barely touch the pedals. On the cross-bar is a woman; the cross-bar itself is wound round with a mat, and on the carrier is a large travelling sack, with a woman's household stool hanging from a corner of it.

AMOPE: Stop here. Stop here. That's his house.
  [*The man applies the brakes too suddenly. The weight leans towards the woman's side, with the result that she props up the bicycle with her feet, rather jerkily. It is in fact no worse than any ordinary landing, but it is enough to bring out her sense of aggrievement.*]
AMOPE [*Her tone of martyrdom is easy, accustomed to use.*]: I suppose we all do our best, but after all these years one would think you could set me down a little more gently.
CHUME: You didn't give me much notice. I had to brake suddenly.
AMOPE: The way you complain—anybody who didn't see what happened would think you were the one who broke an ankle. [*She has already begun to limp.*]
CHUME: Don't tell me that was enough to break your ankle.
AMOPE: Break? You didn't hear me complain. You did your best,

but if my toes are to be broken one by one just because I have
to monkey on your bicycle, you must admit it's a tough life
for a woman.

CHUME: I did my . . .

AMOPE: Yes, you did your best. I know. Didn't I admit it?
Please . . . give me that stool . . . You know yourself that
I'm not one to make much of a little thing like that, but
I haven't been too well. If anyone knows that, it's you.
Thank you [*Taking the stool.*] . . . I haven't been well, that's
all, otherwise I wouldn't have said a thing.
[*She sits down near the door of the hut, sighing heavily, and begins
to nurse her feet.*]

CHUME: Do you want me to bandage it for you?

AMOPE: No, no. What for?
[*Chume hesitates, then begins to unload the bundle.*]

CHUME: You're sure you don't want me to take you back? If it
swells after I've gone . . .

AMOPE: I can look after myself. I've always done, and looked after
you too. Just help me unload the things and place them
against the wall . . . you know I wouldn't ask if it wasn't for
the ankle.
[*Chume had placed the bag next to her, thinking that was all. He
returns now to untie the bundle. Brings out a small brazier covered
with paper which is tied down, two small saucepans . . .*]

AMOPE: You haven't let the soup pour out, have you?

CHUME [*with some show of exasperation.*]: Do you see oil on the
wrapper? [*Throws down the wrapper.*]

AMOPE: Abuse me. All right, go on, begin to abuse me. You
know that all I asked was if the soup had poured away, and it
isn't as if that was something no one ever asked before. I
would do it all myself if it wasn't for my ankle—anyone
would think it was my fault . . . careful . . . careful now . . .
the cork nearly came off that bottle. You know how difficult it
is to get any clean water in this place . . .
[*Chume unloads two bottles filled with water, two little parcels
wrapped in paper, another tied in a knot, a box of matches, a piece of
yam, two tins, one probably an Ovaltine tin but containing something
else of course, a cheap breakable spoon, a knife, while Amope keeps
up her patient monologue, spoken almost with indifference.*]

AMOPE: Do, I beg you, take better care of that jar. . . . I know you didn't want to bring me, but it wasn't the fault of the jar, was it?

CHUME: Who said I didn't want to bring you?

AMOPE: You said it was too far away for you to bring me on your bicycle. . . . I suppose you really wanted me to walk. . . .

CHUME: I . . .

AMOPE: And after you'd broken my foot, the first thing you asked was if you should take me home. You were only too glad it happened . . . in fact if I wasn't the kind of person who would never think evil of anyone—even you—I would have said that you did it on purpose.

[*The unloading is over. Chume shakes out the bag.*]

AMOPE: Just leave the bag here. I can use it for a pillow.

CHUME: Is there anything else before I go?

AMOPE: You've forgotten the mat. I know it's not much, but I would like something to sleep on. There are women who sleep in beds of course, but I'm not complaining. They are just lucky with their husbands, and we can't all be lucky I suppose.

CHUME: You've got a bed at home.

[*He unties the mat which is wound round the cross-bar.*]

AMOPE: And so I'm to leave my work undone. My trade is to suffer because I have a bed at home? Thank God I am not the kind of woman who . . .

CHUME: I am nearly late for work.

AMOPE: I know you can't wait to get away. You only use your work as an excuse. A Chief Messenger in the Local Government Office—do you call that work? Your old school friends are now Ministers, riding in long cars . . .

[*Chume gets on his bike and flees. Amope shouts after him, craning her neck in his direction.*]

AMOPE: Don't forget to bring some more water when you're returning from work. [*She relapses and sighs heavily.*] He doesn't realize it is all for his own good. He's no worse than other men, but he won't make the effort to become something in life. A Chief Messenger. Am I to go to my grave as the wife of a Chief Messenger?

[*She is seated so that the Prophet does not immediately see her when he opens the window to breathe some fresh air. He stares straight out*

*for a few moments, then shuts his eyes tightly, clasps his hands
together above his chest, chin uplifted for a few moments'
meditation. He relaxes and is about to go in when he sees Amope's
back. He leans out to try to take in the rest of her but this proves
impossible. Puzzled, he leaves the window and goes round to the
door which is then seen to open about a foot and shut rapidly.
Amope is calmly chewing cola. As the door shuts she takes out a
notebook and a pencil and checks some figures.
Brother Jeroboam, known to his congregation as Brother Jero, is seen
again at the window, this time with his canvas pouch and divine
stick. He lowers the bag to the ground, eases one leg over the
window.*]

AMOPE [*without looking back.*]: Where do you think you're going?
[*Brother Jero practically flings himself back into the house.*]

AMOPE: One pound, eight shillings, and ninepence for three
months. And he calls himself a man of God.
[*She puts the notebook away, unwraps the brazier, and proceeds to
light it preparatory to getting breakfast.
The door opens another foot.*]

JERO [*Coughs.*]: Sister . . . my dear sister in Christ . . .

AMOPE: I hope you slept well, Brother Jero . . . .

JERO: Yes, thanks be to God. [*Hems and coughs.*] I—er—I hope you
have not come to stand in the way of Christ and his work.

AMOPE: If Christ doesn't stand in the way of me and my work.

JERO: Beware of pride, sister. That was a sinful way to talk.

AMOPE: Listen, you bearded debtor. You owe me one pound,
eight and nine. You promised you would pay me three
months ago but of course you have been too busy doing the
work of God. Well, let me tell you that you are not going
anywhere until you do a bit of my own work.

JERO: But the money is not in the house. I must get it from the
post office before I can pay you.

AMOPE [*fanning the brazier.*]: You'll have to think of something else
before you call me a fool.
[*Brother Jeroboam shuts the door.
A woman trader goes past with a deep calabash bowl on her head.*]

AMOPE: Ei, what are you selling?
[*The trader hesitates, decides to continue on her way.*]

AMOPE: Isn't it you I'm calling? What have you got there?

TRADER [*stops, without turning round.*]: Are you buying for trade or just for yourself?

AMOPE: It might help if you first told me what you have.

TRADER: Smoked fish.

AMOPE: Well, let's see it.

TRADER [*hesitates.*]: All right, help me to set it down. But I don't usually stop on the way.

AMOPE: Isn't it money you are going to the market for, and isn't it money I'm going to pay you?

TRADER [*as Amope gets up and unloads her.*]: Well, just remember it is early in the morning. Don't start me off wrong by haggling.

AMOPE: All right, all right. [*Looks at the fish.*] How much a dozen?

TRADER: One and three, and I'm not taking a penny less.

AMOPE: It is last week's, isn't it?

TRADER: I've told you, you're my first customer, so don't ruin my trade with the ill-luck of the morning.

AMOPE [*holding one up to her nose.*]: Well, it does smell a bit, doesn't it?

TRADER [*putting back the wrappings.*]: Maybe it is you who haven't had a bath for a week.

AMOPE: Yeh! All right, go on. Abuse me. Go on and abuse me when all I wanted was a few of your miserable fish. I deserve it for trying to be neighbourly with a cross-eyed wretch, pauper that you are . . .

TRADER: It is early in the morning. I am not going to let you infect my luck with your foul tongue by answering you back. And just you keep your cursed fingers from my goods because that is where you'll meet with the father of all devils if you don't.

[*She lifts the load to her head all by herself.*]

AMOPE: Yes, go on. Carry the burden of your crimes and take your beggar's rags out of my sight. . . .

TRADER: I leave you in the hands of your flatulent belly, you barren sinner. May you never do good in all your life.

AMOPE: You're cursing me now, are you?

[*She leaps up just in time to see Brother Jero escape through the window.*]

Help! Thief! Thief! You bearded rogue. Call yourself a prophet? But you'll find it easier to get out than to get in.

You'll find that out or my name isn't Amope. . . .

[*She turns on the trader who has already disappeared.*]

Do you see what you have done, you spindle-leg toad?
Receiver of stolen goods, just wait until the police catch up
with you . . .

[*Towards the end of this speech the sound of 'gangan' drums is
heard, coming from the side opposite the hut. A boy enters carrying a
drum on each shoulder. He walks towards her, drumming. She turns
almost at once.*]

AMOPE: Take yourself off, you dirty beggar. Do you think my
money is for the likes of you?

[*The boy flees, turns suddenly, and beats a parting abuse on the
drums.*]

AMOPE: I don't know what the world is coming to. A thief of a
Prophet, a swindler of a fish-seller and now that thing with lice
on his head comes begging for money. He and the Prophet
ought to get together with the fish-seller their mother.

LIGHTS FADE

SCENE III

*A short while later. The beach. A few stakes and palm leaves denote the
territory of Brother Jeroboam's church. To one side is a palm tree, and in the
centre is a heap of sand with assorted empty bottles, a small mirror, and
hanging from one of the bottles is a rosary and cross. Brother Jero is standing
as he was last seen when he made his escape—white flowing gown and a
very fine velvet cape, white also. Stands upright, divine rod in hand, while
the other caresses the velvet cape.*

JERO: I don't know how she found out my house. When I bought
the goods off her, she did not even ask any questions. My
calling was enough to guarantee payment. It is not as if this
was a well-paid job. And it is not what I would call a luxury,
this velvet cape which I bought from her. It would not have
been necessary if one were not forced to distinguish himself

more and more from these scum who degrade the calling of
the Prophet. It becomes important to stand out, to be
distinctive. I have set my heart after a particular name. They
will look at my velvet cape and they will think of my
goodness. Inevitably they must begin to call me . . . the
Velvet-hearted Jeroboam. [*Straightens himself.*] Immaculate
Jero, Articulate Hero of Christ's Crusade . . .

Well, it is out. I have not breathed it to a single soul, but that
has been my ambition. You've got to have a name that
appeals to the imagination—because the imagination is a thing
of the spirit—it must catch the imagination of the crowd. Yes,
one must move with modern times. Lack of colour gets one
nowhere even in the Prophet's business. [*Looks all round him.*]
Charlatans! If only I had this beach to myself. [*With sudden
violence.*] But how does one maintain his dignity when the
daughter of Eve forces him to leave his own house through a
window? God curse that woman! I never thought she would
dare affront the presence of a man of God. One pound eight
for this little cape. It is sheer robbery.

[*He surveys the scene again. A young girl passes, sleepily, clothed
only in her wrapper.*]

JERO: She passes here every morning, on her way to take a swim.
Dirty-looking thing.

[*He yawns.*]

I am glad I got here before any customers—I mean
worshippers—well, customers if you like. I always get that
feeling every morning that I am a shopkeeper waiting for
customers. The regular ones come at definite times.
Strange, dissatisfied people. I know they are dissatisfied
because I keep them dissatisfied. Once they are full, they won't
come again. Like my good apprentice, Brother Chume. He
wants to beat his wife, but I won't let him. If I do, he will
become contented, and then that's another of my flock gone
for ever. As long as he doesn't beat her, he comes here feeling
helpless, and so there is no chance of his rebelling against me.
Everything, in fact, is planned.

[*The young girl crosses the stage again. She has just had her swim
and the difference is remarkable. Clean, wet, shiny face and hair.
She continues to wipe herself with her wrapper as she walks.*]

JERO [*following her all the way with his eyes.*]: Every morning, every
day I witness this divine transformation, O Lord.
[*He shakes his head suddenly and bellows.*]
Pray Brother Jeroboam, pray! Pray for strength against
temptation.
[*He falls on his knees, face squeezed in agony and hands clasped.
Chume enters, wheeling his bike. He leans it against the palm tree.*]

JERO [*not opening his eyes.*]: Pray with me, brother. Pray with me.
Pray for me against this one weakness . . . against this one
weakness, O Lord . . .

CHUME [*falling down at once.*]: Help him, Lord. Help him, Lord.

JERO: Against this one weakness, this weakness, O Abraham . . .

CHUME: Help him, Lord. Help him, Lord.

JERO: Against this one weakness David, David, Samuel, Samuel.

CHUME: Help him. Help him. Help am. Help am.

JERO: Job Job, Elijah Elijah.

CHUME [*getting more worked up.*]: Help am God. Help am God. I say
make you help am. Help am quick quick.

JERO: Tear the image from my heart. Tear this love for the
daughters of Eve . . .

CHUME: Adam, help am. Na your son, help am. Help this your son.

JERO: Burn out this lust for the daughters of Eve.

CHUME: Je-e-esu, J-e-esu, Je-e-esu. Help am one time Je-e-e-e-su.

JERO: Abraka, Abraka, Abraka.
[*Chume joins in.*]
Abraka, Abraka, Hebra, Hebra, Hebra, Hebra, Hebra,
Hebra, Hebra, Hebra . . .

JERO [*rising.*]: God bless you, brother. [*Turns around.*] Chume!

CHUME: Good morning, Brother Jeroboam.

JERO: Chume, you are not at work. You've never come before in
the morning.

CHUME: No. I went to work but I had to report sick.

JERO: Why, are you unwell, brother?

CHUME: No, Brother Jero . . . I . . .

JERO: A-ah, you have troubles and you could not wait to get them
to God. We shall pray together.

CHUME: Brother Jero . . . I . . . I [*He stops altogether.*]

JERO: Is it difficult? Then let us commune silently for a while.
[*Chume folds his arms, raises his eyes to heaven.*]

JERO: I wonder what is the matter with him. Actually I knew it
was he the moment he opened his mouth. Only Brother
Chume reverts to that animal jabber when he gets his spiritual
excitement. And that is much too often for my liking. He is
too crude, but then that is to my advantage. It means he
would never think of setting himself up as my equal.
[*He joins Chume in his meditative attitude, but almost immediately
discards it, as if he has just remembered something.*]
Christ my Protector! It is a good job I got away from that
wretched woman as soon as I did. My disciple believes that I
sleep on the beach, that is, if he thinks I sleep at all. Most of
them believe the same but, for myself, I prefer my bed.
Much more comfortable. And it gets rather cold on the beach
at nights. Still, it does them good to believe that I am
something of an ascetic. . . .
[*He resumes his meditative pose for a couple of moments.*]
[*Gently.*] Open your mind to God, brother. This is the
tabernacle of Christ. Open your mind to God.
[*Chume is silent for a while, then bursts out suddenly.*]

CHUME: Brother Jero, you must let me beat her!

JERO: What!

CHUME [*desperately.*]: Just once, Prophet. Just once.

JERO: Brother Chume!

CHUME: Just once. Just one sound beating, and I swear not to ask
again.

JERO: Apostate. Have I not told you the will of God in this matter?

CHUME: But I've got to beat her, Prophet. You must save me
from madness.

JERO: I will. But only if you obey me.

CHUME: In anything else, Prophet. But for this one, make you
let me just beat am once.

JERO: Apostate!

CHUME: I n' go beat am too hard. Jus' once small small.

JERO: Traitor!

CHUME: Jus' this one time. I no' go ask again. Jus' do me this one
favour, make a beat am today.

JERO: Brother Chume, what were you before you came to me?

CHUME: Prophet . . .

JERO [*sternly.*]: What were you before the grace of God?

CHUME: A labourer, Prophet. A common labourer.

JERO: And did I not prophesy you would become an office boy?

CHUME: You do am, brother. Na so.

JERO: And then a messenger?

CHUME: Na you do am, brother. Na you.

JERO: And then quick promotion? Did I not prophesy it?

CHUME: Na true, prophet. Na true.

JERO: And what are you now? What are you?

CHUME: Chief Messenger.

JERO: By the grace of God! And by the grace of God, have I not seen you at the table of the Chief Clerk? And you behind the desk, giving orders?

CHUME: Yes, Prophet . . . but . . .

JERO: With a telephone and a table bell for calling the Messenger?

CHUME: Very true, Prophet, but . . .

JERO: But? But? Kneel! [pointing to the ground.] Kneel!

CHUME [wringing his hands.]: Prophet!

JERO: Kneel, sinner, kneel. Hardener of heart, harbourer of Ashtoreth, Protector of Baal, kneel, kneel.

[Chume falls on his knees.]

CHUME: My life is a hell . . .

JERO: Forgive him, Father, forgive him.

CHUME: This woman will kill me . . .

JERO: Forgive him, Father, forgive him.

CHUME: Only this morning I . . .

JERO: Forgive him, Father, forgive him.

CHUME: All the way on my bicycle . . .

JERO: Forgive . . .

CHUME: And not a word of thanks . . .

JERO: Out Ashtoreth. Out Baal . . .

CHUME: All she gave me was abuse, abuse, abuse . . .

JERO: Hardener of the heart . . .

CHUME: Nothing but abuse . . .

JERO: Petrifier of the soul . . .

CHUME: If I could only beat her once, only once . . .

JERO [shouting him down.]: Forgive this sinner, Father. Forgive him by day, forgive him by night, forgive him in the morning, forgive him at noon . . .

[A man enters. Kneels at once and begins to chorus 'Amen', or

['Forgive him, Lord', or 'In the name of Jesus (pronounced Je-e-e-sus)'. Those who follow later do the same.]

. . . This is the son whom you appointed to follow in my footsteps. Soften his heart. Brother Chume, this woman whom you so desire to beat is your cross—bear it well. She is your heaven-sent trial—lay not your hands on her. I command you to speak no harsh word to her. Pray, Brother Chume, for strength in this hour of your trial. Pray for strength and fortitude.

[Jeroboam leaves them to continue their chorus, Chume chanting, 'Mercy, Mercy' while he makes his next remarks.]

They begin to arrive. As usual in the same order. This one who always comes earliest, I have prophesied that he will be made a chief in his home town. That is a very safe prophecy. As safe as our most popular prophecy, that a man will live to be eighty. If it doesn't come true,

[Enter an old couple, joining chorus as before.]

that man doesn't find out until he's on the other side. So everybody is quite happy. One of my most faithful adherents—unfortunately, he can only be present at week-ends—firmly believes that he is going to be the first Prime Minister of the new Mid-North-East-State—when it is created. That was a risky prophecy of mine, but I badly needed more worshippers around that time.

[He looks at his watch.]

The next one to arrive is my most faithful penitent. She wants children, so she is quite a sad case. Or you would think so. But even in the midst of her most self-abasing convulsions, she manages to notice everything that goes on around her. In fact, I had better get back to the service. She is always the one to tell me that my mind is not on the service. . . .

[Altering his manner—]

Rise, Brother Chume. Rise and let the Lord enter into you. Apprentice of the Lord, are you not he upon whose shoulders my mantle must descend?

[A woman (the penitent) enters and kneels at once in an attitude of prayer.]

CHUME: It is so, Brother Jero.

JERO: Then why do you harden your heart? The Lord says that you

may not beat the good woman whom he has chosen to be
your wife, to be your cross in your period of trial, and will you
disobey him?

CHUME: No, Brother Jero.

JERO: Will you?

CHUME: No, Brother Jero.

JERO: Praise be to God.

CONGREGATION: Praise be to God.

JERO: Allelu . . .

CONGREGATION: Alleluia.

[*To the clapping of hands, they sing 'I will follow Jesus',
swaying and then dancing as they get warmer.
Brother Jero, as the singing starts, hands two empty bottles to
Chume who goes to fill them with water from the sea.
Chume has hardly gone out when the drummer boy enters from
upstage, running. He is rather weighed down by two 'gangan'
drums, and darts fearful glances back in mortal terror of whatever it
is that is chasing him. This turns out, some ten or so yards later, to be
a woman, sash tightened around her waist, wrapper pulled so high up
that half the length of her thigh is exposed. Her sleeves are rolled
above the shoulder and she is striding after the drummer in no
unmistakable manner. Jeroboam, who has followed the woman's
exposed limbs with quite distressed concentration, comes suddenly to
himself and kneels sharply, muttering.
Again the drummer appears, going across the stage in a different
direction, running still. The woman follows, distance undiminished,
the same set pace, Jeroboam calls to him.*]

JERO: What did you do to her?

DRUMMER [*without stopping.*]: Nothing. I was only drumming and
then she said I was using it to abuse her father.

JERO [*as the woman comes into sight*]: Woman!

[*She continues out. Chume enters with filled bottles.*]

JERO [*shaking his head.*]: I know her very well. She's my
neighbour. But she ignored me . . .

[*Jeroboam prepares to bless the water when once again the
procession appears, drummer first and the woman after.*]

JERO: Come here. She wouldn't dare touch you.

DRUMMER [*increasing his pace.*]: You don't know her . . .

[*The woman comes in sight.*]

JERO: Neighbour, neighbour. My dear sister in Moses . . .

[*She continues her pursuit offstage. Jero hesitates, then hands over his rod to Chume and goes after them.*]

CHUME [*suddenly remembering.*]: You haven't blessed the water, Brother Jeroboam.

[*Jero is already out of hearing. Chume is obviously bewildered by the new responsibility. He fiddles around with the rod and eventually uses it to conduct the singing, which has gone on all this time, flagging when the two contestants came in view, and reviving again after they had passed.*

Chume has hardly begun to conduct his band when a woman detaches herself from the crowd in the expected penitent's paroxysm.]

PENITENT: Echa, echa, echa, echa, echa . . . eei, eei, eei, eei.

CHUME [*taken aback.*]: Ngh? What's the matter?

PENITENT: Efie, efie, efie, efie, enh, enh, enh, enh . . .

CHUME [*dashing off.*]: Brother Jeroboam, Brother Jeroboam . . .

[*Chume shouts in all directions, returning confusedly each time in an attempt to minister to the penitent. As Jeroboam is not forthcoming, he begins, very uncertainly, to sprinkle some of the water on the penitent, crossing her on the forehead. This has to be achieved very rapidly in the brief moment when the penitent's head is lifted from beating on the ground.*]

CHUME [*stammering.*]: Father . . . forgive her.

CONGREGATION [*strongly.*]: Amen.

[*The unexpectedness of the response nearly throws Chume, but then it also serves to bolster him up, receiving such support.*]

CHUME: Father, forgive her.

CONGREGATION: Amen.

[*The penitent continues to moan.*]

CHUME: Father forgive her.

CONGREGATION: Amen.

CHUME: Father forgive am.

CONGREGATION: Amen.

CHUME [*warming up to the task.*]: Make you forgive am. Father.

CONGREGATION: Amen.

[*They rapidly gain pace, Chume getting quite carried away.*]

CHUME: I say make you forgive am.

CONGREGATION: Amen.

CHUME: Forgive am one time.

CONGREGATION: Amen.

CHUME: Forgive am quick quick.

CONGREGATION: Amen.

CHUME: Forgive am, Father.

CONGREGATION: Amen.

CHUME: Forgive us all.

CONGREGATION: Amen.

CHUME: Forgive us all.

[*And then, punctuated regularly with Amens . . .*]

Yes, Father, make you forgive us all. Make you save us from palaver. Save us from trouble at home. Tell our wives not to give us trouble . . .

[*The penitent has become placid. She is stretched out flat on the ground.*]

. . . Tell our wives not to give us trouble. And give us money to have a happy home. Give us money to satisfy our daily necessities. Make you no forget those of us who dey struggle daily. Those who be clerk today, make them Chief Clerk tomorrow. Those who are Messenger today, make them Senior Service tomorrow. Yes Father, those who are Messenger today, make them Senior Service tomorrow.

[*The Amens grow more and more ecstatic.*]

Those who are petty trader today, make them big contractor tomorrow. Those who dey sweep street today, give them their own big office tomorrow. If we dey walka today, give us our own bicycle tomorrow. I say those who dey walka today, give them their own bicycle tomorrow. Those who have bicycle today, they will ride their own car tomorrow.

[*The enthusiasm of the response, becomes, at this point, quite overpowering.*]

I say those who dey push bicycle, give them big car tomorrow. Give them big car tomorrow. Give them big car tomorrow, give them big car tomorrow.

[*The angry woman comes again in view, striding with the same gait as before, but now in possession of the drums. A few yards behind, the drummer jog-trots wretchedly, pleading.*]

DRUMMER: I beg you, give me my drums. I take God's name beg you, I was not abusing your father. . . . For God's sake I beg

you . . . I was not abusing your father. I was only drumming.
. . . I swear to God I was only drumming. . . .
[*They pass through.*]

PENITENT [*who has become much alive from the latter part of the prayers, pointing . . .*]: Brother Jeroboam!
[*Brother Jero has just come in view. They all rush to help him back into the circle. He is a much altered man, his clothes torn and his face bleeding.*]

JERO [*slowly and painfully*]: Thank you, brother, sisters. Brother Chume, kindly tell these friends to leave me. I must pray for the soul of that sinful woman. I must say a personal prayer for her.
[*Chume ushers them off. They go reluctantly, chattering excitedly.*]

JERO: Prayers this evening, as usual. Late afternoon.

CHUME [*shouting after.*]: Prayers late afternoon as always. Brother Jeroboam says God keep you till then. Are you all right, Brother Jero?

JERO: Who would have thought that she would dare lift her hand against a prophet of God!

CHUME: Women are a plague, brother.

JERO: I had a premonition this morning that women would be my downfall today. But I thought of it only in the spiritual sense.

CHUME: Now you see how it is, Brother Jero.

JERO: From the moment I looked out of my window this morning, I have been tormented one way or another by the Daughters of Discord.

CHUME [*eagerly.*]: That is how it is with me, Brother. Every day. Every morning and night. Only this morning she made me take her to the house of some poor man, whom she says owes her money. She loaded enough on my bicycle to lay a siege for a week, and all the thanks I got was abuse.

JERO: Indeed, it must be a trial, Brother Chume . . . and it requires great . . .
[*He becomes suddenly suspicious.*]
Brother Chume, did you say that your wife went to make camp only this morning at the house of a . . . of someone who owes her money?

CHUME: Yes, I took her there myself.

JERO: Er . . . indeed, indeed. [*Coughs.*] Is . . . your wife a trader?

CHUME: Yes, Petty trading, you know. Wool, silk, cloth, and all that stuff.

JERO: Indeed. Quite an enterprising woman. [*Hems.*] Er . . . where was the house of this man . . . I mean, this man who owes her money?

CHUME: Not very far from here. Ajete settlement, a mile or so from here. I did not even know the place existed until today.

JERO [*to himself.*]: So that is your wife . . .

CHUME: Did you speak, prophet?

JERO: No, no. I was only thinking how little women have changed since Eve, since Delilah, since Jezebel. But we must be strong of heart. I have my own cross too, Brother Chume. This morning alone I have been thrice in conflict with the Daughters of Discord. First there was . . . no, never mind that. There is another who crosses my path every day. Goes to swim just over there and then waits for me to be in the midst of my meditation before she swings her hips across here, flaunting her near nakedness before my eyes. . . .

CHUME [*to himself, with deep feeling.*]: I'd willingly change crosses with you.

JERO: What, Brother Chume?

CHUME: I was only praying.

JERO: Ah. That is the only way. But er . . . I wonder really what the will of God would be in this matter. After all, Christ himself was not averse to using the whip when occasion demanded it.

CHUME [*eagerly.*]: No, he did not hesitate.

JERO: In that case, since, Brother Chume, your wife seems such a wicked, wilful sinner, I think . . .

CHUME: Yes, Holy One . . . ?

JERO: You must take her home tonight . . .

CHUME: Yes . . .

JERO: And beat her.

CHUME [*kneeling, clasps Jero's hand in his.*]: Prophet!

JERO: Remember, it must be done in your own house. Never show the discord within your family to the world. Take her home and beat her.

[*Chume leaps up and gets his bike.*]

JERO: And Brother Chume . . .

CHUME: Yes, Prophet . . .

JERO: The Son of God appeared to me again this morning, robed just as he was when he named you my successor. And he placed his burning sword on my shoulder and called me his knight. He gave me a new title . . . but you must tell it to no one—yet.

CHUME: I swear, Brother Jero.

JERO [*staring into space.*]: He named me the Immaculate Jero, Articulate Hero of Christ's Crusade.
[*Pauses, then, with a regal dismissal—*] You may go, Brother Chume.

CHUME: God keep you, Brother Jero—the Immaculate.

JERO: God keep you, brother. [*He sadly fingers the velvet cape.*]

LIGHTS FADE

SCENE IV

As Scene II, i.e. in front of the Prophet's home. Later that day. Chume is just wiping off the last crumbs of yams on his plate. Amope watches him.

AMOPE: You can't say I don't try. Hounded out of house by debtors, I still manage to make you a meal.

CHUME [*sucking his fingers, sets down his plate.*]: It was a good meal too.

AMOPE: I do my share as I've always done. I cooked you your meal. But when I ask you to bring me some clean water, you forget.

CHUME: I did not forget.

AMOPE: You keep saying that. Where is it then? Or perhaps the bottles fell off your bicycle on the way and got broken.

CHUME: That's a child's lie, Amope. You are talking to a man.

AMOPE: A fine man you are then, when you can't remember a simple thing like a bottle of clean water.

CHUME: I remembered. I just did not bring it. So that is that. And now pack up your things because we're going home.
[*Amope stares at him unbelieving.*]

CHUME: Pack up your things; you heard what I said.

AMOPE [*scrutinizing.*]: I thought you were a bit early to get back. You haven't been to work at all. You've been drinking all day.

CHUME: You may think what suits you. You know I never touch any liquor.

AMOPE: You needn't say it as if it was a virtue. You don't drink only because you cannot afford to. That is all the reason there is.

CHUME: Hurry. I have certain work to do when I get home and I don't want you delaying me.

AMOPE: Go then. I am not budging from here till I get my money.

[*Chume leaps up, begins to throw her things into the bag. Brother Jero enters, hides, and observes them.*]

AMOPE [*quietly.*]: I hope you have ropes to tie me on the bicycle, because I don't intend to leave this place unless I am carried out. One pound eight shillings is no child's play. And it is my money not yours.

[*Chume has finished packing the bag and is now tying it on to the carrier.*]

AMOPE: A messenger's pay isn't that much you know—just in case you've forgotten you're not drawing a minister's pay. So you better think again if you think I am letting my hard-earned money stay in the hands of that good-for-nothing.

Just think, only this morning while I sat here, a Sanitary Inspector came along. He looked me all over and he made some notes in his book. Then he said, I suppose, woman, you realize that this place is marked down for slum clearance. This to me, as if I lived here. But you sit down and let your wife be exposed to such insults. And the Sanitary Inspector had a motor-cycle too, which is one better than a bicycle.

CHUME: You'd better be ready soon.

AMOPE: A Sanitary Inspector is a better job anyway. You can make something of yourself one way or another. They all do. A little here and a little there, call it bribery if you like, but see where *you've* got even though you don't drink or smoke or take bribes. He's got a motor-bike . . . anyway, who would want to offer cola to a Chief Messenger?

CHUME: Shut your big mouth!

AMOPE [*aghast.*]: What did you say?

CHUME: I said shut your big mouth.

AMOPE: To me?

CHUME: Shut your big mouth before I shut it for you. [*Ties the mat round the cross-bar.*] And you'd better start to watch your step from now on. My period of abstinence is over. My cross has been lifted off my shoulders by the Prophet.

AMOPE [*genuinely distressed.*]: He's mad.

CHUME [*viciously tying up the mat.*]: My period of trial is over. [*Practically strangling the mat.*] If you so much as open your mouth now . . . [*Gives a further twist to the string.*]

AMOPE: God help me. He's gone mad.

CHUME [*imperiously.*]: Get on the bike.

AMOPE [*backing away.*]: I'm not coming with you.

CHUME: I said get on the bike!

AMOPE: Not with you. I'll find my own way home.

[*Chume advances on her. Amope screams for help. Brother Jero crosses himself. Chume catches her by the arm but she escapes, runs to the side of the house and beats on the door.*]

AMOPE: Help! Open the door for God's sake. Let me in. Let me in . . .

[*Brother Jero grimaces.*]

Is anyone in? Let me in for God's sake! Let me in or God will punish you!

JERO [*sticking his fingers in his ears.*]: Blasphemy!

AMOPE: Prophet! Where's the Prophet?

[*Chume lifts her bodily.*]

AMOPE: Let me down! Police! Police!

CHUME [*setting her down.*]: If you shout just once more I'll . . . [*He raises a huge fist.*]

[*Brother Jero gasps in mock-horror, tut-tuts, covers his eyes with both hands, and departs.*]

AMOPE: Ho! You're mad, You're mad.

CHUME: Get on the bike.

AMOPE: Kill me! Kill me!

CHUME: Don't tempt me, woman!

AMOPE: I won't get on that thing unless you kill me first.

CHUME: Woman!

[*Two or three neighbours arrive, but keep a respectful distance.*]

AMOPE: Kill me. You'll have to kill me. Everybody come and

bear witness. He's going to kill me so come and bear witness. I forgive everyone who has ever done me evil. I forgive all my debtors especially the Prophet who has got me into all this trouble. Prophet Jeroboam, I hope you will pray for my soul in heaven. . . .

CHUME: You have no soul, wicked woman.

AMOPE: Brother Jeroboam, curse this man for me. You may keep the velvet cape if you curse this foolish man. I forgive you your debt. Go on, foolish man, kill me. If you don't kill me you won't do well in life.

CHUME [*suddenly*.]: Shut up!

AMOPE [*warming up as more people arrive*.]: Bear witness all of you. Tell the Prophet I forgive him his debt but he must curse this foolish man to hell. Go on, kill me!

CHUME [*who has turned away, forehead knotted in confusion*.]: Can't you shut up, woman!

AMOPE: No, you must kill me . . .

[*The crowd hub-bubs all the time, scared as always at the prospect of interfering in man-wife palaver, but throwing in half-hearted tokens of concern—*]

'What's the matter, eh?' 'You two keep quiet.'

'Who are they?' 'Where is Brother Jero?' 'Do you think we ought to send for the Prophet?' 'These women are so troublesome! Somebody go and call Brother Jero.'

CHUME [*lifting up Amope's head. She has, in the tradition of the 'Kill me' woman, shut her eyes tightly and continued to beat her fists on the Prophet's doorstep.*]: Shut up and listen. Did I hear you say Prophet Jeroboam?

AMOPE: See him now. Let you bear witness. He's going to kill me . . .

CHUME: I'm not touching you but I will if you don't answer my question.

AMOPE: Kill me . . . Kill me . . .

CHUME: Woman, did you say it was the Prophet who owed you money?

AMOPE: Kill me . . .

CHUME: Is this his house? [*Gives her head a shake.*] Does he live here . . . ?

AMOPE: Kill me . . . Kill me . . .

CHUME [*pushing her away in disgust and turning to the crowd. They retreat instinctively.*]: Is Brother Jeroboam . . . ?

NEAREST ONE [*hastily.*]: No, no. I'm not Brother Jero. It's not me.

CHUME: Who said you were? Does the Prophet live here?

SAME MAN: Yes. Over there. That house.

CHUME [*Turns round and stands stock still. Stares at the house for quite some time.*]: So . . . so . . . so . . . so . . .

[*The crowd is puzzled over his change of mood. Even Amope looks up wonderingly. Chume walks towards his bicycle, muttering to himself.*]

So . . . so . . . Suddenly he decides I may beat my wife, eh? For his own convenience. At his own convenience.

[*He releases the bundle from the carrier, pushing it down carelessly. He unties the mat also.*]

BYSTANDER: What next is he doing now?

CHUME [*mounting his bicycle.*]: You stay here and don't move. If I don't find you here when I get back . . .

[*He rides off. They all stare at him in bewilderment.*]

AMOPE: He is quite mad. I have never seen him behave like that.

BYSTANDER: You are sure?

AMOPE: Am I sure? I'm his wife, so I ought to know, shouldn't I?

A WOMAN BYSTANDER: Then you ought to let the Prophet see to him. I had a brother once who had the fits and foamed at the mouth every other week. But the Prophet cured him. Drove the devils out of him, he did.

AMOPE: This one can't do anything. He's a debtor and that's all he knows. How to dodge his creditors.

[*She prepares to unpack her bundle.*]

LIGHTS FADE

SCENE V

The beach. Nightfall.

A man in an elaborate 'agbada' outfit, with long train and a cap is standing right, downstage, with a sheaf of notes in his hand. He is obviously delivering a speech, but we don't hear it. It is undoubtedly a fire-breathing speech.

The Prophet Jeroboam stands bolt upright as always, surveying him with lofty compassion.

JERO: I could teach him a trick or two about speech-making. He's a member of the Federal House, a back-bencher but with one eye on a ministerial post. Comes here every day to rehearse his speeches. But he never makes them. Too scared. [*Pause. The Prophet continues to study the Member.*] Poor fish. [*Chuckles and looks away.*] Oho, I had almost forgotten Brother Chume. By now he ought to have beaten his wife senseless. Pity! That means I've lost him. He is fulfilled and no longer needs me. True, he still has to become a Chief Clerk. But I have lost him as the one who was most dependent on me. . . . Never mind, it was a good price to pay for getting rid of my creditor. . . . [*Goes back to the Member.*] Now he . . . he is already a member of my flock. He does not know it of course, but he is a follower. All I need do is claim him. Call him and say to him, My dear Member of the House, your place awaits you . . . Or do you doubt it? Watch me go to work on him. [*Raises his voice.*] My dear brother in Jesus! [*The Member stops, looks round, resumes his speech.*] Dear brother, do I not know you? [*Member stops, looks round again.*] Yes, you. In God's name, do I not know you? [*Member approaches slowly.*] Yes indeed. It is you. And you come as it was predicted. Do you not perhaps remember me? [*Member looks at him scornfully.*] Then you cannot be of the Lord. In another world, in another body, we met, and my message was for you . . . [*The Member turns his back impatiently.*]

MEMBER [*with great pomposity.*]: Go and practise your fraudulences on another person of greater gullibility.

JERO [*very kindly, smiling.*]: Indeed the matter is quite plain. You are not of the Lord. And yet such is the mystery of God's ways that his favour has lighted upon you . . . Minister . . . Minister by the grace of God . . .

[*The Member stops dead.*]

Yes, brother, we have met. I saw this country plunged into strife. I saw the mustering of men, gathered in the name of peace through strength. And at a desk, in a large gilt room, great men of the land awaited your decision. Emissaries of foreign nations hung on your word, and on the door leading into your office, I read the words, Minister for War . . . .

[*The Member turns round slowly.*]

. . . It is a position of power. But are you of the Lord? Are you in fact worthy? Must I, when I have looked into your soul, as the Lord has commanded me to do, must I pray to the Lord to remove this mantle from your shoulders and place it on a more God-fearing man?

[*The Member moves forward unconsciously. The Prophet gestures him to stay where he is. Slowly—*]

Yes . . . I think I see Satan in your eyes. I see him entrenched in your eyes . . .

[*The Member grows fearful, raises his arms in half-supplication.*]

The Minister for War would be the most powerful position in the Land. The Lord knows best, but he has empowered his lieutenants on earth to intercede where necessary. We can reach him by fasting and by prayer . . . we can make recommendations. . . . Brother, are you of God or are you ranged among his enemies . . . ?

[*Jeroboam's voice fades away and the light also dims on him as another voice—Chume's—is heard long before he is seen. Chume enters from left, downstage, agitated, and talking to himself.*]

CHUME: . . . What for . . . why, why, why, why 'e do am? For two years 'e no let me beat that woman. Why? No because God no like am. That one no fool me any more. 'E no be man of God. 'E say 'in sleep for beach whether 'e rain or cold but that one too na big lie. The man get house and 'e sleep there every night. But 'in get peace for 'in house, why 'en no let me get peace for mine? Wetin I do for am? Anyway, how they come meet? Where? When? What time 'e know say na my wife? Why 'e dey protect am from me? Perhaps na my woman dey give am chop and in return he promise to see say 'in husband no beat am. A-a-a -ah, give am clothes, give am food and all comforts and necessities, and for exchange, 'in go see that 'in husband no beat am . . . Mmmmmm.

[*He shakes his head.*]

No, is not possible. I no believe that. If na so, how they come quarrel then. Why she go sit for front of 'in house demand all 'in money. I no beat am yet . . .

[*He stops suddenly. His eyes slowly distend.*]

Almighty! Chume, fool! O God, my life done spoil. My life done spoil finish. O God a no' get eyes for my head. Na lie. Na big lie. Na pretence 'e de pretend that wicked woman! She no' go collect nutin! She no' mean to sleep for outside house. The Prophet na 'in lover. As soon as 'e dark, she go in go meet 'in man. O God, wetin a do for you wey you go spoil my life so? Wetin make you vex for me so? I offend you? Chume, foolish man, youu life done spoil. Your life done spoil. Yeah, ye . . . ah ah, ye-e-ah, they done ruin Chume for life . . . ye-e-ah, ye-e-ah, . . .

[*He goes off, his cries dying offstage.*

Light up slowly on Jero. The Member is seen kneeling now at Brother Jero's feet, hands clasped, and shut eyes raised to heaven . . .]

JERO [*his voice gaining volume.*]: Protect him therefore. Protect him when he must lead this country as his great ancestors have done. He comes from the great warriors of the land. In his innocence he was not aware of this heritage. But you know everything and you plan it all. There is no end, no beginning . . .

[*Chume rushes in, brandishing a cutlass.*]

CHUME: Adulterer! Woman-thief! Na today a go finish you!

[*Jero looks round.*]

JERO: God save us! [*Flees.*]

MEMBER [*unaware of what is happening.*]: Amen.

[*Chume follows out Jero, murder-bent.*]

MEMBER: Amen. Amen. [*Open his eyes.*] Thank you, Proph . . .

[*He looks right, left, back, front, but he finds the Prophet has really disappeared.*]

Prophet! Prophet! [*Turns sharply and rapidly in every direction, shouting.*] Prophet, where are you? Where have you gone? Prophet! Don't leave me, Prophet, don't leave me!

[*He looks up slowly, with awe.*]

Vanished. Transported. Utterly transmuted. I knew it. I knew I stood in the presence of God. . . .

[*He bows his head, standing. Jeroboam enters quite collected, and points to the convert.*]

JEROBOAM: You heard him. With your own ears you heard him. By tomorrow, the whole town will have heard about the miraculous disappearance of Brother Jeroboam. Testified to and witnessed by no less a person than one of the elected Rulers of the country. . . .

MEMBER [*goes to sit on the mound.*]: I must await his return. If I show faith, he will show himself again to me. . . . [*Leaps up as he is about to sit.*] This is holy ground. [*Takes off his shoes and sits. Gets up again.*] I must hear further from him. Perhaps he has gone to learn more about this ministerial post. . . . [*Sits.*]

JEROBOAM: I have already sent for the police. It is a pity about Chume. But he has given me a fright, and no prophet likes to be frightened. With the influence of that nincompoop I should succeed in getting him certified with ease. A year in the lunatic asylum would do him good anyway.

[*The Member is already nodding.*]

Good . . . He is falling asleep. When I appear again to him he'll think I have just fallen from the sky. Then I'll tell him that Satan just sent one of his emissaries into the world under the name of Chume, and that he had better put him in a strait-jacket at once . . . And so the day is saved. The police will call on me here as soon as they catch Chume. And it looks as if it is not quite time for the fulfilment of that spiteful man's prophecy.

[*He picks up a pebble and throws it at the Member. At the same time a ring of red or some equally startling colour plays on his head, forming a sort of halo. The Member wakes with a start, stares open-mouthed, and falls flat on his face, whispering in rapt awe—*]

'Master!'

BLACKOUT

THE END

JERO'S METAMORPHOSIS

Characters

BROTHER JEROBOAM

SISTER REBECCA

ANANAIAS

CHIEF EXECUTIVE OFFICER

CLERK TO THE TOURIST BOARD

CHUME

MAJOR SILVA

SHADRACH

CALEB

ISAAC

MATTHEW

A POLICEWOMAN

} *and other Beach Prophets*

SCENE I

Brother Jero's office. It is no longer his rent-troubled shack of The Trials *but a modest whitewashed room, quite comfortable. A 'surplus-store' steel cabinet is tucked in a corner. On a cloth-covered table is an ancient beat-up typewriter of the oldest imaginable model but functioning. A vase of flowers, the usual assortment of professional paraphernalia—bible, prayer-book, chasuble, etc., etc.*

On the wall, a large framed picture of a uniformed figure at a battery of microphones indicates that Jero's diocese is no longer governed by his old friends the civilian politicians. As Jero dictates, striding up and down the room, it is obvious that he has his mind very much on this photograph. A demure young woman, quite attractive, is seated at a table taking the dictation.

JERO: . . . in time of trouble it behoves us to come together, to forget old enmities and bury the hatchet in the head of a common enemy . . . no, better take that out. It sounds a little unchristian wouldn't you say?

REBECCA [*her voice and manner are of unqualified admiration*]: Not if you don't think it, Brother Jeroboam.

JERO: Well, we have to be careful about our brother prophets. Some of them might just take it literally. The mere appearance of the majority of them, not to mention their secret past and even secret present . . . ah well, stop at 'bury the hatchet'.

REBECCA: Whatever you say, Brother Jeroboam.

JERO: Not that I would regret it. We could do with the elevation to eternity of some of our dearly beloved brother prophets on this beach, and if they choose the way of the hangman's noose or elect to take the latest short cut to heaven facing a firing squad at the Bar Beach Show,[1] who are we to dispute such a divine solution? Only trouble is, it might give the rest of us a bad name.

REBECCA: Nothing could give you a bad name, Brother Jero. You stand apart from the others. Nothing can tarnish your image, I know that.

1. Popular expression for the new fashion of public executions in Lagos, capital of Nigeria.

JERO: You are indeed kind, Sister Rebecca. I don't know what I would do without you.

REBECCA: You won't ever have to do without me, Brother Jero. As long as you need me, I'll be here.

JERO: Hm, yes, hm. [*The prospect makes him nervous.*] I thank you, Sister. Now we must get back to work. Read me the last thing I dictated.

REBECCA: . . . in time of trouble it behoves us to get together, to forget old enemies and bury the hatchet in the head . . . no, we stop at 'hatchet'.

JERO: Good. I have therefore decided to summon—no, invite is better wouldn't you say? The more miserable they are the more touchy and proud you'll find them. The monster of pride feeds upon vermin, Sister Rebecca. The hole in a poor man's garment is soon filled with the patchwork of pride, so resolutely does Nature abhor a vacuum.

REBECCA: Oh Brother Jero, you say such wise things.

JERO: I have but little gifts, Sister Rebecca, but I make the most of them. Yes, let the phrase read—after much prayer for guidance, I am inspired to invite you all to a meeting where we shall all, as equals before God and servants of his will, deliberate and find a way to stop this threat to our vocation. In our own mutual interest—underline that heavily—in our own mutual interest, I trust that all shepherds of the Lord whose pastures are upon this sandy though arable beach will make it their duty to be present.

[*He shakes his head as if to clear it, goes to a small cupboard and brings out a bottle. Pouring a drink.*]

The gall is bitter, Sister Rebecca. The burden is heavy upon me.

REBECCA: It has to be done, Brother Jero. The end will justify the means.

JERO: To fraternize with those cut-throats, dope-pedlars, smugglers, and stolen goods receivers? Some of them are ex-convicts do you know that? Some of them are long overdue for the Bar Beach Spectacular.

REBECCA: The more noble of you in sinking your pride and meeting with them in the service of God.

JERO [*offering a glass.*]: You will join me, Sister Rebecca?

REBECCA: No, Brother Jero, but you must have one.

JERO: You are sure it is not wrong?

REBECCA: All things are God's gifts. It is not wrong to use them wisely.

JERO: You comfort me greatly, Sister Rebecca. The times are indeed trying. Believe me, it is no time for half-measures.

REBECCA: Brother Jero, you promised . . .

JERO: Oh I didn't mean this half-measure. [*Tosses down drink.*]

REBECCA: Forgive me, I . . .

JERO: A natural error. No, I was referring to our present predicament. To survive, we need full-bodied tactics.

REBECCA: I know you will find a way.

JERO: It seems to me that in our upward look to heaven for a solution we have neglected what inspiration is afforded us below. Yes, indeed we have.

REBECCA: Has earth anything to offer the true Christian, Brother Jero? How often have you said yourself . . .

JERO: That was before I read this precious file which you brought to Christ as your dowry. An unparalleled dowry in the history of spiritual marriages Sister Rebecca. And before . . . [*He takes down the picture on the wall, inspects it at arm's length nodding with satisfaction.*] . . . yes, I think we have neglected our earthly inspirations.

REBECCA: But Brother Jero . . .

JERO: Trust me, Sister Rebecca.

REBECCA: I do, Brother Jero, I do.

JERO: The voice of the people is the voice of God, did you know that Sister?

REBECCA: I trust you. I follow wherever you lead me, Brother Jeroboam.

JERO: I shall lead you to safety, you and all who put their faith in me.

REBECCA: Instruct me, Brother Jero.

JERO [*hanging up the picture.*]: Distribute those invitations at once. Go to my tailor and ask him to deliver my order tonight. Prepare everything for the spiritual assembly. When the moment comes, all shall be made plain.

REBECCA: I am with you to the end.

JERO: When the tailor delivers the order, you will understand.

REBECCA [*looking at the notes.*]: You did not fix a time for the meeting.

JERO: Tonight, Sister, at eight. We have no time to lose.

[*He picks up his chasuble, drapes it round his neck, his holy rod, bible, etc. Then he picks up the file again, opens it at a page and smiles, nodding with satisfaction, pats the file tenderly.*]

Our secret weapon, Sister Rebecca. We must take good care of it.

[*Locks it up in a cabinet.*]

REBECCA: You are going out Brother Jero?

JERO: Preparations, Sister, preparations. If we must fight this battle well, there is a certain ally we cannot do without. I must go and seek him.

[*He stops. Benevolent smile.*]

But we shall win, Sister Rebecca, we shall win. Because I have already the best ally on my side. Here, in this room.

[*Going, hesitates, moves towards the vase of flowers and raises it to his face, sniffing delicately with his eyes shut.*]

And I thank you for brightening up my humble shack with these flowers, even as you have lightened my life with your spiritual lamp.

[*Goes out rapidly, leaving Sister Rebecca coy, enraptured, confused, and overwhelmed all at once.*

Once outdoors Brother Jero slips round the side and observes her through a window. The woman's condition obviously uplifts him for he moves off with even jauntier step and a light adjustment to his chasuble. He is immediately confronted by a fellow prophet, Ananaias, one of the poorer specimens of the brotherhood but built like a barrel.]

ANANAIAS: What are you up to now, Jero? Spying on your own little nest?

JERO [*clamps his hand on Ananaias and drags him off.*]: S-sh.

ANANAIAS: Take your hands off me. [*Shakes him off easily but follows him.*] So who have you got in there? The bailiffs?

JERO: Bailiffs like all sinners are welcome in my church, Brother Ananaias. But I do not welcome them in my humble abode.

ANANAIAS: That's enough of that pious nonsense. I know you.

JERO: Just what do you know of me, Brother?

ANANAIAS: Eh, come off it. If it's bailiffs . . .

JERO: Bailiffs do not even know my dwelling Ananaias.

ANANAIAS: That's because you're a clever man, Jero. Not even your worst enemy will deny you that.

JERO: Will you kindly say what business brought you here? I'm a busy man.

ANANAIAS: All right, then. I came to tell you you're going to need all that cunning of yours very soon. The City Council have taken a final decision. They're going to chuck us out. Every last hypocritical son of the devil.

JERO: That is old news, Ananaias. And for some of us it doesn't matter of course. The Lord will provide. But for those with no true vocation . . .

ANANAIAS: Like you.

JERO: I said vocation. You wouldn't know what that is. The beach for you is just a living, nothing else.

ANANAIAS: You haven't done badly out of it yourself I notice.

JERO: It is written that the good Lord shall feed his true servants. What are you going to do when you wake up one morning and find yourself face to face with a bulldozer?

ANANAIAS [flexing his muscles.]: Let them try that's all, let them try.

JERO: Wrestling is one thing but a bulldozer is another. Not even you can wrestle with a bulldozer. And let me tell you, you are getting no younger.

ANANAIAS: Am I a born fool? There's a man drives those clumsy beasts isn't there? I leave the machine alone and drag him out by the scruff of his neck. When I've dipped him in the sea a few times he will emerge a good Christian and learn how to leave holy prophets alone.

JERO: That's not the way to fight them.

ANANAIAS: What's the way then? Stand by? Let them run me out of this land of milk and honey? I was doing quite well as a wrestler before I got the call and came into the service of the Lord. Gave all that up for this barren waste and now I can't even call it my own?

JERO: A moment ago it was a land of milk and honey.

ANANAIAS: Spiritual milk and honey of course. Otherwise barren waste. Look at it yourself.

JERO: Violence will not help us. I am calling a meeting tonight at which all these matters will be discussed. The good Lord shall help us find a way.

ANANAIAS: Calling a meeting? You already have something up your sleeve or you wouldn't be calling a meeting. Come on, let's have it. Let's be partners, you and me.

JERO: Tonight.

ANANAIAS: Now. Or I'll go in that room and tell whoever is there you were hiding and spying on them. I'll shout and tell them you're right here.

JERO [*folding his arms.*]: Go ahead, then.

ANANAIAS: Hey?

JERO: I said go ahead.

ANANAIAS: You're bluffing you know.

JERO: Call my bluff then. And by the way, when the battle is over and we have won our rights, I shall run you off this beach without lifting a finger.

ANANAIAS: You can't do that to me. I've got as much right as you to be here.

JERO: Not you.

ANANAIAS: You can't do it. I'm a holy man same as you.

JERO [*contemptuously.*]: Wrestling. Were you also wrestling in Kiri-kiri Prisons?

ANANAIAS [*clamping his hand over Jero's mouth in turn, and staring wildly round.*]: You're the devil himself you are. How come you know that?

JERO: I know.

ANANAIAS [*suddenly.*]: What of it? So I did a bit of thieving before and got nabbed. But I've been straight ever since. Earned my living wrestling for pick-ups clean and honest. And then I got the call. I'm reformed. What's wrong with a reformed sinner?

JERO: Reformed sinner? Hm. You didn't by any chance thug for a certain businessman just this last week did you? A little trade war over the monopoly of the whisky retail trade. Whisky Ananaias, whisky!

ANANAIAS [*dignified.*]: I beg your pardon, Brother Jero. I never was no thug in all my life. Bodyguard, yes. Bodyguard I was, and whoever says that is not a respectable position, internationally recognized, I'd just like to meet him that's all.

JERO: The police still have the fingerprints of the man who set fire to the store of one of the trade rivals. Bottles of spirits exploding all night and injuring innocent people. And the dumb, gross, incompetent all-muscle-and-no-brain petty criminal left a hefty thumbprint on the kerosene tin and then threw the kerosene tin on a refuse heap near by. They also know that that dirty great print matches the thumbprint of a certain ex-convict. The only thing they don't know is where he is hiding out after crimes of arson, unlawful wounding, attempted murder . . .

ANANAIAS [*swallowing hard.*]: Brother Jero . . .

JERO: Even the tin of kerosene was stolen from a near-by shop . . . that was robbery. Did you also use violence, Ananaias?

ANANAIAS: I swear to God, Brother Jero . . .

JERO: You are known to be a violent man. The Prosecutor can make it robbery with violence. And you know what that means.

ANANAIAS: I mean to say, Brother Jero, you are pretty hard on a man. You know yourself business is slow. . . . A man must eat. . . .

[*Jero lets him squirm a little.*]

JERO: Tonight at the meeting I shall put forward certain plans. . . .

ANANAIAS: I'll support you, Brother, depend on my vote any time. [*Getting warmer.*] And if there's anyone you'd prefer to take a walk outside on his head for making trouble . . .

JERO: I don't need your violence thank you. [*Going.*] And keep away from this place until meeting time.

ANANAIAS [*running after him.*]: I say Brother, Brother . . .

JERO: Well?

ANANAIAS: Brother Jero. Could you lend me a shilling or two till the meeting? You know I wouldn't ask if . . . you . . . well you see how it is yourself. Things haven't been going well lately. No contribution, nothing at all. The congregation have shrunk to nothing and even them as comes, all I get is the story of their family troubles. They no longer pay tithes.

JERO: You were greedy, Brother Ananaias. If every man of a hundred congregation paid a tithe at the end of every month he is going to notice very soon that a tithe from everyone means several times what each man is earning. And all that for one man—you—alone! That's why they stopped coming.

ANANAIAS: Heh?

JERO: Yes, that's how you lost your little flock.

ANANAIAS: From a hundred to nothing!

JERO: From a hundred to nothing, except those who come to borrow money.

ANANAIAS: But how come such an idea enter their head? I would never have thought of it.

JERO [*handing him a shilling.*]: Perhaps *somebody* put it in their head. Good day, Ananaias.

ANANAIAS: Heh? [*Stands open-mouthed, gaping at the retreating Jero.*]

[*From the opposite side, the Chief Executive Officer of the Tourist Board of the City Council emerges, rumpled and dusty from his hiding place. He is followed by the Clerk to the Board and a policewoman. Ananaias hides and observes.*]

CLERK: This is the place, sir.

EXECUTIVE [*angrily brushing his bowler hat and suit. The Clerk helps him.*]: About time too. I shall deal very rigorously with all of you who subjected me to this most humiliating adventure. Come all this way to lose not only a confidential file but a Confidential Secretary. Why I should be the one to be saddled with their recovery . . .

CLERK: Sir, it is the only way . . .

EXECUTIVE: Nothing unbecoming to a man's dignity is ever the only way. Bear that in mind.

CLERK: To achieve results sir . . .

EXECUTIVE: Kindly stop arguing with me. It is not in my character to skulk and hide until a mere charlatan is out of the way. I prefer to confront him squarely even if he's the devil himself.

CLERK: Sir, please let's enter and get the business over. He may return any time.

EXECUTIVE: If you are planning for me to escape through the window if he returns suddenly . . .

CLERK: Nothing of the sort, sir, nothing of the sort. I only say time is money, sir. Let's go in.

[*He knocks on the door but the Chief Executive barges in. Rebecca looks startled at their entrance. Ananaias creeps closer. The policewoman waits by the door.*]

EXECUTIVE: Is this the woman?

CLERK: Yes, sir. Miss Denton, this is the Chief Executive Officer of the Tourist Board of the City Council. Miss Denton, sir.

EXECUTIVE: Miss Denton . . .

REBECCA: My name is Rebecca.

EXECUTIVE: I do not believe, young lady, that we are on Christian name terms.

REBECCA: I do not believe that you are on Christian terms at all, sir. Your soul is in danger.

EXECUTIVE [*splutters badly and explodes.*]: My religious state is no concern of yours, young woman.

REBECCA: But it is, sir, it is. I am my brother's keeper. The state of your soul distresses me, sir.

CLERK: That's how it started, sir. That's how it started.

EXECUTIVE: That is how what started?

CLERK: That was how the prophet got her. He wasn't even addressing her at all but the C.E.O. who came to serve him notice. He kept preaching at him all the time but she was the one who got the message. Christ, sir, you should have seen her convulsions!

EXECUTIVE: Why the hell did he bring her in the first place?

REBECCA: Hell is true sir. I was living in hell but did not know it until Brother Jero pointed the path of God to me.

EXECUTIVE: I was not addressing you, woman.

CLERK: She was his private secretary . . .

EXECUTIVE: I know she was his private secretary, damn you . . .

REBECCA: He will not be damned sir, the Lord is merciful. . . .

EXECUTIVE: Can't anyone shut up this religious maniac? I asked, why bring her along? Do you see me here with my private secretary?

REBECCA: I shall answer that question. When you are saved, you are no longer afraid to tell the truth. My boss asked me to come with him to take notes, but in my heart I knew that he was planning to seduce me.

EXECUTIVE: What! You dare slander a senior government official of my department in my presence? I shall order an investigation and have you charged with . . .

CLERK: Don't, sir. It's the truth. The C.E.O. has had his eye on her a long time. Wouldn't let her alone in the office, making her

do overtime even if there was no work to do, just to try
and . . .

EXECUTIVE: That's enough thank you. I don't need the whole
picture painted in bold and dirty colours.

CLERK: Yes, sir, I mean, no, sir.

REBECCA: Do not distress yourself for that poor sinner. I pray for
the salvation of his soul every day.

EXECUTIVE: And we are praying for you to come to your senses.
And for a start just hand me the file you had with you. And be
thankful I am not having you charged for keeping an official
file after office hours.

CLERK: And a confidential file don't forget that, sir. Very
confidential.

EXECUTIVE: Quite right. The file, young lady. We will overlook
the offence since you weren't really in possession of your
senses.

REBECCA: I was never more clearly within my senses as now.

EXECUTIVE: You call this a sensible action? You, an intelligent
young girl, a fully trained Confidential Secretary . . .

CLERK: Eighty words per minute, sir, one hundred and twenty
shorthand . . .

EXECUTIVE: Did I ask you to supply me statistics?

CLERK: Beg pardon, sir. Just saying what a waste it is.

EXECUTIVE: Of course it's a bloody waste. Eighty words per
minute and a hundred and twenty shorthand. You had enough
will-power to resist the revolting advances of a lecherous Chief
Eviction Officer on the rampage, you are trusted sufficiently to
be assigned an official duty which is most essential to our
national economy and what happens—you permit yourself to
be bamboozled by a fake prophet, a transparent charlatan . . .

REBECCA [pitying.]: It is the devil which speaks in you sir, it's the
devil which makes you call Prophet Jeroboam all those bad
names.

EXECUTIVE: He deserves more than a bad name. He deserves a
bad end and he will come to it yet.

REBECCA: Fight the devil in you, sir, let us help you fight and
conquer him.

EXECUTIVE: Can't you see Jeroboam is the devil, damn you? All
the prophets on this beach are devils. . . .

REBECCA: The devil is in you, sir, I can see him.

EXECUTIVE: They have to be evicted. They stand in the way of progress. They clutter up the beach and prevent decent men from coming here and paying to enjoy themselves. They are holding up a big tourist business. You know yourself how the land value has doubled since we started public executions on this beach.

REBECCA: Shameless sinners who acquire wealth from the misfortunes of others? Will you make money off sin and iniquity? Oh sir, you must let Brother Jero talk to you about the evil in your plans. To make money out of sin is to bring sin upon the dwellers of your city. Not Sodom nor Gomorrah shall suffer as this city of yours when the wrath of the Lord descends upon it and the walls are wiped off the surface of the earth. The Lord speaks in me. I am the mouthpiece of his will. Give up this plan and let the prophets continue the blessed task of turning men back to the path of goodness and decency. . . .

EXECUTIVE: Shut her up. For God's sake shut her up.

REBECCA [*sudden joy.*]: Praise the Lord! A change has begun in you already. When you first came in you called on hell and you damned your fellow man. Now you call out in God's name. Hallelujah! Hallelujah! Hallelujah! Come to me, said the Lord. Call my name and I shall answer. Hallelujah! Hallelujah! Call his name and he shall heed you. Come to me, said the Lord, come to me. Come to me, said the Lord, come to me. Come to me, said the Lord, come to me. Call my name, and I shall heed you. Turn from sin and I shall feed you. Turn from filth and I shall cleanse you. Turn from filth and I shall cleanse you.
[*She approaches the Executive Officer with outstretched arms as if to embrace him. He retreats round the room but she follows him. She gets progressively 'inspired'.*]
Give up the plan, said the Lord, give up the plan. What avails all the wealth of the world, if your soul is lost. What avails your cars and houses if you'll burn in hell. Save this sinner, Lord save his soul. Burn out the greed of his heart, burn out the greed.
[*The Chief Executive makes the door but Ananaias with a roar of 'Hallelujah' steps out and blocks it. The Chief Executive flings*]

himself back into the room, bang into the arms of Rebecca who with
a shout of 'Hallelujah' holds him in an unbreakable embrace. His
bowler hat is knocked off and he soon parts company with his
umbrella. The Clerk retreats to the corner of the room on seeing
Ananaias, while the policewoman who tries to squeeze past
Ananaias is herself swept up with one arm and held there
by Ananaias.]

ANANAIAS: And this sinner, Lord, and this sinner!

REBECCA: Hallelujah!

ANANAIAS: From her labour of sin, oh Lord, from her labour of sin.

REBECCA: Hallelujah!

ANANAIAS: Policework is evil, oh Lord, policework is evil.

REBECCA: Halle-Halle-Hallelujah. [*And continues the chorus.*]

ANANAIAS: Save this sinner, Lord, save this sinner. Protect her from bribery, oh Lord! Protect her from corruption! Protect her from iniquities known and unknown, from practices unmentionable in thy hearing. Protect her from greed for promotion, from hunger for stripes, from chasing after citations with actions over and beyond the call of duty. Save her from harassing the innocent and molesting the tempted, from prying into the affairs of men and nosing out their innocent practices. Take out the beam in thine own eye, said the Lord.

REBECCA: Hallelujah!

ANANAIAS: Take out the beam in thine own eye!

REBECCA: Hallelujah!

ANANAIAS: Take out the beam in thine own eye, for who shall cast the first stone sayeth the Lord! Let him that hath no sin cast the first stone! Let him that hath no sin make the first arrest! Vengeance is mine saith the Lord, I shall recompense. Vengeance is mine, take not the law into your own hands! Verily I say unto you it is easier for a camel to pass through a needle's eye than for a police man or woman to enter the kingdom of heaven. We pray you bring them into the kingdom of heaven Lord. Bring them into the kingdom of heaven Lord. Bring them into the kingdom of heaven Lord. Bring them all into the kingdom of heaven. Save them from this hatred of their fellow men, from this hatred of poor weak

vessels who merely seek a modest living. Oh bring them into
the kingdom of heaven Lord. Right up to the kingdom of
heaven Lord. Right into the kingdom of heaven . . .
[*Rebecca's ecstacy has reached such proportions that she is
trembling from head to foot. Suddenly she flings out her arms,
knocking off the glasses of the Executive Officer.*]

REBECCA: Into the kingdom of heaven Lord, into the kingdom of
heaven . . .
[*Executive Officer seizes his freedom on the instant, dives through
the window headfirst. The Clerk is about to help him pick up his
fallen bowler and umbrella but changes his mind as Ananaias steps
forward. He follows his master through the window. Ananaias in
making for the fallen trophy lets go the policewoman who makes for
safety through the door. Rebecca is completely oblivious to all the
goings-on, only gyrating and repeating 'into the kingdom of
heaven . . .'. Ananaias picks up the umbrella and bowler, looks in
the cupboard and pockets a piece of bread he finds there, sniffs the
bottle and downs the contents. Finding nothing else that can be
lifted, he shrugs and starts to leave. Stops, takes another look at the
yet ecstatic Rebecca, goes over to a corner of the room and lifts up a
bucket of water, throws it on Sister Rebecca. She is stopped cold and
shudders. Exit Ananaias, taking the bucket with him.*]

SCENE II

*A portrait of the uniformed figure, in a different pose, hangs over the veranda
of the house where Chume lives in rented rooms. He is practising on a
trumpet, trying out the notes of 'What a friend we have in Jesus'. His
Salvation Army uniform is laid out carefully on a chair, stiffly starched and
newly ironed. Enter Major Silva, also of the Salvation Army.*

SILVA [*his accent is perfect RP plus a blend of Oxford.*]: Good day,
Corporal Chummy. I'm afraid the Captain could not come
today, but I will do my humble best to deputize for him.
[*Points to the trumpet and the sheet music.*] I am glad to notice
that you at least do some homework.
[*Chume looks at him with a mixture of suspicion and hostility.*]

CHUME: How can? You don't yourself blow trumpet.

SILVA: That indeed is true, but I do understand music and that really is what I intend to teach. Well, shall we begin?

CHUME: Where is Captain Winston?

SILVA: I have told you, he is unable to come. Now, if you will just tell me how far you have progressed with him we shall er, see what we can do eh?

CHUME [obviously dissatisfied.]: It is much better for man to have only one teacher. I begin get used to Captain Winston and then somebody else comes. Captain Winston understand how to teach me.

SILVA: Well, if you gave me a chance, Chummy, I think I may be able to fill Captain Winston's shoes for a lesson at least, with God's help. Well now . . .

CHUME: I think . . . well, we can wait. I mean I can just practise by myself until . . .

SILVA: Now, now, Chummy, we haven't got all day you know. Here, let's start with this shall we? Let's hear you play this piece, enh. [Selecting a sheet from the pile.] Then I can form some sort of idea. Right? Just play it once through.

CHUME: No, I don't want to play that one.

SILVA: Oh? All right. What do you wish to play? Pick out another one . . . anything you like. What hymn did you last practise with the Captain?

CHUME: I don't know. We just dey practise that's all.

SILVA: Well, play me what you last practised then.

CHUME: We practise hymn upon hymn. Er—one hymn like that, but I don't remember the name.

SILVA: Well, give me the first few bars and we will go from there. Right?
[Chume, obviously still uncomfortable, lifts the trumpet to his lips.]
Good. After four. One—Two—Three—Four.
[Chume sets upon 'What a friend we have in Jesus', Silva listens, registers mild surprise and shrugs. He waits for Chume to finish a verse.]
But that is the music I picked for you. I thought you said you didn't want to play it.

CHUME: En-hen? I change my mind.

SILVA: All right. Now, Chummy, this time try and play what is written down here. Stick it on your trumpet please. You see, you cannot give church hymns your own rhythm. You have to play what has been put down, so please read the score and play.

CHUME: I no talk so? I say is better to wait for Captain Winston. You can't understand how to teach me properly.

SILVA: Now, now, let's stop all this silliness. Here, let's have another go. It's all a matter of tempo, Chummy, tempo—Tam. ta. ra. ta. ra. ta. tam . . . tam . . . tam . . . ta. ra. ta. ra. ta. tam . . . Sharp and precise, Chummy, not like high life or juju music. Now shall we try again? This time, follow the score. [*He hands the sheet to Chume who sticks it on his trumpet.*] Now, are we ready? One—Two—Three . . . Tam . . . ta. ra . . . [*Chume plays the tune in the same swingy beat and Silva stops him.*]

SILVA: No, no, tempo, Chummy, tempo . . . good God! [*Coming round to point out the score.*] Corporal, do you always read music upside down?

CHUME: Hm? [*Guiltily begins to re-set the card, Silva looks at him with increasing suspicion.*] No wonder . . . en-hen, that's better.

SILVA [*severely.*]: Corporal Chummy, can you read music notation at all?

CHUME [*angrily.*]: I no talk so? You done come with your trouble. I say I go wait for Captain Winston you say you go fit teach me. Now you come dey bother me with music notation. Na paper man dey take trumpet play abi na music?

SILVA: Can you read music or not, Brother Chummy?

CHUME: Can you play trumpet or not, Major Silva?

SILVA: Really this is too much. How can Captain Winston expect me to teach you anything when you are musically illiterate.

CHUME: So I am illiterate now? I am illiterate? You are illiterate yourself. Illiterate man yourself.

SILVA: What! All right let us keep our temper.

CHUME: I have not lost my temper, it is you who don't know where you leave your own. You no even sabbe call my name correct and you dey call man illiterate. My name na Chume, no to Chummy.

SILVA [*with superhuman effort.*]: Anger, the Christian soldier's anger must be reserved only for the enemies of God and righteousness. It has no place within the army of God itself. Please bow your head, Corporal Chummy. I beg your pardon—Choo-may.

[*He strikes an attitude of prayer and Chume obediently does likewise. They remain silent for several moments.*]

May God give us strength against the sin of false pride and the devil of wrath, Amen.

CHUME: Amen.

SILVA: And now we shall begin all over again. [*Taking off the music card.*] We will forget all about this for the moment shall we? Captain Winston said that you were a natural on the trumpet and I suppose he is right. But there are certain things still to be learnt otherwise you will be like a lone voice crying in the wilderness. Now, shall we try again? I want you to watch me and try and follow the er, the movement of my hands—like this. Watch, watch . . . Tam . . . ta. ra. ta. tam. ta. ra . . . tam and so on. Got it?

CHUME [*assertively*.]: Yes, yes. That is how Captain Winston is teaching me.

SILVA: Good. Now are we ready? One—Two—Three . . .
[*Continues to talk as he plays.*]
That's better. Always remember that the tunes of the Army must be martial in colour and tempo. We march to it remember, not dance. No, no. Stop. No flourishes please, no flourishes. Especially not with a march. Most especially not with a march.

CHUME: Which one be flourish again?

SILVA: Beg your pardon?

CHUME: I say which one be flourish?

SILVA: Oh, flourish. Well, flourish is er . . . extra, you know, frills, decoration. What we want is pure notes, pure crystal clear notes. [*Chume looks blank.*] Look, just play the first bar again will you.

CHUME [*more mystified still.*]: Bar?

SILVA: Yes, the first . . . all right, start from the beginning again will you and I will stop you when you come to the flourish. . . .
[*Chume plays. Silva stops him after a few notes.*]
That's it. You played that bit Ta-a-ta instead of ta-ta.

CHUME: Oh you mean the pepper.

SILVA: Pepper?

CHUME: Enh, pepper. When you cook soup you go put small pepper. Otherwise the thing no go taste. I mean to say, 'e go taste like something. After all, even sand-sand get in own taste. But who dey satisfy with sand-sand? If they give you sand-sand to chop you go chop?

SILVA [*beginning to doubt his senses.*]: Mr. Chume, if I tell you I understand one word of what you're saying I commit the sin of mendacity.

CHUME: What! You no know wetin pepper be? Captain Winston, as soon as I say pepper 'e knows wetin I mean one time.

SILVA: I do not know, to use your own quaint expression, wetin musical pepper be, Mr. Chume.

CHUME: And condiments? Iru? Salt? Ogiri? Kaun? And so on and so forth?

SILVA: Mr. Chume, I'm afraid I don't quite see the relevance.

CHUME: No no, no try for *see* am. Make you just *hear* am. [*Blows a straight note.*] Dat na plain soup. [*Blows again, slurring into a higher note.*] Dat one na soup and pepper. [*Gives a new twist.*] Dat time I put extra flavour. Now, if you like we fit lef' am like that. But suppose I put stockfish, smoke-fish, ngwam-ngwam . . .

SILVA: If you don't mind I would just as soon have a straightforward rehearsal. We have no time for all this nonsense.

CHUME: Wait small, you no like ngwam-ngwam or na wetin? Na my traditional food you dey call nonsense?

SILVA: I had no intention whatsoever to insult you, Mr. Chume.

CHUME: If nonsense no to big insult for man of my calibre, den I no know wetin be insult again.

SILVA: Brother Chume, please. Do remember we have an important date at tomorrow's executions. We must rehearse!

CHUME [*blasts an aggressive note on the trumpet.*]: Stockfish! [*Another.*] Bitter-leaf! I done tire for your nonsense. [*Throws down cap, blows more notes.*] Locust bean and red pepper! [*Kicks off shoes.*] If you still dey here when I put the ngwam-ngwam you go sorry for your head.
[*Throws himself into the music now, turning the tune into a traditional beat and warming up progressively. His legs begin to*

slice into the rhythm and before long his entire body is caught up with it. He dances aggressively towards Silva who backs away but cannot immediately escape as Chume's dance controls the exit. Finally when Chume leaps to one side he seizes his chance and takes to his heels. Chume continues dancing and does not notice Brother Jero who enters and, after a despairing shake of his head, with his usual calculating gesture, steps into the dance with him. Chume becomes slowly aware that other legs have joined his, his movement peters to a stop and he follows the legs up to the smiling, benevolent face of Brother Jero. Chume backs off.]

JERO [*holds out his arms.*]: It is no ghost, Brother Chume. It is no apparition that stands before you. Assure yourself that you are well again and suffer no more from hallucinations. It is I, your old beloved master the Prophet Jeroboam. Immaculate Jero. Articulate Hero of Christ's Crusade.

CHUME [*He stands stock still.*]: Commot here before I break your head.

JERO: Break my head? What good will my broken head do you?

CHUME: It will make compensation for all de ting I done suffer for your hand. I dey warn you now, commot.

JERO: Suffer at my hands? You, Brother Chume? Suffer at my hands.

CHUME: You tell the police say I craze. Because God expose you and your cunny-cunny and I shout am for the whole world . . .

JERO: Brother Chume . . .

CHUME: I no be your Brother, no call me your brother. De kin' brother wey you fit be na the brotherhood of Cain and Abel. The brotherhood of Jacob and Esau. Eat my meat and tief my patrimony . . .

JERO: You do me great injustice, Brother Chume.

CHUME: Na so? And de one you do me na justice? To lock man inside lunatic asylum because you wan' cover up your wayo. You be wayo man plain and simple. Wayo prophet! [*Warming up.*] Look, I dey warn you, commot here if you like your head! [*Advancing.*]

JERO: You raised your hand once against the anointed of the Lord, remember what it cost you.

CHUME: Which anointed of the Lord? You?

JERO: You raised a cutlass against me Brother Chume, but I forgave you.

CHUME: Dat na forgiveness? Three month inside lunatic asylum!
Na dat den dey call forgiveness for your bible?

JERO: Was that not better than a life sentence for attempted
murder?

CHUME: If to say I get my cutlass inside your head that time this
world for done become better place. They can hang me but I
for become saint and martyr. I for die but de whole world go
call me Saint Chume.

JERO: But look round you, Brother Chume, look around you.
You want to make this world a better place? Good! But to get
hanged in the process? And perhaps in public? For whom? For
the sake of people like Major Silva? People who don't even
understand the musical soul which the Lord has given you?
Are they worth it, Brother Chume? Oh I was watching you
for some time you know—that man is an enemy believe me.
An enemy. He does not understand you. I am sure they are all
like that.

CHUME: They are not all like that. Captain Winston . . .

JERO: A white man. He is not one of us. And you know yourself
he's a hypocrite. All white men are hypocrites.

CHUME: Na him come save me from that lunatic asylum, not so?
If dat na hympocrisy then thank God for hympocrites.

JERO: He needed a trumpeter.

CHUME: Before that time I no fit play trumpet. I no sabbe hol' am
self.

JERO: But you were playing on a penny flute and he heard you. I
know the whole story, Brother Chume. He and his band came
round to comfort you unfortunate inmates . . .

CHUME [*violently*.]: I am not unfortunate inmate. Na you tell them
to lock me inside dat place with crazemen. The day I fust meet
you, dat day na my unfortunate.

JERO [*going progressively into a 'sermonic' chanting style*.]: Brother
Chume, you should thank the good Lord, not blame him for
the situation in which you found yourself. When he, in his
wisdom saw fit to place wings on my feet and make me fly
upon the deserted beach away from your flaming cutlass of
wrath, it was not, be assured, my life upon which he set such
value. No, Brother Chume, it was yours. Yours! Consider, if
you had indeed achieved your nefarious intention and

martyred me upon the sands, would not your soul be damned for ever? Picture my blood sinking into the sand and mingling with the foam, your feet sinking into the gruesome mixture and growing heavy with the knowledge of eternal damnation. What man, be he so swift of foot can run unaided upon a sandy shore? Could you think to escape the hounds of God's judgement and the law? See yourself as you would be, a fugitive from man and God, a dark soul lost and howling in the knowledge of damnation. Or would you fling yourself upon the waves and seek to drown yourself? If you succeeded, you were doubly damned. If you failed and the sea rejected you, flung your tainted body back upon the shore, think what a life of rejection yours would be, unable to seek solace even in death! Did you not yourself mention the moral tale of Cain and Abel only this minute? Was Cain not damned for ever? Was he not cursed by the Almighty himself? But I knew it was not in you to perform such an evil act. It was, obviously, the work of the devil. Your mind was turned away from the light of reason and your judgement clouded for a while. Was it then wrong of me to protect you the only way I could? For three months you received tender care and treatment. Your good woman, Amope, seeing her husband in danger of losing his reason proved once again that a heart of gold beat beneath her shrewish nature. For the first time since your marriage, Brother Chume, you saw that a voice of honey may lurk beneath the sandy tongue of a termagant. She showed you the care and love which she had denied you these many years. And so at last, seeing that you had recovered your reason, the good Lord sent unto you a deliverer just as he did deliver Nebuchadnessar of old from the horror of darkness and insanity. Oh, Brother Chume, Brother Chume, great is the Lord and full of kindness. Let us kneel down and praise his name. Praise the Lord, Brother Chume, praise the Lord. Praise the Lord for the gift of reason and the gift of life. Then praise him also for your coming promotion, yes, your coming promotion for this is the glad tidings of which I am the humble bearer.

CHUME [*hesitant.*]: Promotion?

JERO: Of whose glad tidings I am made humble bearer. I send *you*,

Prophet Jero, said the Lord. Blessed are the peacemakers for they shall inherit the kingdom. Make your peace with Brother Chume and take with you this peace-offering, the good tidings of his coming promotion.

CHUME: Promotion? How can?

JERO [*sternly*.]: Do you doubt, Brother Chume? Do you doubt my prophecy? Has your sojourn among lunatics made you forget who prophesied war and have we not lived to see it come to pass? Do you trust in me and praise the Lord or do you confess yourself a waverer at this hour of trial.

CHUME: Praise the Lord.

JERO: In his new image, Brother, sing his praise.

CHUME: Sing his praise.

JERO: Through blood has he purged us, as prophesied by me.

CHUME: Sing his praise.

JERO: Sing his praise, hallelujah, sing his praise.

CHUME: Hallelujah!

JERO: Out of the dark he brought you, into the light.

CHUME: Hallelujah!

JERO [*going all out to truly arouse Chume's 'rhythmic rapport'*.]: Out of the dark he brought you, into the light!

CHUME: Hallelujah!

JERO: Never again to stumble, never again.

CHUME: Hallelujah!

JERO: Sent him off howling, praise Him, fire in his tail.

CHUME: Hallelujah!

JERO: Praise the Lord Hallelujah praise the Lord.

CHUME: Hallelujah!

JERO: Praise the Lord, Brother, praise the Lord.

CHUME: Praise the Lord, Brother, praise the Lord.

JERO: Praise the Lord, Brother, praise the Lord.

CHUME: Hallelujah! Hallelujah, praise the Lord, Hallelujah! Praise the Lord. Hallelujah, praise the Lord, Hallelujah! Praise the Lord . . .

[*With Jero clapping in rhythm and Brother Chume swaying and chanting on his knees.*]

JERO [*moves aside and detachedly observes Chume in ecstasy.*]: I had my doubts for a while but I should have known better. These Salvation Army brothers may be washed in the red blood of the Lord, but the black blood of the Bar Beach brotherhood proves stronger every time. [*Sudden shout, turning to Chume.*] Hallelujah, Brother, Hallelujah!

[*He joins Chume for a few more moments, then taps him on the shoulder.*]

JERO: Brother Chume. Brother Chume. [*He shakes him a little.*] Brother Chume. Brother Chume!

[*Picks up the trumpet and blows a blast in Chume's ear.*]

CHUME [*starts out of his ecstasy.*]: Here, Brother Jero.

JERO [*with excitement.*]: The trumpet of the Lord, Chume! It sounds the clarion to duty. There is a time for everything, so says the Lord. A time for laughing and time for crying; a time for waking and a time for sleeping; a time for praying and a time for action. This is a time for action.

CHUME: Action?

JERO: Yes, action. Rise, Brother Chume, and follow me. The Lord hath need of thee.

CHUME [*getting up, hastily pulls himself together.*]: Of me, Brother Jero?

JERO: Yes, of you. You have stayed too long among the opposition. Cheated. Humiliated. Scorned. It is time for your elevation. Pick up your trumpet and follow me. I shall explain it all on our way to meet your—[*He pauses for deliberate emphasis.*]—brother *Prophets*.

CHUME [*open-mouthed.*]: Brother Prophets, Brother Jero? But me na . . .

JERO: Not any longer, Chume. From now you are a holy prophet in your own light. No, no, that is *not* the promotion. It is only the first taste. Your full elevation takes place tonight, before the assembled brotherhood of the beach. You have gone through the fires of hell and emerged a strong servant of the Lord. You are saved, redeemed, inspired, and re-dedicated. From now on, a true brother, an equal; no longer a servant of mine. Kneel, Brother Chume.

CHUME [*kneeling groggily.*]: But prophet . . . me na only poor . . .

JERO: I perform only the good Lord's commands, nothing more. [*With his holy rod he taps him on both shoulders.*] Arise Prophet Chume, serve the Lord and fight his cause till eternity. [*Turns the rod round and offers him the 'hilt'.*] Until you obtain yours and it is consecrated you may use mine.

CHUME [*overwhelmed.*]: Dis kindness too much, Brother Jero.
JERO: I am only the instrument of the Lord's will. [*Briskly.*] Now
get up and let's go. The others are awaiting and we have
much to do.

BLACKOUT

SCENE III

The front space of Brother Jero's headquarters. Loud chatter among a most
bizarre collection of prophets. Sister Rebecca emerges from the house carrying
the portrait from the office and hangs it against the outer wall. The desk
and chair have already been moved out of the office for the meeting. Rebecca
takes a chair to a most unbending individual who stares straight ahead and
keeps his arms folded. He is the only one who seems to abstain from the
free-flowing drinks, the effect of which is already apparent on one or two.

SHADRACH: No, Sister, we refuse to sit down. We refuse to sit
down. We have been slighted and we make known our protest.
We have been treated with less courtesy than becomes the
leader of a denomination twenty thousand strong. Brother
Jero, at whose behest we have presented ourselves here at great
inconvenience, is not himself here to welcome us. We protest
his discourtesy.
CALEB: Hear hear. [*Hiccups.*] Hardly the conduct of a gentleman
prophet.
REBECCA: Brother Shadrach, I assure you he was held up by
matters which concern this very affair you have come to
discuss.
ISAAC: He is very long about it then.
SHADRACH: Much much too long, Sister Rebecca. To make us
wait is an act of indignity thrust upon us.
ANANAIAS: Oh sit down, you fatuous old hypocrite.
SHADRACH [*turns to go.*]: We take our leave.
CALEB: Hear hear. [*Hiccup.*] Let's all stage a dignified walk-out.
Nobody walks out these days. Not since the parliamentarians
vanished.

ISAAC: Good old days those. Good for the profession.

CALEB: Come on, old Shad, give us a walk-out. [*With much difficulty on the word.*] An ecclesiastically dignified walk-out.

REBECCA: Brother Shadrach, please . . .

SHADRACH: No, we take our leave. For the third time tonight we have been insulted by a common riff-raff of the calling. We take our leave.

CALEB: Hear hear. The honourable member for . . .

REBECCA: Pay no attention Brother. I apologize on their behalf. Forgive us all for being remiss.

SHADRACH: I forgive you, Sister. [*Sits down.*]

ANANAIAS [*leans over the back of his chair.*]: You will burst, Shadrach, you will burst like the frog in the swamp.

CALEB: Like the frog in the adage, Brother. [*Hiccup.*] Frog in the adage.

SHADRACH [*without losing his poise, whips his hand round and seizes that of Ananaias by the wrist and brings it round front. The hand is seen to contain a purse.*]: Mine, I believe, Ananaias?

ANANAIAS: It dropped on the ground. Is that the thanks I get for helping you pick it up?

SHADRACH: I accuse no one, Ananaias. [*Returning wallet into the recesses of his robes.*] We are all met, I hope, in a spirit of brotherhood. The lesson reads, I am my brother's keeper Ananaias, not, I am my brother's pursekeeper.

ANANAIAS [*turns away.*]: Lay not your treasures upon earth says the good book. Verily verily I say unto you, it is easier for a camel and so on and so forth.

CALEB [*raising his mug.*]: Sister Rebecca, my spirits are low.

REBECCA [*rushing to fill it.*]: Forgive me, Brother Caleb.

CALEB: Upliftment is in order, God bless you.

ISAAC: So where is this Jeroboam fellow? When is he coming to tell us why he has made us forsake our stations to wait on his lordship?

REBECCA: In a moment, Brother Matthew. [*Going to fill his mug.*]

ISAAC: I am not Brother Matthew . . .

REBECCA: I beg your pardon, Brother.

CALEB: A clear case of mistaken identity, Sister Rebecca.

ISAAC: I am not Brother Matthew, sister, and I beg you to note that fact.

MATTHEW [*nettled.*]: May one ask just what you have against being
  Brother Matthew?

ISAAC: I know all about Brother Matthew, and that should be
  enough answer for anyone with a sense of shame.

REBECCA: Forgive my unfortunate error. Don't start a quarrel on
  that account.

ISAAC: And to think he has the nerve to show his face here. Some
  people are utterly without shame.

CALEB: Hear hear.

MATTHEW: And others are poor imitation Pharisees.

CALEB: Hear hear.

ISAAC: Better an imitation Pharisee than a sex maniac.

MATTHEW: I take exception to that!

ISAAC: Very good. Take exception.

MATTHEW: Dare repeat that and see if it doesn't land you in
  court for slander. Go on, we are all listening. I have witnesses.
  Come on I dare you.

ISAAC: I don't have to. We all know the truth. You may have been
  acquitted but we know the truth.

MATTHEW: Coward!

ISAAC: Fornicator.

MATTHEW: Drunkard, con-man. Forger.

CALEB: Three to one. Foul play.

REBECCA [*getting between them as they head for a clash.*]: Brothers, in
  the name of our common calling I beg of you . . .
  [*Jero and Chume enter. Rebecca sighs with relief.*]
  Oh, Brother Jero, you are truly an answer to prayers.

JERO: Welcome, Brothers, welcome all of you and forgive me for
  arriving late at my own meeting. [*Hands Rebecca a key.*] Unlock
  the safe and bring out our secret weapon, Sister.

ISAAC: We have waited two hours, Brother.

ANANAIAS: You have not been here a half-hour Isaac. I saw you
  come in.

JERO: A-ah, I see empty mugs. No wonder our brothers are
  offended. Sister Rebecca, we require better hospitality.

REBECCA [*emerging with the file.*]: Do you think that wise, Brother
  Jero? They are already quite . . .

JERO: Trust me, I know what I am doing Sister. [*Loudly.*] More
  drinks for our brothers. Fill up the cups Sister Rebecca.

SHADRACH: We do not drink. We came here for a serious
　　discussion, so we were informed. We have not come here to
　　wine and dine.

JERO: We will not quarrel. I admit the fault is mine. Sister
　　Rebecca, some snuff for Brother Shadrach.

REBECCA: I shall get it at once, Brother Jero.

JERO [*turns and beams on the gathering.*]: And now, dear brother
　　shepherds of the flock, let us waste no more time. We are
　　mostly known to one another so I shall not waste time on
　　introductions. The subject is progress. Progress has caught up
　　with us. Like the oceantide it is battering on our shore-line, the
　　doorstep of our tabernacle. Projects everywhere! Fun fairs!
　　Gambling! Casinos! The servants of Mammon have had their
　　heads turned by those foreign fleshpots to which they are
　　drawn whenever they travel on their so-called economic
　　missions. And our mission, the mission of the good Lord
　　Jehovah shall be the sacrificial lamb, on the altar of Mammon.
　　Oh when you see smoke rising on that grievous day, know that
　　it rises from these shacks of devotion which we have raised to
　　shelter the son of God on his Visitation on that long-awaited
　　day. And what shall he find? What shall he find when he comes
　　over the water, that great fisherman among men, thinking to step
　　on to the open tabernacle which we, you and I, have founded
　　here to await his glorious coming? *THIS!* [*With a flourish he
　　pulls out a sheaf of photographs from his bag.*] This, my brothers!
　　[*Jero observes their reactions as the photos of luscious scantily-clad
　　bathers are circulated. Reactions vary from Shadrach who turns
　　away in calculated disgust to Ananaias who finds them lewdly
　　hilarious and Matthew who literally drools.*]

SHADRACH: It must never happen here!

ISAAC: Never. We must organize.

CALEB: I concur. Rally the union. No business sharks in our
　　spirituous waters.

ISAAC: All legitimate avenues of protest must be explored.

MATTHEW: What for?

ANANAIAS: What do you mean, what for?

MATTHEW: I said what for? These photos reveal strayed souls in
　　need of salvation. Must we turn away from suchlike? Only the
　　sick have need of the physician.

ISAAC: Not your kind of physick, Brother Matthew.

SHADRACH: If we take Brother Jeroboam's meaning correctly, and we think we do, the intention is to exclude . . . er . . . us, the physicians from this so-called resort is it not, Brother?

MATTHEW: We don't know that for certain.

JERO [*hands him the file at an open page.*]: Read this, Brother Matthew. These are the minutes of the meeting of Cabinet at which certain decisions were taken.

MATTHEW [*shrinks away.*]: What file is that?

JERO: Read it.

MATTHEW: It says Confidential on that paper. I don't want any government trouble.

ISAAC: Very wise of you, Brother Matthew. Mustn't risk your parole. [*Takes the file.*] I'll read it. [*At the first glance he whistles.*] How did you get hold of this, Jero?

JERO: The Lord moves in mysterious ways . . .

ANANAIAS: . . . His wonders to perform. Amen.

ISAAC [*reading.*]: 'Memorandum of the Cabinet Office to the Board of Tourism. Proposals to turn the Bar Beach into a National Public Execution Amphitheatre.' Whew! You hadn't mentioned that.

JERO: I was saving it for a surprise. It is the heart of the whole business enterprise.

SHADRACH: We don't understand. Does this mean . . . ?

JERO: Business, Brother Shadrach, big business.

MATTHEW: Where do we come in in all this?

JERO: Patience, we're coming to it. Brother Isaac, do read on. Go down to the section titled Slum Clearance.

ISAAC [*His expression clouds in fury.*]: Hn? Hn? Hng!!!

MATTHEW: What is it? What is it?

ISAAC: Riff-raff! They call us riff-raff!

JERO: Read it out, Brother Isaac.

ISAAC: 'Unfortunately the beach is at present cluttered up with riff-raff of all sorts who dupe the citizenry and make the beach unattractive to decent and respectable people. Chiefest among these are the so-called . . .' Oh may the wrath of Jehovah smite them on their blasphemous mouths!

JERO [*taking back the file.*]: Time is short, Brothers. We cannot afford to be over-sensitive. [*Reads.*] '. . . the so-called prophets and evangelists. All these are not only to be immediately expelled but steps must be taken to ensure that they never at any time find their way back to the execution stadium.'

SHADRACH: Fire and brimstone! Sodom and Gomorrah!

JERO: Patience Brothers, patience. 'It is proposed however, that since the purpose of public execution is for the moral edification and spiritual upliftment of the people, one respectable religious denomination be licensed to operate on the Bar Beach. Such a body will say prayers before and after each execution, and where appropriate will administer the last rites to the condemned. They will be provided a point of vantage where they will preach to the public on the evil of crime and the morals to be drawn from the miserable end of the felons. After which their brass band shall provide religious music.'

ISAAC: A brass band? That means . . .

JERO: Yes, the Salvation Army.

SHADRACH: Enough. We have heard all we need to know of the conspiracy against us. The question now is, what do we do to foil them?

JERO: Organize. Band together. Brother Matthew is right: the sick have need of healing. We must not desert the iniquitous in their greatest hour of need.

SHADRACH [looking towards Caleb, then Ananaias.]: We foresee problems in banding together with certain members of the calling.

JERO: All problems can be overcome. The stakes are high, Brother Shadrach.

SHADRACH: The price is also high.

ANANAIAS: Oh shut up, you fatuous hypocrite!

SHADRACH: Ananaias!

JERO: Peace, Brothers, peace. Ananaias, I shall require greater decorum from you.

ANANAIAS: You have it before you ask, Brother Jero. Anything you say.

MATTHEW: What does Jeroboam have in mind, exactly? You didn't call us together without some idea in your head.

JERO: Quite correct, Brother Matthew. I have outlined certain plans of action and have even begun to pursue them. The time is short, in fact, the moment is now upon us. The Bar Beach becomes the single execution arena, the sole amphitheatre of death in the entire nation. Where at the moment we have spectators in thousands, the proposed stadium will seat hundreds of thousands. We must acquire the spiritual monopoly of such a captive congregation.

CALEB: Hear, hear!

ISAAC [*impatiently*.]: Yes, but how?

JERO: We form ONE body. Acquire a new image. Let the actuality of power see itself reflected in that image, reflected and complemented. We shall prophesy with one voice, not as lone voices crying in the wilderness, but as the united oracle of the spiritual profession.

CALEB: Brother Jero, I hand it to you. I couldn't have phrased it better and I pride myself on being a bookish sort of fellow.

MATTHEW: What image then?

JERO: Such an image as will make our outward colours one with theirs.

CALEB: Show them up in their true colours you mean. [*He splutters with laughter until he is coughing helplessly, near-choking*.]

JERO: Brother Caleb, I think that remark was in very bad taste.

MATTHEW [*wildly*.]: And dangerous. Very dangerous. I refuse to remain one moment longer if such remarks are permitted. We are not here to look for trouble. I dissociate myself from that remark.

ISAAC: Still watching your parole, Brother Matthew?

CALEB [*leans over drunkenly*.]: Psst. Is it true the magistrate was a sidesman in your church?

JERO: Brothers, Brothers, this is no time for our private little quarrels. We must not envy Brother Matthew his spiritual influence in er . . . certain fortunate quarters when we are on the threshold of bringing the highest and the mightiest under our spiritual guidance.

SHADRACH: Are you day-dreaming? In a day or two you will not even have a roof over your head and you speak of . . .

JERO: Yes Brother Shad, the highest and mightiest, I assure you, will come under our spiritual guidance.

SHADRACH: Success has swelled your head, Brother Jero.

CALEB: That's why he thinks big. [*Roars off alone into laughter*.]

JERO: Suppose I tell you, Shadrach, that it has come to the ears of the rulers that a certain new-formed religious body has prophesied a long life to the régime? That this mysterious body has declared that the Lord is so pleased with their er . . . spectacular efforts to stamp out armed robbery, with the speed of the trials, the refusal of the right to appeal, the rejection of silly legal technicalities, and the high rate of executions, that all these things are so pleasing to the Lord that he has granted eternal life to their régime?

SHADRACH: They won't believe you.

JERO: They have already. The seed was well planted and it has taken root. Tomorrow the Tourist Board shall propose a certain religious body for the new amphitheatre. The Cabinet will be informed that it is the same body which has made the prophecy. Our spiritual monopoly shall be approved without debate—Does anyone doubt me?

SHADRACH: The Shadrach-Medrach-Abednego Apostolic Trinity has a twenty-thousand strong congregation all over the country. These include men from all walks of life including very high ranks within the uniformed profession. We propose therefore that our Apostolic Trinity absorb all other denominations into its spiritual bosom. . . .

[*The proposal is greeted with instant howls of rejection.*]

JERO: No, Brother Shadrach. As you see, it just will not do. Are there any other proposals?

[*They all shrug at one another.*]

ISAAC: All right Jero, let's have your proposal.

JERO: You all know Brother Chume. Prophet Chume I ought to say.

MATTHEW: But he's the one who went off his head.

ANANAIAS: Looks saner than you or me. Cleaner anyway.

JERO: Prophet Chume has left the ranks of the enemy and cast his lot among us. With his help, with the intimate knowledge which he has acquired of the workings of that foreign body to which he once belonged we shall re-create ourselves in the required image. We shall manifest our united spiritual essence in the very form and shape of the rulers of the land. Nothing, you will agree could be more respectable than that. [*Rises.*] Sister Rebecca, bring out the banner!

REBECCA [*runs out with the flag, flushed with excitement.*]: Is this the moment, Brother Jero?

JERO: The moment is now, Sister. Witness now the birth of the first Church of the Apostolic Salvation Army of the Lord! [*Chume begins the tune of 'Are you washed in the Blood of the Lamb'. Rebecca sings lustily, deaf to the world.*] Behold the new body of the Lord! Forward into battle, Brothers!

ISAAC: Against what?

JERO: Precisely.

SHADRACH [*disdainfully.*]: Precisely what? He asks, against what? You say, precisely.

JERO: Precisely. Against what? We don't know any more than our secular models. They await a miracle, we will provide it.

SHADRACH [*indicating Chume.*]: With lunatics like him. You fancy yourself an empire builder.

JERO: A spiritual empire builder, Brother Shadrach. Those who are not with us, are against us. This is the Salvation Army with a difference. With pepper and ogiri. With ngwam-ngwam. Right, Brother Chume?

[*Chume nods vigorously without stopping the music.*]

ISAAC: Hey, you haven't said who is to be head of this Army.

CALEB: Good point. Very good point.

JERO: We come in as equals. We form a syndicate.

SHADRACH: Everybody needs a head.

CALEB [*solemnly.*]: Old Shad is de-ee-eep. [*Hiccups.*]

JERO: A titular head. He gives the orders and keeps close watch on the church treasury. Purely ceremonial.

ISAAC: Yes, but who? Who do you have in mind for Captain?

JERO: Captain, Brother Isaac? No no, not captain. We must not cut our image small in the eyes of the world. General, at least.

SHADRACH: And who would that be, you still haven't said.

JERO: Whoever has the secrets of the Tourist Board in his hands. Whoever can guarantee that the new body does obtain nomination from the Tourist Board.

ANANAIAS: I knew it. I knew he was keeping something to himself.

ISAAC: You have thought of everything, haven't you?

JERO: You may say I am divinely inspired, Brother Isaac.

SHADRACH: And you, we presume, are in possession of the aforesaid secrets?

JERO: Have we a united body or not?

ANANAIAS: Christ! Those fat pockets begging to be picked while their owners are laughing at the poor devil at the stake. It's a sin to be missing from this garden of Eden. [*Throws Jero a salute.*] General! Reporting for duty, sir.

JERO [*saluting in turn.*]: Sergeant-major! Go in the room and find a uniform that fits you.

ISAAC: Millionaire businessmen! Expensive sinners coming to enjoy the Bar Beach show.

JERO: Who else is for the Army of the Lord?

ISAAC: It's Sodom and Gomorrah. The milk is sour and the honey is foul.

JERO: Who is for the Army of the Lord?

ISAAC: What rank do you have in mind for me?

JERO: Major. [*Gestures.*] In there. You'll find a uniform that fits you.

[*As he goes in Ananaias returns singing lustily and banging a tambourine. He is uniformed in what looks like a Salvation Army outfit except for the cap which is the 'indigenous' touch, made in local material and 'abetiaja' style. The combination is ludicrous.*]

MATTHEW [*takes another look at the picture of a curvaceous bathing belle and decides.*]: I used to play the flute a little, Brother Jer . . . I mean General Jeroboam. In fact I was once in my school band.

JERO: You'll find a uniform in there, Captain.

SHADRACH: The uniform will not change you. You will still be the same Bar Beach riff-raff no matter what you wear. Nobody will give you a monopoly.

CALEB: Wrong on all counts, Brother Shad. By the cut of his tailor shall a man be known. Uniform maketh man.

JERO: Very soon the syndicate will be closed. The Army hierarchy is for foundation members only. We hold office by divine grace, in perpetuity. Join now or quit.

SHADRACH: Overreacher. We know your kind, Jeroboam. Continue to count your chickens.

CALEB: Wrong again, Shad. You don't know the worthy Jero it seems. If he says he'll get the monopoly, he will. A thorough methodical man, very much after my heart.

JERO: What rank do you want, Caleb?

CALEB: I'll stick out for Colonel. I may be slightly [*Hiccups.*] see what I mean, but I know what's what. I'm an educated man and that's a rare commodity in this outfit. Present company naturally excepted, General.

JERO: Lieutenant-Colonel.

CALEB: General, I'm thinking that instead of merely preaching at the assembly we could do a morality play, you know, something like our Easter or Christmas Cantata. I'm quite nifty at things like that—The Rewards of Sin, The Terrible End of the Desperado . . . and so on. Well er . . . that sort of specialized duties deserves a higher rank don't you think, mon General?

JERO [*firmly.*]: Lieutenant-Colonel.

CALEB [*throws a drunken salute.*]: So be it, mon General.

[*Goes in. The others are coming out, uniformed.*]

JERO: You are alone, Shadrach.

SHADRACH: We are never alone. We proceed this minute to the Chairman of the Tourist Board, there to put an end to our ambitions. The much-respected aunt of the Chairman is a devout member of our flock.

JERO [*looks at his watch.*]: If you wish to see the Chief Executive Officer in person he will arrive in a few minutes. He was invited to this meeting.

SHADRACH: Here?

JERO: He will negotiate for the other side.

SHADRACH: Bluff! The only officer you'll see here is the Eviction Officer.

ANANAIAS [*looking out.*]: My General, the enemy is without!

JERO: Let him pass freely.

ANANAIAS: What do they want? [*Going to the door.*] You're back are you? Lucky for you the General gives you safe conduct.

EXECUTIVE: You have a nerve summoning us here at this time of night. [*Blocking his ears.*] Will you tell them to stop that lunatic din!

JERO: Colonel Chume . . .

ANANAIAS: He won't hear. I'll stop him for you.

[*Goes over, salutes, and takes the trumpet from his mouth.*]

JERO: Sit down.

EXECUTIVE: I demand . . .

JERO: Seat him down Sergeant-Major.

ANANAIAS: My pleasure, General, sir.

[*Forces down the Chief Executive into a chair. The Clerk quickly scurries into a seat.*]

JERO: Excuse me while I get ready for the negotiations.

[*He picks up the file off the table with deliberate movements. The Executive Officer stares at the file fascinated. He exchanges looks with the Clerk who quickly looks down.*

Jero goes into the room.]

SHADRACH: We are, we presume, in the presence of the Chief Eviction Officer of the Tourist Board.

CLERK: No, that's C.E.O. II. This is C.E.O. I, Chief Executive Officer. C.E.O. III is still to be appointed—that's the Chief Execution Officer, a new post.

EXECUTIVE [*turns to inspect Shadrach slowly, like a strange insect.*]: And who might you be?

SHADRACH: Leader of the Shadrach-Medrach-Abednego Apostolic flock, twenty-thousand strong.

EXECUTIVE [*wearily.*]: Another fanatic.

SHADRACH: It is our hope that you have come here to put an end to the schemes of this rapacious trader on piety who calls himself . . .

EXECUTIVE: Oh Christ!

[*Enter Jero, resplendent in a Salvation Army General uniform. Chume blares a fanfare on the trumpet.*]

JERO: The file, Sister Rebecca.

EXECUTIVE: And now I hope you will . . .

JERO: You came, I trust, alone as requested.

EXECUTIVE: Yes I foolishly risked my life coming without protection to this haunt of cut-throats.

JERO: It was entirely in your own interests.

EXECUTIVE: So you said. And now perhaps you will kindly tell me what my interests are.

JERO: They are such as might be unsuitable for the ears of a policeman. That is why I suggested that you leave your escort behind.

EXECUTIVE: Come to the point.

JERO [*takes a seat, carefully brushing his creases.*]: You will remember that when the Chief Eviction Officer was compelled, as a result of the violent spiritual conversion of Colonel Rebecca . . .

EXECUTIVE: Colonel who?

JERO: Colonel Rebecca of the Church of the Apostolic Salvation Army. CASA for short. Do you know that Casa means home? In this case, spiritual home. I am sure you approve our new image.

[*Enter Rebecca with file. She is now in uniform.*]

EXECUTIVE: Your image does not interest me in the slightest.

JERO: And your own image Chief Executive Officer?

[*Hands him two sheets of paper from the file.*]

Great is the Lord and Mighty in his ways. He led your Chief Eviction Officer to my door in the company of one He had marked down for salvation; she overwhelmed him with the onslaught of such hot holiness that he fled leaving his documents in the possession of a woman possessed.

EXECUTIVE: What do you want? Just say what you want?

JERO: Monopoly is the subject of your file No. I.B.P. stroke 537 stroke 72A. Beauty parlours, supermarkets, restaurants, cafés and ice-cream kiosks, fair-grounds, construction and hiring of beach huts, amusement gadgets, gambling machines and dodgems and roundabouts and parking facilities—for the new National Amphitheatre to be built on the Bar Beach. Mr. Executive Officer, the list is endless, but what is of interest to the good Lord whose interests I represent is the method of awarding these very superabundant contracts.

EXECUTIVE: No need to talk so loud. [*Looks round nervously.*] Just say what you want.

JERO: Render unto Caesar what is Caesar's, and unto God what is God's.

EXECUTIVE: What does that mean in plain Caesar's language?

JERO: A monopoly on spirituality.

EXECUTIVE: What's that?

JERO: Made out to the Church of the Apostolic Salvation Army. CASA.

SHADRACH: We on this side place our trust in your integrity not to accede to any such request.

EXECUTIVE: Will someone tell me who this fellow is?

JERO: Colonel Rebecca has been kind enough to prepare the letter. It requires only your signature she tells me.

EXECUTIVE [*taking the letter, incredulous.*]: Is that all? Just a monopoly on the rights to hold religious rallies here?

JERO: It's enough.

EXECUTIVE: Not even a monopoly on some small business enterprise?

JERO: We are already in business. Of course we expect you to declare that all land actually occupied as of now by the various religious bodies would from now on be held in trust, managed and developed by the newly approved representative body of all apostolic bodies, CASA . . .

EXECUTIVE: What!

SHADRACH: Mr. Executive Officer . . .

EXECUTIVE: What has that to do with monopoly on spirituality?

JERO: Spirituality, to take root, must have land to take root in.

EXECUTIVE: Yes, yes, of course, I—er—see your point.

JERO: Our image also conforms on all levels. We are not fanatics. Our symbol is blood. It washes all sins away. *All* sins, Mr. Tourist Board.

EXECUTIVE: Yes, indeed. A point decidedly in your favour.

SHADRACH: We protest, sir. We strongly protest!

EXECUTIVE: Who is this man?

JERO: An apostate. Ignore him. [*Shadrach splutters speechlessly. Jero pushes a piece of paper to the official.*] The declaration. It says nothing but the truth. You are present at the meeting for apostolic union. You see yourself the new body which has emerged, fully representative.

SHADRACH: Thieves! Robbers! Rapists and cut-throats!

JERO: We did not include you, Brother Shadrach.

[*The Executive Officer signs, then Jero pushes it to the Clerk.*] Witness it. [*The Clerk looks at Executive Officer.*]

EXECUTIVE: Sign the damn thing and let's get out of here.

JERO [*hands the paper to Rebecca.*]: Are those their genuine signatures, Colonel?

EXECUTIVE [*offended.*]: I don't double-deal. I am a man of my word.

JERO: It isn't that I don't trust you.

REBECCA: It is their signatures, my General.

EXECUTIVE: And now may I have . . .

JERO: Your list of contracts? Just one more paper to be signed. The attachment. The survey map which indicates what portions of the beach are referred to as trust property of CASA.

EXECUTIVE: This is impossible. We have allocated some of the land squatted on by your . . .

JERO: Please give me the credit of having done my home-work. You forget we have had a formidable ally in the person of Colonel Rebecca, your former Confidential Secretary. And we have drawn on that precious file which your Eviction Officer so generously loaned us. There is no duplication, check it if you wish.

EXECUTIVE: All right, all right. [*About to sign.*]

SHADRACH: Don't sign your soul away to the devil, sir!

EXECUTIVE: Can't you shut him up?

JERO: Sergeant-major!

ANANAIAS: My pleasure sir. Come on, Shad.
[*Holds him expertly by the elbow and ejects him.*]

SHADRACH: We protest most strenuously at this barefaced conspiracy. We shall pursue it to the highest level. The leader of a flock twenty-thousand strong is not to be taken lightly we promise you . . .

EXECUTIVE: Are you sure he won't make trouble later? [*He signs.*]

JERO: Leave him to us. The testimony of the Salvation Army will weigh against that of a disgruntled charlatan anywhere. [*Takes the map and returns the incriminating papers.*] Your documents, sir. I hope you take better care of them next time.

EXECUTIVE [*grabs them quickly, glances through and stuffs them in his pockets.*]: And now to go and deal with that stupid Eviction Officer.

JERO: Blame him not. The power of the spirit on murky souls overcomes the strictest civil service discipline.

EXECUTIVE: Don't preach at me, humbug.

JERO: On the contrary we will preach at you. Every Tuesday at twelve o'clock the Church of Apostolic Salvation Army will preach outside your office. The subject of our sermons shall be, the evils of corruption—of the soul. We intend to restrict ourselves to spiritual matters. We will not contradict the secular image.
[*The Clerk bursts out laughing. The Executive eyes him balefully and the laughter dries on his face.*]

EXECUTIVE: You report to me in my office first thing tomorrow morning. You and the Eviction Officer. [*Storms out.*]

ANANAIAS [*as the Chief Clerk hesitates.*]: Hey you, follow your master.

CLERK: Er . . . Brother . . . I mean . . . er—General, you wouldn't . . . I mean . . . by any chance . . . what I mean to say is . . . even a Lance-Corporal would do me.

REBECCA: Glory be! [*Rushes forward to embrace him.*] I think there is a uniform just his size, my General.

JERO: As you wish Colonel, Lance-Corporal it is then.

ANANAIAS: What next, my General?

JERO: No time like the present. We march this moment and show the flag. Brother Chume, kneel for your second christening. Or third. I'm beginning to lose count. [*Chume kneels. Jero anoints his head.*] Go down, Brother Chume, rise Brigadier Joshua!

SEVERALLY [*amidst embraces.*]: God bless you, Joshua. God bless Brigadier Joshua.

CHUME [*overwhelmed.*]: Oh Brother—sorry General—Jero. I am so unworthy . . .

JERO: Nonsense, Chume, you are the very ornament of your rank. Stand to action Brigade. Brigadier Joshua will lead, blowing the trumpet. Sergeant Ananaias!

ANANAIAS: My General?

JERO: When Joshua blows the trumpet, it will be your duty to make the miracle happen. The walls shall come tumbling down or you will have some explaining to do.

ANANAIAS: Leave it to me, my General.

JERO: Just lean on the rotting walls Ananaias and the Lord will do the rest. By dawn the entire beach must be cleansed of all pestilential separatist shacks which infest the holy atmosphere of the united apostolate of the Lord. Beginning naturally with Apostate Shadrach's unholy den. The fire and the sword, Ananaias, the fire and the sword. Light up the night of evil with the flames of holiness! Consecrate the grounds for the Bar Beach Spectacular!

ANANAIAS: Apostolic Army of the Lord, Atten . . . tion! Forward, Banner of the Lord! [*Rebecca takes up position.*] Forward, Trumpet of the Lord! [*Chume positions himself.*] Sound the

Trumpet! By the left, Quick . . . Swing against Corrup . . . tion!

[*Chume blasts the first bar of 'Joshua Fit the Battle of Jericho' in strict tempo, then swings elated into a brisk indigenous rhythm to which the Army march-dance out into the night. Jero, with maximum condescension acknowledges the salute of the army. As the last man disappears, he takes a last look at the framed photo, takes it down and places it face towards the wall, takes from a drawer in the table an even larger photo of himself in his present uniform and mounts it on the wall. He then seats himself at the table and pulls towards him a file or two, as if to start work. Looks up suddenly and on his face is the amiable-charlatan grin.*]

JERO: After all, it is the fashion these days to be a desk General.

BLACKOUT

THE END

MADMEN
AND SPECIALISTS

The first version of *Madmen and Specialists* was performed at the 1970 Playwrights' Workshop Conference at the Eugene O'Neill Theater Center, Waterford, Connecticut, U.S.A. The first complete version, printed here, had its première at the University of Ibadan, Nigeria, in March 1971, with the University Theatre Arts Company. The cast was as follows:

AAFAA		*Femi Johnson*
BLINDMAN		*Femi Osofisan*
GOYI	*Mendicants*	*Wale Ogunyemi*
CRIPPLE		*Tunji Oyelana*
SI BERO *Sister to Dr. Bero*		*Deola Adedoyin*
IYA AGBA		*Nguba Agolia*
IYA MATE	*Two old Women*	*Bopo George*
DR. BERO *Specialist*		*Nat Okoro*
PRIEST		*Gbenga Sonuga*
THE OLD MAN *Bero's Father*		*Dapo Adelugba*

Designed and directed by the author.

Characters

AAFAA		IYA AGBA
BLINDMAN		IYA MATE } Two Old Women
GOYI	} Mendicants	DR. BERO Specialist
CRIPPLE		PRIEST
SI BERO Sister to Dr. Bero		THE OLD MAN Bero's Father

The action takes place in and around the home surgery of Dr. Bero, lately returned from the wars.

PART ONE

Open space before Bero's home and surgery. The surgery is down in a cellar. The level ground in the fore and immediate front space serves as drying space for assorted barks and herbs. The higher structure to one side is a form of semi-open hut. Inside it sit Iya Agba and Iya Mate. Iya Agba is smoking a thin pipe. Iya Mate stokes a small fire.

By the roadside is a group of mendicants—Cripple, Goyi, Blindman and Aafaa. Aafaa's St. Vitus spasms are designed to rid the wayfarer of his last pennies in a desperate bid to be rid of the sight. Goyi is held stiffly in a stooping posture by a contraption which is just visible above his collar. The Cripple drags on his knees. They pass the time by throwing dice from the gourd rattle.

The Cripple has just thrown the dice.

AAFAA: Six and four. Good for you.

CRIPPLE: Your turn, Blindman. [*Gives the dice and gourd to Blindman.*]

[*Blindman throws.*]

Five and five, Someone is going to give us fivers.

GOYI: Fat chance of that. [*He throws.*]

AAFAA: Three and two, born loser. What did you stake?

GOYI: The stump of the left arm.

CRIPPLE: Your last?

GOYI: No, I've got one left.

BLINDMAN: Your last. You lost the right stump to me yesterday.

GOYI: Do you want it now or later?

BLINDMAN: Keep it for now.

CRIPPLE: When do I get my eye, Aafaa?

AAFAA: Was it the right or the left?

GOYI: Does it matter?

AAFAA: Sure it does. If it's the right one he can take it out now. The left is my evil eye and I need it a while longer.

CRIPPLE: It was the right.

AAFAA: I've just remembered the right is my evil eye.

CRIPPLE: I'll make you an offer. Let me throw against both of you for Goyi's stumps. I'll stake the eye Aafaa lost to me.

GOYI: Why leave me out? I still want to try my luck.

BLINDMAN: You have nothing left to stake.

CRIPPLE: You're just a rubber ball, Goyi. You need a hand to throw with, anyway.

GOYI: I can use my mouth.

AAFAA: To throw dice? You'll eat sand my friend.

BLINDMAN: Sooner or later we all eat sand.

CRIPPLE: Hey, you're beginning to sound like the Old Man.

AAFAA [*voice change.*]: Did you eat sand, my friend? We'll make you the Ostrich in our touring circus.

BLINDMAN: The limbless acrobat will now perform his wonderful act—how to bite the dust from three classic positions.

GOYI: Upright, take off, and prone.

CRIPPLE: We'll never go on that tour.

AAFAA: Roll up—roll up. Presenting the Creatures of As in the timeless parade.

BLINDMAN: Think we'll ever make that tour?

AAFAA: We will. But until the millions start rolling in, we better not neglect the pennies. [*He nudges them, pointing to Si Bero.*] [*Si Bero approaches, carrying a small bag from which protrude some twigs with leaves and berries. The Mendicants begin their performance as soon as they sense her approach. Blindman is alms collector, Goyi repeats a single acrobatic trick, Aafaa is the 'dancer'. Blindman shakes the rattles while the Cripple drums with his crutches and is lead singer.*]

SI BERO [*as Aafaa moves to intercept her.*]: Don't try that nonsense with me. I live in this neighbourhood, remember?

AAFAA [*His spasms ceasing abruptly. The others also stop playing.*]: Don't they say charity begins at home?

SI BERO: Your preaching is so good it's a wonder you can't find yourself a congregation.

AAFAA [*stiffening.*]: What congregation, woman? Who said I was ever a preacher?

SI BERO: You were never anything. Go and find some decent work to do.

AAFAA: With this affliction of mine?

SI BERO: It comes and goes, not so? You can work in between.

AAFAA: And this one? And that? And that? [*Pointing lastly to Goyi.*] If it weren't for the iron rod holding up his spine he

would collapse like a toad you step on. Just what sort of work
do you want him to do?

GOYI: A penny or two, Si Bero. We haven't eaten today.

BLINDMAN: And that is God's truth. Aafaa, why do you pick a
quarrel with her? Just ask her for a few pennies, you know
she treats us well.

CRIPPLE: The lane is deserted. Nobody comes and goes any
more.

GOYI: Something is driving them away from here. If there isn't
something going on, then this isn't an iron I have in my back.

AAFAA: It is your neighbourhood, you say, Si Bero. What are you
doing to drive people away?

SI BERO: Perhaps your mother's ghost is haunting the place. Why
don't you ask her the next time she visits you?

AAFAA: Why do you always pick on me, old woman? What has
my mother done to you?

SI BERO: She gave birth to you for a start. [*She throws a penny to
the Cripple who tosses it into the gourd.*] If you want more
than that, you know where to come. I still need people to sort
out my herbs.

AAFAA: Herbs! Herbs! Herbs! Always—come and sort out herbs
to earn yourself a decent coin.

SI BERO: And eat. You can have work and eat. The two go
together.

[*She goes out.*]

CRIPPLE [*rattling the coin in the gourd, calls after her.*]: God bless
you, Si Bero.

BLINDMAN: He shall, he will, he must.

GOYI: He'd better or I'll know the reason why.

CRIPPLE: Your turn, Aafaa.

AAFAA: What for?

CRIPPLE: A penny is something.

AAFAA: Not for me.

GOYI: Give her a pennyworth, then.

AAFAA: Can't be bothered.

BLINDMAN: Go on. Don't be mean.

CRIPPLE: You're the priest, after all.

AAFAA [*suddenly grinning.*]: A penny's worth, you say?

CRIPPLE: That's only fair.

AAFAA [*shouting after the now distant woman.*]: God bless your
  brother!
  [*They all break out guffawing.*]

GOYI: More grease to his elbow.

AAFAA: Not forgetting his armpits.

BLINDMAN: More power to his swagger-stick!

CRIPPLE: May light ever shine . . .

AAFAA: From his braids and buttons.

GOYI: May he come home safely . . .

AAFAA: To your loving arms.

CRIPPLE: Not to mention his Daddy's.

GOYI: God help her, that is some brother she has. You may say he
  is . . . dutiful.

CRIPPLE: Him a dutiful son? You're crazy.

BLINDMAN: I know what he means. [*He points an imaginary gun.*]
  Bang! All in the line of duty!
  [*Goyi clutches his chest, slumps over.*]

AAFAA: Did we try him?

CRIPPLE: Resurrect, you fool. Nobody tried you yet.

AAFAA [*in a ringing voice.*]: You are *accused*.

BLINDMAN: Satisfied?

CRIPPLE: Fair enough.

BLINDMAN: Bang!
  [*Goyi slumps.*]

AAFAA [*rinsing his hands.*]: Nothing to do with me.

BLINDMAN: Fair trial, no?

AAFAA: Decidedly yes.

BLINDMAN: What does he say himself?

GOYI: Very fair, gentlemen. I have no complaints.

BLINDMAN: In that case we permit you to be buried.

GOYI: You are generous, gentlemen. I have a personal aversion to
  vultures.

BLINDMAN: Oh, come come. Nice birds they are. They clean up
  after the mess.

CRIPPLE: Not like some bastards we know. [*He spits.*]

AAFAA [*posing.*]: In a way you may call us vultures. We clean up
  the mess made by others. The populace should be grateful for
  our presence. [*He turns slowly round.*] If there is anyone here
  who does not approve us, just say so and we quit. [*His hand*

makes the motion of half-drawing out a gun.] I mean, we are not here because we like it. We stay at immense sacrifice to ourselves, our leisure, our desires, vocation, specialization, et cetera, et cetera. The moment you say, Go, we . . .
[*He gives another inspection all round, smiles broadly, and turns to the others.*] They insist we stay.

CRIPPLE: I thought they would. Troublesome little insects but . . . they have a sense of gratitude. I mean, after all we did for them.

GOYI: And still do.

BLINDMAN: And will continue to do.

CHORUS: Hear hear hear hear. Very well said, sir.

GOYI: Oh, come on. Shall we follow the woman or yap here all day? Let's get spying.

AAFAA: She's a devil, that's my complaint. She was born with a stone in her stomach.

GOYI: What's wrong? It's the job we are here to do, isn't it?

AAFAA: I still don't like messing about with her herbs.

BLINDMAN: Herbs are herbs, not so? Let's get going.

AAFAA: That woman's herbs are not just herbs. She hoards them and treats them like children. The whole house is full of twigs. If it's a straightforward business, why doesn't she use them? Or sell them or something?

GOYI: But everyone knows she's mad. They get that way after a while living alone. I've known a woman in my village who collects potsherds. Any piece of broken pot would do. Just let an old woman live by herself for a short while and she gets up to all sorts of things. Boxes, cupboards, trunks, every nook and corner. You couldn't walk on the floor without crunching pottery under your foot. Then she would scream curses at you.

CRIPPLE: What are we to do?

GOYI: There must be some way to stay nearer the house most of the day. We can't spend the whole day sorting herbs.

AAFAA: She's a witch. When she spirits out a foetus from the belly of a pregnant woman she pickles it in the herbs and it goes in a bottle for her brother's experiments.

BLINDMAN: For a so-called chaplain you talk plenty of nonsense.

AAFAA: Listen to the blind fool. What do you know about it?

CRIPPLE: Are we going to argue or follow her home?

GOYI: I don't like the whole business. She has been good to us.

AAFAA: With the pennies she throws as if she's feeding a dog? I spit on that kind of goodness!

CRIPPLE: I still don't like it. Why is he doing it? His own family too, what's he up to?

GOYI: He's a specialist.

AAFAA: Amen.

GOYI: What?

AAFAA: Amen. He is a specialist. That takes care of everything, not so?

GOYI: There is bound to be something in it for us.

BLINDMAN: Something like burnt fingers?

GOYI: What do you mean?

BLINDMAN [*shrugs.*]: When things go wrong it's the lowest who get it first.

AAFAA: There is money at the bottom of it.

CRIPPLE [*places Blindman's hand on his shoulder and starts off in the direction of the house.*]: And we are at the bottom. So, let's go and make sure the woman doesn't stumble on any official secrets.

AAFAA [*checks.*]: Rem Acu Tetigisti.

CRIPPLE: What? I don't get you.

AAFAA: R.A.T.! R.A.T.! I smell a rat.

GOYI: Is he having an attack?

CRIPPLE: What's up, Aafaa?

AAFAA: You said it yourself—Official Secrets. Official rat is what I smell. Yessir! We'll get paid something decent. Secret Service funds and all that. Let's celebrate.

GOYI: Nonsense. It's just a simple family vendetta.

AAFAA: Christ! Every one of you freaks will have ideas! And where did you pick up that word, anyway?

GOYI: Where you pick up yours, leave me alone.

AAFAA [*haughtily.*]: One thing I disapproved of in the Old Man was he didn't discriminate. Talk of casting pearls before swine. Vendetta my foot. I tell you the Cripple has Rem Acu Tetigistied it. Official Secrets that's what at the bottom of it. Bottomless account. We'll get overtime and risk allowance.

GOYI: It's not going to be risky, is it?

AAFAA: I know you have none, but I'll be risking my conscience. That needs compensation.

CRIPPLE: What do you think, Blindman?

BLINDMAN: Hm. Aafaa may be right. For once.

AAFAA: Never mind the cleverness. You agree.

BLINDMAN: R.A.T. You have touched the matter with a needle.

GOYI: Where? I'm still lost.

AAFAA: Where? I'll soon show you, dumbclod. [*He lunges for Goyi's crotch.*]

GOYI [*protecting himself.*]: No!

AAFAA: Why not? You got any more use for it?

BLINDMAN: Maybe he wants to continue the line.

AAFAA: What! This crooked line? It would be a disservice to humanity.

CRIPPLE: Hey. Think he'll do that to his own father?

BLINDMAN: When the Specialist wants results badly enough . . .

CRIPPLE: Yes, but what results?

AAFAA: Does it matter? [*Voice change. He points a 'needle' held low, at Goyi.*] Say anything, say anything that comes into your head but SPEAK, MAN! [*Twisting the needle upwards.*]
[*Goyi, hand over crotch, yells.*]

BLINDMAN [*solemnly.*]: Rem Acu Tetigisti.

AAFAA: Believe me, this hurts you more than it hurts me. Or— vice versa. Truth hurts. I am a lover of truth. Do you find you also love truth? Then let's have the truth. THE TRUTH!
[*He gives another push. Goyi screams.*]

CRIPPLE: } Rem Acu Tetigisti.
BLINDMAN: }

AAFAA: Think not that I hurt you but that Truth hurts. We are all seekers after truth. I am a Specialist in truth. Now shall we push it up all the way, all the way? Or shall we have all the truth all the truth. [*Another push. Goyi screams, then his head slumps.*] Hm, the poor man has fainted.

CRIPPLE: } Rem Acu Tetigisti.
BLINDMAN: }

[*Aafaa makes a motion of slapping his face several times. Goyi revives.*]

GOYI: Where am I?

CRIPPLE: Within the moment of truth, dear friend.

AAFAA [*chanting.*]: Rem Acu . . .

OTHERS: Tetigisti, tetigisti.

ALTOGETHER: Rem Acu Tetigisti.

AAFAA: You have touched it with a . . .

OTHERS: Fine needle, fine, fine needle.

ALL: You have touched it with a fine fine.

AAFAA: Rem Acu . . .

> [*They repeat the song, Aafaa singing 'Rem Acu Tetigisti' in counterpoint to the others 'You have touched it with a needle'.*]
> Hey. [*He taps Goyi on the shoulder.*] Are you recovered? Good. Here we go again.

CRIPPLE: Perhaps he needs a drink of water.

AAFAA: Really? Well, give him one, then. We are no monsters here. No one will charge me with heartlessness. Give him a drink of water. A large one.

> [*Blindman hands Goyi a 'bowl' of water. Goyi drains it while they all watch avidly.*]
> Satisfied? Happy? More? No. [*He takes the bowl and hands it to Blindman.*] Anything else? Perhaps you would like to use the conveniences? The toilet? [*Goyi nods.*] Over there. Be my guest.
> [*Goyi turns, his hand goes to his fly, he stops, turns round slowly. A big grin appears on the faces of the other three.*]
> What's the matter? No wan' pee-pee? Pee-pee pee-pee? No more pee-pee? I know what it is. [*Chanting.*] Rem Acu . . .

OTHERS: Tetigisti, tetigisti . . .

> [*As they go through the chant again Si Bero reappears with a small bunch of herbs. They quickly stop singing.*]

CRIPPLE: Are we to come now, Si Bero? We need the work.

SI BERO: Wait here. I'll tell you when I'm ready.

> [*They watch her pass. She goes into the Old Women's hut and Aafaa sneaks near a moment later, to try to eavesdrop. The others pass the time throwing dice.*]
> [*In the Old Women's hut.*]

IYA MATE: A-ah, you have a good eye, daughter.

IYA AGBA: Where did you find it?

SI BERO: Not far from where I went yesterday. Someone had emptied a pile of rubbish near by, that's why I missed it.

> [*The two Old Women move nearer the light, examining the berries.*]

IYA MATE: The berries are all right too. Birds attack them quite early. You are lucky.

IYA AGBA: I wasn't expecting her to find any berries.

SI BERO [*dipping in the bag.*]: I brought you some tobacco. And snuff for you, Iya Mate.

IYA MATE: You are a good woman. Some menfolk leave the home and never know whether they will come back to a dung-heap or worse.

IYA AGBA: Weeds growing through the window and bats hanging from the rafters. That is when they find out that some women carry a curse in their breasts.

IYA MATE: Your menfolk are lucky. There will be leaves in their living-room—but not the kind that places the handprint of death on a man's heart. Now, you leave these here.

IYA AGBA [*suddenly.*]: Let me see that. Let me see it!

IYA MATE: What's the matter?

IYA AGBA: Bring it here. It's not the right one at all.

IYA MATE: Here. Look for yourself. No one can tell me my eyes are failing.

IYA AGBA: Just now I remember what you said—birds haven't attacked it. Usually it's the poison kind they don't go near. [*She breaks the stalk.*] I thought so. This is the twin. Poison.

SI BERO: Poison! But . . .

IYA MATE: It can't be poison.

IYA AGBA: They don't grow much. Haven't seen one in—oh, since I was a child. Farmers destroy them as soon as they see them. But it's the poison twin all right. Except for that red streak along the stalk you wouldn't tell them apart.

IYA MATE: I didn't even know there was the poison kind.

IYA AGBA: You don't see them much. Once in a lifetime. Farmers don't let them live, you know. Burn out the soil where they find it growing, just to kill the seeds. Foolishness. Poison has its uses too. You can cure with poison if you use it right. Or kill.

SI BERO: I'll throw it in the fire.

IYA MATE: Do nothing of the sort. You don't learn good things unless you learn evil.

SI BERO: But it's poison.

IYA MATE: It grows.

IYA AGBA: Rain falls on it.

IYA MATE: It sucks the dew.

IYA AGBA: It lives.

IYA MATE: It dies.

IYA AGBA: Same as any other. An-hn, same as any other.

SI BERO: That means I still have to find the right one.

IYA AGBA: It will be in the same place. They grow together most
of the time.

SI BERO: I'll go tomorrow.

IYA MATE: Take some rest. Or . . . is he on his way home?

SI BERO: There is no news at all. I am beginning to . . .

IYA AGBA: Beginning to worry like every foolish woman. He'll
come back. He and his father. There is too much binds them
down here. They will take root with their spirit, not with their
bodies on some unblessed soil. Let me see your hands. [*She
scrutinizes the hands carefully, bursts suddenly into a peal of
laughter.*] These hands are not yet ready to wind shrouds. We
shall drink palm wine soon, very soon when someone returns.
[*She takes Si Bero by both hands and begins to shuffle with her,
singing.*]
Ofe gbe wa de'le o—Ofe . . .
Ofe gbe wa de'le o—Ofe
Oko epo epa i runa
Gbe wa de'le o
Ofe gbe wa de'le[1]
[*The Mendicants look at one another, begin to beat time with
them, then join the singing in a raucous, cynical tone. The women
stop, amazed and offended. The Old Women fold their arms,
retire deeper into the hut while Si Bero dashes out, furious.*]

SI BERO: Stop that noise! Did I ask you here for entertainment?

CRIPPLE: No offence, Si Bero, no offence. We only thought you
had forgotten us.

SI BERO: And thought your horrible voices the best way of
reminding me.

---

1. 'Wind-spirit, bear us home, wind-spirit
   Wind-spirit, bear us home, wind-spirit
   The boat that bears oil of the ground-nut avoids the naked flame
   Bear us home
   Wind-spirit, bear us home'

GOYI: It's not our fault our voices are no better.

AAFAA: We can't all have voices like choiring angels, you know.

SI BERO: That's enough from you. Come along if you still want to work, only keep your voices down and stop frightening the neighbourhood.

[*They follow her to the front of the house.*]

CRIPPLE: So here we are, Si Bero. Bring out the herbs and let us catch the smell of something in your kitchen while we are about it.

AAFAA: How much are we getting today? Let's decide that first.

SI BERO: Depends how hard you work.

GOYI: Let's start work. It's a hot day and a man may as well stay close to shelter.

SI BERO: I have a whole sack my buyer brought in yesterday.

[*She takes hold of Blindman's hand.*]

You can give me a hand, the sack is heavy. [*Aafaa immediately positions himself to accompany her.*] Not you, damn your forwardness. Did I talk to you?

AAFAA: He's not much use. He'll trip over and break his neck.

SI BERO: And that's his business not yours.

[*She leads Blindman into the house.*]

AAFAA: Did you see that?

GOYI: I am sure even the Blindman did.

CRIPPLE: She didn't want any of us three, that was certain, but I . . .

AAFAA: Picks the one who can't see a thing.

CRIPPLE: I saw.

AAFAA: I told you it's funny business.

CRIPPLE: I am trying to tell you I saw. I saw the herbs.

AAFAA: Where? Where?

CRIPPLE: From here. From down here I could see through a gap in the door when she opened it.

AAFAA: What then? What did you see?

CRIPPLE: Herbs. Roots. Nothing but dried plants. The shelves are right up to the ceiling and they were full of leaves. All browned and crinkled.

GOYI: What kind?

CRIPPLE: All kinds.

GOYI: What is she going to do with all that forest?

AAFAA: Perhaps now you will learn to listen to me.

CRIPPLE: She must be slightly crazy. Living all alone, I suppose.

AAFAA: S-sh. They're coming. See if you can sneak another look.

[*Si Bero and Blindman enter, carrying a heavy sack between them.*]

SI BERO [*entering backwards, she stumbles against the Cripple who is trying to see through a crack.*]: Get out of the way, will you. Are you now the doorstep that I must step on you to get out of my own house?

CRIPPLE [*forced to retreat.*]: You are in a bad mood today, Si Bero.

SI BERO: Your mother is in a bad mood, not me. Now get working instead of dragging yourself in people's way. Get busy. You know how I like them sorted out.

AAFAA: Yes, we know.

GOYI: First the roots.

CRIPPLE: Then peel the barks.

AAFAA: Slice the stalks.

CRIPPLE: Squeeze out the pulps.

GOYI: Pick the seeds.

AAFAA: Break the pods. Crack the plaster.

CRIPPLE: Probe the wound or it will never heal.

BLINDMAN: Cut off one root to save the other.

AAFAA: Cauterize.

CRIPPLE: Quick-quick-quick-quick, amputate!

[*Blindman lets out a loud groan.*]

AAFAA: What do you mean, sir! How dare you lie there and whine?

GOYI: Cut his vocal chords.

AAFAA: 'Before we operate we cut the vocal chords.'

BLINDMAN: That's only for the dogs.

CRIPPLE: Your case is worse. You are an underdog.

GOYI: Rip out his vocal chords.

[*Blindman lets out another scream.*]

AAFAA: We don't want you in this fraternity.

CRIPPLE: Fool! You should see the others and thank your stars.

BLINDMAN: I can't see them to thank.

AAFAA [*snatches his stick.*]: Shall I put them on his head? He can have them in all colours.

CRIPPLE: Leave him for now, we'll simply expel him.

BLINDMAN [*screaming again.*]: Oh God!

GOYI: Who's got the flaming sword?

AAFAA: Right here, Lord, right here.

GOYI: Show him the door.

AAFAA: Out of the garden, bum, don't ever show your face in here again.

BLINDMAN: I appeal.

CRIPPLE: Who to?

BLINDMAN: As.

AAFAA: In the name of As of the beginning, out!

BLINDMAN: No!

AAFAA: Out!

BLINDMAN: No!

AAFAA: One—Two—Three—Four—

BLINDMAN [*druggedly*.]: Five—Six—Seven—Eight—Nine—

AAFAA: Out!

BLINDMAN [*wearily*.]: Out! [*His head drops down. Aafaa raises the 'sword'.*]

SI BERO: Have you all gone mad?

AAFAA: No. I'm quite good at it, actually. One stroke and—clean through the tendons. Bang through the ball-and-socket, believe me. I never touch the marrow.

GOYI: Heh, stop. The woman.

SI BERO: I said have you gone mad? Are you here to work or fool around?

CRIPPLE: Oh, never mind us. Come on.

[*They settle down quickly. As the sack is emptied on the ground, Si Bero, already about to turn into the house, stops, goes over and picks out a bunch of roots which she turns about in her hand, inspecting it. The Mendicants cannot contain their curiosity, directly observing her action. Blindman listens intensely into the silence. Finally she starts towards the Old Women's hut.*]

AAFAA: We can sort that bunch if you like. And give it a scraping. It seems dirty enough.

SI BERO [*turns slowly on him.*]: Not half as dirty as your anus. The day you scrape that you can tell me what needs scraping and what doesn't.

AAFAA [*raising his stick.*]: You go too far with that mouth of yours! [*Si Bero looks him up and down contemptuously. She continues on her way.*]

I have a mind to set fire to every single herb in that house.

BLINDMAN: Why don't you learn to leave her alone?

AAFAA: What did I do? What did I say? Just because of one stinking root. She has a mouth like a running gutter.

BLINDMAN: Leave the woman alone. She minds her own business, you mind yours.

AAFAA: And that's enough from you, Mr. Blind Advocate. I don't have to listen to you take her side all the time. One more word from you . . .

[He feints a slap across Blindman's face. Blindman, alert, springs suddenly backwards and grasps his staff. Aafaa looks at him a moment, then bursts out laughing.]

Do you see what I see? The man actually wants to fight me. Did you see? Did you see him? He has no eyes but he actually wants to fight. Hm? Is it really a fight you're looking for, Blind One?

[He kicks aside his staff but Blindman immediately closes in on Aafaa, reaches for his arms and imprisons them. They strain against each other.]

CRIPPLE: Bloody fools!

GOYI: Look! The specialist.

[He points to the spot where they were first seen. Standing there is Bero, uniformed, carrying a holdall. He watches. The Cripple tugs at the clothes of the struggling men.]

CRIPPLE: Better stop that, he's here.

GOYI: He's waiting for us. Come on.

[The two men break apart, Aafaa is panting heavily. The Cripple dashes quickly and brings Blindman his stick. Somewhat sheepishly they troop towards Bero.]

BERO [gives them a long cold stare.] Was that what I sent you to do in that house?

AAFAA: He started it. And the woman.

CRIPPLE: Aafaa hit him first. Knocked off his stick. A blind man too. [He spits.]

AAFAA: If people know they have a handicap then they shouldn't open their mouths to provoke their betters.

CRIPPLE: Hits a blind man. [He spits again.]

AAFAA: If you think just because you are a cripple you won't get it from me if you go beyond bounds, just try it and see.

CRIPPLE: A blind man. [*He spits again.*]

AAFAA [*raises the rattle threateningly.*]: Don't think because of him being here I can't . . .

[*The Cripple counters immediately by raising his crutch.*]

BERO: Shut up! Shut up all of you. I didn't send you to the house to fight. I asked you to keep your eyes open and keep her from going down. [*He looks at them with contempt, then jerks his thumb in the direction of the cellar.*] What about him. Is he staying quiet?

AAFAA [*jerking his thumb at Blindman.*]: Ask him. He is the only one who got to enter the house. Ask Blindman what he saw.

BERO: I have no time for fooling.

BLINDMAN: He was quiet. I don't think the woman knows anything.

BERO: What room did you enter?

BLINDMAN: The one with the herbs. I don't think there are any bare walls in there; it's all covered with herbs. From the floor to the ceiling, it's all full of herbs very carefully laid and touched and dusted every day of her life. I could tell that as soon as I entered.

CRIPPLE: I saw it. I caught a glimpse.

AAFAA: Last night when we got him into that underground place she was fast asleep. We didn't make a noise.

BLINDMAN: Excuse me, I wish to say something.

BERO: Yes?

BLINDMAN: I can only tell you what I felt—in that room where I stood with her. There is more love in there than you'll find in the arms of a hundred women. I don't know what unhappiness you intend for her but . . .

BERO: That's enough. You don't know a thing about anything, so shut up.

[*Blindman shrugs and retires to one side.*]

GOYI: My feeling is, I can't help agreeing with him. In any case we are not much use to anyone.

BERO: I said that's enough. You're under orders.

AAFAA: I am not. And I haven't eaten today.

BERO: Very good.

AAFAA: Enh? Say that again. Which of what is very good?

BERO: The fact that you haven't eaten today. If you fall down on the job you know you will go back to being hungry.

AAFAA: Good. I am glad to hear where we stand. We've done one thing already and don't think it was easy getting him in that hole without waking the neighbours or your sister. So what about for now? Have we already fallen down on the job that we see nothing of what you promised?

BERO [*studies him for a while, then turns to the others.*]: Have you told him who I am exactly?

AAFAA: Oh yes, Dr. Bero. I know who you are. The specialist. We all do. So what about it? You say we are under orders but I tell you I am not. I know these three are discharged. As for me, I have never even taken orders from you before.

BERO: These are no longer discharged and you now take orders from me. You either get that into your twisted mind or get out now.

AAFAA: You can't tell me to get out. We teamed together without your help and we are not doing badly as it is. You can't come here and break us up. If we have anybody to thank it's him down there. Not that I care. I always thought he was crazy. But just don't you forget we are a team—one for all and all for one.

BERO: You prefer that? Begging for pennies and getting spat upon?

AAFAA: That's what you think. Ho ho, that's a good one, isn't it? Isn't it? You don't know anything about us, do you? Think we spent all that time with your old man without learning a thing or two? You can't specialize in everything, you know.

GOYI: Shut up, Aafaa.

CRIPPLE: You talk too much, shut your mouth.

BERO: He's saying nothing I don't know already.

AAFAA: You know nothing, Dr. Bero. You can't bluff me.

BLINDMAN: You really are a fool, Aafaa.

CRIPPLE [*whining.*]: Pay no attention to him. We do nothing really bad, just one or two things to eke out the droppings of charity.

BERO: Save that for your customers. I'm not interested in what you've done. But from now on you stop taking any risks. I don't want to have to look for you in every filthy gaol.

CRIPPLE: If you'll make up for our losses, sir . . . we were on our way to greater things.

GOYI: I'll say that for us. We were just beginning.

BERO: To do what?

CRIPPLE: Well, you know . . . your Old Man did come up with some ripe ideas . . .

BERO: You'll be taken care of. That's a promise.

CRIPPLE: Then as I said before, that's all right by me.

GOYI: Me too.

AAFAA: No, it isn't. I don't mind the risks we are taking right now. . . .

BERO: I said, no more risks.

AAFAA: That's for us to decide until you say how much. What does he know about risks anyway? Even if I was only a chaplain to the men out there I knew what risk was. I nearly had it once or twice. Quite different from working for Intelligence where all you had to do was sift through papers full of lies and know how to slap people around. . . .

[Bero cuts him across the face with his swagger stick. Aafaa staggers back, clutching the wound. Bero stands still, watching him. At the sound of pain Iya Agba looks out of the hut and impassively observes the scene.]

BERO: That should remind you I do know how to slap people around. And you'd better remember some other things I know. You weren't just discharged because of your—sickness. Just remember that . . . and other things.

[He stands gazing towards the house for a while.]

I am due home now. You know when to follow. Just remember to carry out my instructions to the letter.

[He walks purposefully to the house. As he passes by the Old Women's hut Iya Agba leans back to avoid being seen by him. A moment later Si Bero emerges, sees Bero and shouts, running towards him. Iya Mate joins the other woman to watch the reunion.]

SI BERO: Bero! Bero! [She embraces him, then tears herself off and shouts.] He's home! He's back!

BERO: Don't do that!

SI BERO [rushing about, she doesn't hear.]: He's home! He's . . .

BERO [chases after and restrains her.]: Be quiet!

SI BERO: What?

BERO: I don't want my return announced.

SI BERO: Why not? [Suddenly suspicious.] You're not going back again, are you?

BERO: It isn't that. I want some quiet, that's all.

SI BERO: Oh! how thoughtless I was. But they will be disappointed.

BERO: Who will?

SI BERO: Our neighbours. All your old patients.

BERO: Corpses.

SI BERO: What? I said your old patients.

BERO: I said corpses. Oh, forget it.

SI BERO: I can't. [*She scans his face anxiously.*] They haven't forgotten you.

BERO: They still exist, do they?

SI BERO [*again puzzled.*]: Who? I don't understand.

BERO: I'm tired. Let's talk of something else.

SI BERO: Oh yes, you must be. Come inside. No, wait. You mustn't come in yet. Be patient now, Bero. [*Hurrying into the house.*] Don't move from there. Stand still.

[*Bero looks slowly round him, he gazes as if he is trying to pierce through walls into neighbouring homes. The expression on his face is contempt.*

Si Bero reappears with a gourd of palm wine, pours it on the ground in front of the doorstep. Then she moves to unlace his boots.]

BERO: You still keep up these little habits.

SI BERO: I like to keep close to earth.

BERO [*stepping back to prevent her from taking off his boots.*]: Bare feet, wet earth. We've wetted your good earth with something more potent than that, you know.

SI BERO: Not you. Neither you nor Father. You had nothing to do with it. On the contrary.

BERO: What, on the contrary?

SI BERO: Were you together? Did you manage to work together?

BERO: We were together. For some time.

SI BERO: Is he going to stay with us?

BERO: We'll . . . discuss him later.

SI BERO [*suddenly fearful.*]: What is it, Bero? Is he . . . ?

BERO [*stares back at her, letting the pause hang.*]: Well, is he—what?

SI BERO [*laughing.*]: Stop trying to frighten me.

BERO: Who's trying to?

SI BERO: Where are you hiding him? I bet he's waiting round the corner.

BERO: He'll rejoin us in his own time.

SI BERO [*disappointed.*]: Oh. But he's safe.

BERO [*impatiently.*]: Of course he is.

SI BERO [*takes his hand.*]: Come with me. I must show you to the Old Women and tell them also Father is safe.

BERO: What Old Women?

SI BERO: Over there in the hut.

BERO: Who are they?

SI BERO: Herbalists. They helped me with your work.

BERO: But why bring them here? Why camp them on my doorstep?

SI BERO: They were good to me. I couldn't have done a thing without them. Come and talk to them.

[*Bero does not move. Immediately, the Old Women start to speak. Bero and Si Bero remain still, Bero looking towards the Old Women's hut while Si Bero watches him.*]

IYA AGBA: Well, has it been worth it, do you think?

IYA MATE: It's good to see her face bubbling like froth on good wine.

IYA AGBA: Not her, him!

IYA MATE: Oh, him. Well, you never can tell with seeds. The plant may be good . . . but we'll know, we'll know.

IYA AGBA: I hope it's a good seed. That was two lives we poured into her hands. Two long lives spent pecking at secrets grain by grain.

IYA MATE: More than two. What she took from us began with others we no longer call by name.

IYA AGBA: She sucked my head dry.

IYA MATE: She is a good woman.

IYA AGBA: Yes, but what about him?

IYA MATE: You sense something wrong in him?

IYA AGBA: It's my life that's gone into his. I haven't burrowed so deep to cast good earth on worthless seeds.

IYA MATE: Nor she. Tramping through all those bushes, finding the desolate spots only we remember.

IYA AGBA: She was stubborn, others would have given up early. [*She giggles.*] I did my best to put her off. Sent her on those fruitless errands, hoping she'd give up. Others would have done.

IYA MATE: Oh, you are wicked.

IYA AGBA: She proved herself, there's no denying it. She proved herself. If she'd wanted it easy or simply out of greed I would have guided her feet into quicksands and left her there.

IYA MATE: You would, I know you, you would.

IYA AGBA: So let him watch it. I haven't come this far to put my whole being in a sieve.

[*She turns abruptly and returns into the hut. Iya Mate remains for a while.*]

SI BERO: They told me what to look for, where to look for it. How to sort them and preserve them.

BERO [*nods.*]: You haven't wasted your time. I still need things from my former vocation.

SI BERO: Former vocation?

BERO: A means, not an end.

SI BERO: We heard terrible things. So much evil. Then I would console myself that I earned the balance by carrying on your work. One thing cancels out another. Bero, they're waiting. Go and greet them Bero. They held your life together while you were away.

BERO: What is that supposed to mean?

SI BERO: I never feared for you while they were here.

BERO: You really disappoint me. You are supposed to be intelligent. It was you I asked to do my work, not some stupid old hags. I suppose they filled your head with all that evil stuff. You've been pretty free with that word.

SI BERO: Not you yourself Bero, but guilt contaminates. And often I was afraid . . . [*Suddenly determined.*] Bero, where is Father?

BERO: Safe.

SI BERO [*stubbornly.*]: But you must know when he's coming.

BERO: Sometime.

SI BERO: When? Why didn't you return together?

BERO: He's a sick man. He is coming home to be cured.

SI BERO: Sick? Wounded?

BERO: Mind sickness. We must be kind to him.

SI BERO: How long, Bero? How long had he been sick?

BERO: Ever since he came out. Maybe the . . . suffering around

him proved too much for him. His mind broke under the
strain.

SI BERO [*quietly.*]: How bad? Don't hide anything, Bero. How bad
is he?

BERO: He started well. But of course we didn't know which way
his mind was working. Madmen have such diabolical cunning.
It was fortunate I had already proved myself. He was
dangerous. Dangerous!

SI BERO: What do you mean? Did he endanger you?

BERO: Did he! He was in a different sector, working among the
convalescents. I wouldn't have known what was going on if I
had still been with the Medical Corps.

SI BERO: If you had still been?

BERO: I told you. I switched.

SI BERO: But how? You have your training. How does one
switch, just like that?

BERO: You are everything once you go out there. In an
emergency . . . [*He shrugs.*] The head of the Intelligence Section
died rather suddenly. Natural causes.

SI BERO: And that's the new vocation?

BERO: None other, sister, none other. The Big Braids agreed I was
born into it. Not that that was any recommendation. They are
all submental apes.

SI BERO [*studying him avidly, a slow apprehension beginning to show on
her face.*]: But you have . . . you have given that up now.
You are back to your real work. Your practice.

BERO [*turns calmly to meet her gaze.*]: Practice? Yes, I intend to
maintain that side of my practice. A laboratory is important.
Everything helps. Control, sister, control. Power comes from
bending Nature to your will. The Specialist they called me,
and a specialist is—well—a specialist. You analyse, you
diagnose, you—[*He aims an imaginary gun.*]—prescribe.

SI BERO [*more to herself.*]: You should have told me. I have made
pledges I cannot fulfil.

BERO: Pledges? What are you talking about?

SI BERO: I swore I was sure of you, only then would they help me.

BERO: Who? The Old Women?

SI BERO: They held nothing back from me.

[*The Priest enters, hails them from a distance.*]

PRIEST: A-ah, there you are. Bero, my boy, welcome home. I
     caught a glimpse of you from my vestry and I said, No, it's
     not him, it can't be. But of course, who else could it be
     looking so handsome and imposing. Your prayers are
     answered, I said to myself, your prayers are answered, you
     doubting Thomas. And how is the little lady, the courageous
     one who kept the fort in the absence of brother and father?
     Overjoyed, I am sure, overjoyed. So are we all.
     [*He observes nothing of Bero's cold attitude nor the fact that Bero has
     moved casually away from the patronizing arm which he tried to
     place on his shoulder.*]
     I meant to call on one or two neighbours on the way but
     that's just the selfish sinner I am, may God forgive me. No, I
     decided, I'll just have him all to myself for a little bit.

BERO: That's rather lucky.

PRIEST: Beg your pardon?

SI BERO: He's tired, Pastor. Don't let it out he's back yet.

PRIEST: Of course not. I wouldn't dream of doing such a thing.
     We all have our human failings of course, but I do know how
     inconsiderate people can be in their joys. Wouldn't think a
     man who's just returned from the seventh outpost of hell
     would want a little time to himself. I've suffered from my old
     complaint, you know, my boy, but I can suffer a little longer.
     Just get settled, son, just get settled and give yourself a
     well-deserved rest.

SI BERO: Pastor, you know I offered you . . .

PRIEST: Not quite the same thing, young lady, not quite the same
     thing. The doctor used to make those extracts with his own
     hand and . . .

SI BERO: It was the same one he made before he left.

PRIEST: No, no, I could tell the difference. Oh yes, I could tell.

SI BERO: It was the same.

PRIEST: Good of you to try, but no. You just didn't make it the
     same. I could tell the difference at once. As soon as you're
     rested, my boy, as soon as you've rested . . . oh dear me. How
     shameful. Here I am complaining of my little fits and I
     haven't even asked news of my good friend. When is your
     father coming, my lad?

BERO: Soon.

SI BERO: Bero was just telling me . . .

PRIEST: Soon. How soon?

BERO: Soon enough.

PRIEST: Not soon enough for me, boy, not soon enough. I can't wait to take issue with him on all our old debates. Such an argumentative man, your father, such an argumentative man. And he'll have some stories to tell me, I'm sure. Really looking forward to our long evenings together. What an experience he must have had, what an experience! You know, it's strange how these disasters bring out the very best in man—and the worst sometimes. In your father's case, of course, the very best. Truly noble. I couldn't believe my ears when he got up one day and said he was going to join you. At your age, I said, you doddering old thing? I used to call him that, you know, and he would call me the mitred hypocrite. All in play, of course, only in play. So he . . . where was I? Something about your father, I believe. Oh yes, he suddenly got up one evening, right in the midst of our argument and said, I am going to see what's going on. He was just reading me a letter from you and he got all worked up. It can't be, he shouted. And then he leapt up and said—right out of the blue—we've got to legalize cannibalism. Yes, right out of the blue. What do you mean, I said, thinking he only wanted to start another argument. But no, he repeats it over and over and of course, I took him on. Legalize cannibalism? It's a damnable and heathenish idea. Yes, that's how we started the argument. Warmest session we ever had together. He wouldn't yield one foot and I wouldn't budge one inch. Not one fraction of an inch. My polemical spirit was aroused. Not to talk of Christian principles. For three hours I fought him foot by foot. Never been in better form. Nearly all night we argued, if you please, and then in the morning he was gone. What do you make of that?

SI BERO: Pastor, I think Bero is a little tired . . .

PRIEST: Had only one letter from him all that time. Told me he was doing recuperative work among some disabled fellows. No forwarding address, if you please. I couldn't even continue our old debate by post. Strange man, your father, very strange. You didn't run into him out there, did you? I'm really anxious to know if he still intends to legalize cannibalism.

BERO: He does.

PRIEST: I knew it. A stubborn man, once he gets hold of an idea. You won't believe it but he actually said to me, I'm going to try and persuade those fools not to waste all that meat. Mind you he never could stand wastage, could he? I remember he used to wade into you both if he caught you wasting anything. But human flesh, why, that's another matter altogether.

BERO: But why, Pastor. It's quite delicious, you know.

PRIEST: Just what I say. It's . . . what did you say?

BERO [*reaches out and pulls out the Priest's cheek.*]: This. Delicious.

PRIEST [*struggles free.*]: You're joking, of course.

BERO: No. Your friend will confirm it when he comes.

PRIEST [*increasingly horrified.*]: You mean he . . .

BERO: No, not him. He never meant anything. At least, not that way. But we found it delicious just the same.

PRIEST: You?

BERO: I give you the personal word of a scientist. Human flesh is delicious. Of course, not all parts of the body. I prefer the balls myself.

PRIEST [*vehemently.*]: I don't believe you.

BERO: You don't? Well, then, why don't you stay to dinner?

PRIEST: Dinner? [*Cheering up.*] Of course. I see all you want is an argument like your old man. Delighted, of course. Only too delighted to oblige . . . [*He is stricken by a sudden doubt.*] Er . . . dinner . . . did you say dinner?

BERO: Dinner. I came well-laden with supplies.

[*The Priest glances at Bero's bulging briefcase lying near by, gulps.*]

PRIEST: I . . . er . . . I am wondering if I haven't got a little christening to attend to. I . . . er . . . couldn't simply come for drinks afterwards?

BERO: A christening so late in the evening?

PRIEST: Well, you know, the blessing at home and all that. The christening was this morning. [*He is already retreating.*] God bless you, my children both. I shall hurry back as soon as it's all over. Can't get rid of these extra parish duties . . . welcome back once again, my boy . . .

[*They watch him take flight.*]

SI BERO [*laughing.*]: You know, for a moment I nearly believed you.

BERO: Oh? [*Turns and looks at her pityingly.*] You didn't?

[*Pause. They look each other in the face. Her laughter dies slowly.*]

SI BERO: Oh God.

BERO: Out of your world, little sister, out of your little world. Stay in it and do only what I tell you. That way you'll be safe.

SI BERO [*vehemently.*]: Abomination!

BERO: Delicious, you heard me say.

SI BERO: Abomination!

BERO [*deliberate cruelty.*]: Delicious. The balls, to be exact. I thought I told you to stay in your little world! Go and take tea with the senile pastor or gossip with your old women. Don't come out from where you're safe. [*Quietly.*] Or sane.

SI BERO: But at least tell me why? In God's name why?

BERO: No, not in God's name—in the name of As!

SI BERO: What?

BERO: The new god and the old—As.

SI BERO: What are you trying to be, Bero—evil?

BERO: Does it sound that bad? It was no brain-child of mine. We thought it was a joke. I'll bless the meat, he said. And then— As Was the Beginning, As is, Now, As Ever shall be . . . world without . . . We said amen with a straight face and sat down to eat. Then, afterwards . . .

SI BERO: Yes?

BERO: He told us. [*Pause. He laughs suddenly.*] But why not? Afterwards I said why not? What is one flesh from another? So I tried it again, just to be sure of myself. It was the first step to power you understand. Power in its purest sense. The end of inhibitions. The conquest of the weakness of your too too human flesh with all its sentiment. So again, all to myself I said Amen to his grace.

SI BERO: I don't follow you, Bero. Who said grace? Whose words are these?

BERO: Father's part of the liturgy of his bed-ridden audience. Wait a minute. [*Pointing to the Mendicants.*] They can tell you more about it.

SI BERO: Who? These? What have they to do with . . . ?

BERO: Have you never thought how they came to beg so close to here? At the beginning, that is. Before I found out about them.

SI BERO: Oh, is that it? You mean he sent them? But you know him—Liberty House. It's not a crime. I found them work to do.

BERO [*heatedly*.]: It's not his charitable propensities I am concerned with. Father's assignment was to help the wounded readjust to the pieces and remnants of their bodies. Physically. Teach them to make baskets if they still had fingers. To use their mouths to ply needles if they had none, or use it to sing if their vocal chords had not been shot away. Teach them to amuse themselves, make something of themselves. Instead he began to teach them to think, think, THINK! Can you picture a more treacherous deed than to place a working mind in a mangled body?

SI BERO: Where is he?

BERO: Where? Here.

SI BERO: Here?

BERO [*pointing to the Mendicants*.]: There. When they open their mouths you can hear him. You! Come here! Tell her. Would you call yourself sane?

[*The Mendicants have approached, Aafaa in the lead.*]

AAFAA: Certainly not, sir.

BERO: You got off lightly. Why?

AAFAA: I pleaded insanity.

BERO: Who made you insane?

AAFAA [*by rote, raising his eyes to heaven.*]: The Old Man, sir. He said things, he said things. My mind . . . I beg your pardon, sir, the thing I call my mind, well, was no longer there. He took advantage of me, sir, in that convalescent home. I was unconscious long stretches at a time. Whatever I saw when I came to was real. Whatever voice I heard was the truth. It was always him. Bending over my bed. I asked him, Who are you? He answered, The one and only truth.

CRIPPLE: Hear hear.

GOYI: Same here.

AAFAA: Always at me, he was, sir. I plead insanity.

CRIPPLE: Hear hear.

GOYI: Same here.

AAFAA [*pointing to Blindman.*]: Even him.

BLINDMAN: Once I even thought I could see him.

GOYI: Oh, but you did, you did.

BLINDMAN: No, not really.

CRIPPLE: You did, you did. The picture forms in the mind, remember?

GOYI: His very words. But any fool knows they form on the eye.

AAFAA: Lord, he mixed us up.

BLINDMAN: You can see me, he said, you can see me. Look at me with your mind. I swear I began to see him. Then I knew I was insane.

CRIPPLE: Hear hear.

GOYI: Same here.

AAFAA: We all did.

CRIPPLE: And getting me all choosy!

BLINDMAN: Poor you.

CRIPPLE: Beggars can't be choosers, we all knew that.

AAFAA: Yet he got you choosy.

CRIPPLE: I was mad.

BLINDMAN [changing his voice.]: Remember, even if you have nothing left but your vermin, discriminate between one bug and the next.

CRIPPLE: Some bugs are friendly, others wild.

GOYI: The one sucks gently, the other nips.

BLINDMAN: If you must eat a toad . . .

CRIPPLE: . . . pick the fat one, with eggs in its belly.

AAFAA: Listen to the fool. It's you he's calling a toad.

[The Cripple advances on him.]

GOYI: No, it wasn't. Don't listen to him.

AAFAA [voice change.]: You'll listen now or you'll listen later!

SI BERO: Where is Father?

AAFAA: Where is he, where is he? As is everywhere.

CRIPPLE [picking a flea from his rags.]: Got him!

SI BERO [turning sharply.]: What!

CRIPPLE [throwing it in his mouth.]: A fat one.

GOYI: Greedy beggar.

AAFAA: Did you choose it?

CRIPPLE: It chose me.

BLINDMAN: Chose? An enemy of As.

AAFAA: Sure? Not a disciple.

BLINDMAN: An enemy. Subversive agent.

AAFAA: Quite right. As chooses, man accepts. Had it sucked any blood?

CRIPPLE: It tasted bloody.

GOYI: Accept my sympathies.

CRIPPLE: Not needed. The blood is back where it belongs.

AAFAA: The cycle is complete?

CRIPPLE: Definitely.

GOYI: Then you can't complain.

SI BERO: What is this, Bero? Where is Father?

AAFAA: Within the cycle.

BLINDMAN: That's good. The cycle of As. Tell the Old Man that—he'll be pleased.

SI BERO: Where is he?

AAFAA: Where the cycle is complete there will As be found. As of the beginning, we praise thee.

SI BERO [shutting her ears.]: Oh God!

BERO [pointing to the Mendicants.]: Do you still want to see him?

AAFAA: As—Was—Is—Now.

SI BERO: Shut up, you loathsome toads!

   [There is a brief silence. They all look at her.]

AAFAA [grinning.]: Toads again. You hear that?

CRIPPLE: She was looking at you.

AAFAA: What! I must say I feel insulted.

CRIPPLE: A man must have some pride.

GOYI: My pride is—As.

AAFAA: And all in the line of duty. Sir, I demand protection.

BERO: That's enough. Open the surgery. [He turns to Si Bero.] You want to see him? You shall.

MENDICANTS [already moving towards the surgery.]: As—Was—Is—Now—As Ever Shall Be . . .

   Bi o ti wa

   Ni yio se wa

   Bi o ti wa

   Ni yio se wa

   Bi o ti wa l'atete ko se . . .[1]

---

1. Even as it was
  So shall it be
  Even as it was
  So shall it be
  Even as it was at the beginning of the act . . .'

SI BERO: And what in God's name is that?

BERO: One of their chants. [*He grabs her arm as she tries to run after the Mendicants.*] Now listen, and always remember this—he is wholly in my charge.

SI BERO: How long? How long has he been home?

BERO: Home? What home? I tell you he is here in my charge. It was either this or . . . Do not interfere!

[*He holds her with his eyes for a few moments, then moves to follow the Mendicants. He stops when he sees that she has made no attempt to follow.*]

You want to see him? Come on.

[*Pause. Si Bero looks at him with increasing horror and disbelief. She turns and runs towards the Old Women who receive her at the door of the hut. Bero goes on into the clinic where the light has come on, revealing the Old Man seated in the midst of the chanting Mendicants. Lights fade slowly.*]

PART TWO

The surgery, below the ground floor of the house. An examination couch
assortment of a few instruments and jars in a locked glass case, a chromium
sterilizing unit, etc., etc., a table, swivel chair, etc. A white smock hang.
against a shelf, with surgical mask and gloves tucked in the pockets. The
Mendicants are crouched, standing, stooping in their normal postures,
humming their chant and listlessly throwing dice. The Old Man's attitude
varies from boredom to tolerant amusement.

AAFAA: A. As is Acceptance, Adjustment. Adjustment of Ego to
the Acceptance of As . . . hm. Not bad. B . . . B . . . [*His eye
roams over the room for inspiration, falls on the Blindman.*] Of
course, B, Blindness. Blindness in As. I say this unto you, As is
all-seeing; All shall see in As who render themselves blind to
all else. C . . . C? [*He looks at the others one by one but ends up
shaking his head.*] No, nothing from you lot this time. Can't
see how I can ask the flock to get crippled for some reward in
As. C . . . No, I'll have to skip it for now. D—good—I
don't have to go far for that. D, Divinity. That's us. For
Destiny too. In fact Destiny first, then Divinity. Destiny is the
Duty of Divinity. D-D-D—Destiny in 3-Dimension. We the
Divinity shall guide the flock along the path of Destiny.
E . . .

BLINDMAN: Epilepsy?

AAFAA [*sharply.*]: Watch your mouth!

BLINDMAN: For your Divinity to have control, the flock must be
without control. Epilepsy seems to be the commonest form—at
least, I have witnessed much that is similar.

GOYI: I know what you mean. Taken by the spirit, they call it.
It's a good circus turn any day. Aafaa should know.

AAFAA: You are not suggesting I exploited human infirmities, are
you?

CRIPPLE: I wish I had the power. Gives a man a sense of power to
watch others twitch like so many broken worms. Broken
worms, ah, that's a fine thing to come from my mouth.

AAFAA: Before we get to Z I promise you your private and personal consolation. F . . . F . . . F . . .

GOYI: As farts, damn you! [*He turns his rear and gestures obscenely.*]

AAFAA: I was going to suggest Fulfils. As fulfils.

GOYI: And I say Farts.

AAFAA: Are you going to confront your Destiny with a fart?

GOYI: I have done before. I did it in that place where they treated us. Treatment! No doctor. Only nurses who couldn't tell a man's end from their own. Hey, listen, and let me tell you, it was the cleverest thing I ever thought all those sweet times we spent with the Old Man. With him saying this and saying that to us and me on my side—couldn't turn on my back and couldn't turn on my belly—and the sun would come up one day and I wouldn't see it again until it come up the next. One thing he told us—remember that day?—he told us the earth goes round and round, which if you remember was just too much for someone like me to swallow. So, the following morning when the sun came round again, I said to myself well, I suppose the Old Man must be right. I don't know what makes the world go round but I do know what goes round the world. It's wind. And I broke it loudly and felt better.

CRIPPLE: Dirty pig.

GOYI: It's all very well for you to talk. You could get around even then. I sometimes think God made you out of rubber or something.

AAFAA [*who has been thinking his own thoughts, gives a sudden shout.*]: God, that's it. Godhead! What a real pagan I've become if that took me so long. G, As is Godhead. I is next.

BLINDMAN: I am I, what more do you want?

AAFAA [*chews it over.*]: I am I, thus sayeth As. No . . . that might cause trouble.

BLINDMAN: What kind of trouble?

AAFAA: Think of it yourself. Sooner or later someone is going to say it and leave out 'so sayeth As'. And that means trouble.

GOYI: I don't follow.

CRIPPLE: Ask the Old Man. He'll settle the question.

[*They turn towards the Old Man, but he is still motionless, unresponsive.*]

AAFAA: Old Man, what do you think of the I matter?

[*Again they wait in vain for his response.*]

All right, if that doesn't interest you, at least give us something between I and Z. That is still a long way to go and already I can feel my brain giving out. Not to talk of the others. Anything you like, your forgotten wishes, your deepest cravings, your pet dreams . . .

GOYI: S-sh!

CRIPPLE: Why do you keep making fun of him? Leave him alone.

AAFAA [*looks genuinely surprised.*]: But I . . .

GOYI: That's what he used to say. You were using his very words just to mock him.

AAFAA: Well I didn't mean to.

[*His apparent contrition leaves the others a little flat. They steal furtive glances at the Old Man who does not move.*]

CRIPPLE: I have a pet dream.

AAFAA: We know what that is, so shut up!

BLINDMAN: I want to hear his pet dream.

AAFAA: Can't you guess what it is by seeing where he scratches himself at night?

BLINDMAN: No I cannot see.

[*A brief pause.*]

CRIPPLE: I'll tell you. Every night we sleep in this place I have that dream. It's what makes me stay on. It is what makes me . . . assist . . .

AAFAA: Collaborate.

CRIPPLE: I don't know what the big word means.

BLINDMAN [*gently.*]: No. Don't bother with it. Continue with your dream.

CRIPPLE: It is what makes me continue to obey the specialist.

[*Pause.*]

OLD MAN [*unnoticed, he has turned round to face them.*]: Go on, your dream.

CRIPPLE [*for a moment he, with the rest, shows confusion.*]: I . . . dream he tells me to get on that table. He says, I could not attend to you before but there were other things . . . one thing at a time, certain things are more important than others. So he operates on my back and in another moment he's finished, wipes his hands and says . . .

AAFAA: Arise, throw off thy crutches and follow me.

CRIPPLE [*lowering his eyes as if in abashment.*]: Yes, more or less the same words. But just as I want to get up, I wake up from the blasted dream!

AAFAA [*with explosive disgust.*]: That's a permanent dream if ever I heard one. You think the specialist has time for your petty little inconvenience? You're getting to be quite important in your mind to afford dreams like that. I wouldn't dare. Would you? [*Turning to Goyi, he sees him turn his head in confusion.*] Oh, you too? What have we here? A conspiracy of the élite? I suppose you too have been dreaming you'll get back your sight from him? No, I should have known you better. Just these two. [*Explosively.*] You are just the kind of people who make life impossible for professionals. Miracle, Miracle! That's all we ever get out of your smelly mouths. Because you blackmailed one Christ into showing off once in a while you think all others are suckers for that kind of showmanship. Well, you've met your match this generation. Turn left, turn right, turn right about again, you'll find everyone you meet is more than a match for you.

[*A short pause.*]

BLINDMAN: Isn't it time for his food?

AAFAA: The little woman will knock when it's ready. And let him starve a bit anyway, why not? He got us into this mess. If there is one thing I can't stand it's amateurs. Even there I didn't like him all that much. Now the specialist—that's a professional. You only need to remember it's father and son. Human beings both of them. Who is my neighbour, you know—all that stuff and sentiment.

[*A knock on the door. They all fall silent. The three seeing Mendicants dart a look at the Old Man. The knock is repeated.*] All right, we heard. Put down the tray and go back to your hole. Go on. Get going.

[*They listen to the footsteps retreat out of hearing.*]

[*He chants at the Old Man.*] Lord, now lettest thou thy servant depart in peace, according to thy word. [*To Blindman.*] Are you going to open the door?

[*Blindman sighs, gets up, followed by Goyi. He unbolts the door and Goyi exits. He bolts it again, Aafaa watching every movement.*]

Chop time, Old Man. Your food is on the way.

OLD MAN: Did you take my watch? [*He stirs and feels in his breast pocket.*]

AAFAA: It was broken. I sent it for repairs.

OLD MAN: You have it on your wrist.

AAFAA: Mistaken identity. [*Holding up his wrist.*] Take a look if you like.

OLD MAN: You took my glasses also.

AAFAA [*dips into his pocket.*]: Try these. No? They might just fit you never can tell. They used to belong to him. [*Pointing to Blindman.*] Are you sure you wouldn't try them? After the blast took off his eyes—that's how we first met—it was my job to go round comforting the poor fools—or burying them. Anyway—and that's the strange thing; the glasses were knocked off all right, but not a scratch on them. So he says, take my glasses from that bedside cupboard in case someone else needs them. I've kept them ever since. Are you sure you won't try them?

OLD MAN: Let me see that watch again.

AAFAA: It won't tell you anything.

OLD MAN: Which of you took my glasses?

AAFAA: What does it matter?

OLD MAN: I want to see what's in the food. What are you giving me to eat?

AAFAA: Leave that to us.

[*A sudden peremptory knock on the door. Enter Bero, followed by Goyi bearing a tray of food.*]

BERO: I thought I would join you for dinner.

OLD MAN [*rounding on him.*]: Will you tell me just what is going on?

BERO: Nothing Old Man, nothing.

OLD MAN: I wish to write a letter.

BERO: Who to?

OLD MAN: To your superiors.

BERO [*winces, but recovers his poise.*]: There isn't such a thing.

OLD MAN: Your superiors, I said. I demand the right to send to them at once.

[*Pause. Finally.*]

BERO: You shall.

OLD MAN: I wish to write them at once. Now!

BERO [*turns to Aafaa.*]: Fetch some writing material. Go to the nearest stationers.

OLD MAN: Why all the way to look for a store? Isn't there any in the house?

BERO: None that belongs to you. Perhaps you would give him money for your requirements?

[*The Old Man starts to take money from his pockets, slows down in suspicion, and looks at Bero. Then, slowly, he dips into all his trouser pockets.*]

OLD MAN: You know you took my money. Or ordered it removed.

BERO: I don't know anything of the sort.

OLD MAN [*violently.*]: You know I have no money here!

BERO: I don't know anything. You on the contrary appear to know everything. Isn't that right? You know everything.

[*To Aafaa.*] The Old Man appears to have no money. Obviously he can have no writing paper. Perhaps you would like to send a verbal message?

OLD MAN: You can take your verbal message to—[*He looks at him scornfully, then sits down.*]

BERO: I tried to help. You will, of course, be given the best of everything you need. Need. [*Pause.*] Your food will get cold.

OLD MAN: I need my pipe.

BERO [*appears to consider it.*]: Why not? In this case I raise my idea of your need to coincide with your want.

[*He opens a cabinet, gives him his pipe and tobacco.*]

That gentlemen there will offer you a light whenever you—need it.

[*The Old Man begins to stuff his pipe, normally at first, then slower and slower. When the pipe is filled he holds it by the bowl, waiting. Aafaa dips his hand in his pocket as if about to pull out matches, pauses, slowly holds out a closed fist then opens it suddenly to reveal the hand empty. He breaks into silent laughter.*]

OLD MAN: I need a light.

BERO: And your watch. And glasses. And money. And paper. But do you really? I promised you the best of everything and this will prove to you I mean it. [*He takes a packet of cigarettes from his pocket and offers it.*] They are the best cigarettes on the market.

[*He takes out a packet of matches, holds out both matches and*

*cigarettes in one hand, holds out the other hand, inviting him to
return the pipe and tobacco.*]

OLD MAN: I prefer . . . my pipe.

[*Bero does not move. A long pause. The Old Man looks round at
the Mendicants avidly watching. Finally he returns the pipe and
pouch, accepts the cigarettes and matches, but moves the packet
against his face to read the brand name.*]

BERO: You can't see to read.

[*The Old Man snatches the box away from his face, opens the box
and takes out a cigarette, lights it, then breaks into a slow smile.*]

OLD MAN: You would, wouldn't you? You would try that on me.
Me! Shall I teach you what to say? Choice! Particularity!
What redundant self-deceptive notions! More? More?
Insistence on a floppy old coat, a rickety old chair, a moth-eaten
hat which no certified lunatic would ever consider wearing,
a car which breaks down twenty times in twenty minutes, an
old idea riddled with the pellets of incidence. Enough? More?
Are you cramming it up fast for the next victim? A perfect
waterproof coat is rejected for a patched-up heirloom that
gives the silly wearer rheumatism. Is this an argument for
freedom of choice? Is it sensible to cling so desperately to bits
of the bitter end of a run-down personality? To the creak in
an old chair, the crack in a cup, a crock of an old servant, the
crick in the bottleneck of a man's declining years . . . [*Pause.
His voice changes.*] But it did come to the test and I asked you
all, what is one meat from another? Oh, your faces then,
your faces . . .

BERO: You still boast of that? You go too far, Old Man.

OLD MAN: After all, what's meat for the ranks should be meat for
the officers . . . [*Chuckles.*] It could happen I said, it will
happen. But I never really believed it.

BERO: They would have killed you, you know that? If I hadn't
had you hidden away they would have killed you slowly.

OLD MAN [*still on his own.*]: No. I've asked myself over and over
again. I said it would happen, I knew it would happen, but I
never really believed it.

BERO: They wanted to kill you, mutilate you, hang you upside
down then stuff your mouth with your own genitals. Did you
know that? [*His explosiveness breaks in on the Old Man.*]

OLD MAN: Why do you hesitate?

BERO: To do what?

OLD MAN: I said, why do you hesitate? [*Pause.*] Once you begin there is no stopping. You say, ah, this is the last step, the highest step, but there is always one more step. For those who want to step beyond, there is always one further step.

BERO: Nothing more is needed.

OLD MAN: Oh yes, there is. I am the last proof of the human in you. The last shadow. Shadows are tough things to be rid of. [*He chuckles.*] How does one prove he was never born of man? Of course you could kill me . . .

BERO: Or you might just die . . .

OLD MAN: Quite possible, quite possible.

BERO: You're lucky you've lasted this far.

OLD MAN: I *have* lasted, but the question of being lucky . . . ?

BERO: There is a search for you everywhere.

OLD MAN: I thought that was over. Tenacious gods they worship, don't they?

BERO: And you?

OLD MAN: Or maybe they are the tenacious gods.

BERO: And the god you worship?

OLD MAN: Abominates humanity—the fleshy part, that is.

BERO: Why As?

OLD MAN: Because Was—Is—Now . . .

BERO: Don't!

OLD MAN: So you see, I put you all beyond salvation.

BERO: Why As?

OLD MAN: A code. A word.

BERO: Why As?

OLD MAN: It had to be something.

BERO: Why As?

OLD MAN: If millions follow . . . that frightened you all.

BERO: Why As?

OLD MAN: Are you going to reopen the files? The case is closed. Insane, the verdict, thanks to you.

BERO: Why As?

OLD MAN: Why not?

BERO: Why As?

OLD MAN: Who wants to know?

BERO: I. Why As?

OLD MAN: What's in it for you?

BERO: *I* am asking questions! Why As?

OLD MAN: We went through this before.

BERO: I took a chance saving you.

OLD MAN: Risked your neck, yes. Compromised your position.

BERO: I didn't do that for nothing.

OLD MAN: It won't be for nothing. As my next-in-line you
are my beneficiary. Legal. These of course are my natural
heirs.

BERO: To what?

OLD MAN: As. What else?

BERO: I could turn you out and let them find you.

OLD MAN: The file is closed.

BERO: Is it? They are still looking for you.

OLD MAN: They should be looking for themselves. I robbed them
of salvation.

BERO: Oh yes, you are good at quibbling.

OLD MAN: Oh, their faces! That was a picture. All those faces
round the table.

BERO: If they hadn't been too surprised they would have shot you
on the spot.

OLD MAN: Your faces, gentlemen, your faces. You should see your
faces. And your mouths are hanging open. You're drooling
but I am not exactly sure why. Is there really much difference?
All intelligent animals kill only for food, you know, and you
are intelligent animals. Eat-eat-eat-eat-eat-Eat!

BERO [*raises his arm.*]: Stop it!

OLD MAN [*turns and holds him with his eyes.*]: Oh yes, you rushed
out and vomited. You and the others. But afterwards you
said I had done you a favour. Remember? [*Bero slowly lowers
his arm.*] I'm glad you remember. Never admit you are a
recidivist once you've tasted the favourite food of As.
[*Pause.*]

BERO: That's your last meal. Eat.
[*Going out.*]

OLD MAN: Because it's *your* last chance? [*Bero stops but doesn't turn
round.*] I guessed it. You have to prove you have not
yourself been contaminated. But suppose you find no answer

to take back, what then? [*Pause, smiling.*] The—choice—is
simple. *Be* contaminated!
[*Bero exits, slamming the door.*]

AAFAA [*dashes towards the food tray, opens the lid and sniffs.*]:
Inspiration! C, Contentment. A full belly. [*He starts to pick at
the Old Man's food. The others join him, wolfing down huge
chunks of meat. Aafaa gnaws at a huge bone.*] A full belly comes
and goes; for half the people I know it never comes. H—
Humanity! Humanity the Ultimate Sacrifice to As, the
eternal oblation on the altar of As . . . I say, I get better all
the time!

GOYI [*irritated.*]: At what? You're just a parrot.

AAFAA: I take exception to that. I'm a good pupil. The Old Man
himself admits it. The quickest of the underdogs, he always said.

GOYI: Yes, underdogs. First the Old Man tells us we are the
underdogs, then his blasted son makes us his watchdogs!

AAFAA [*shrugs.*]: Makes life a little more amusing you'll admit . . .
[*They continue to eat.*]

[*Bero and Si Bero meet in front of the house.*]

BERO: What is it? Are you spying on me?

SI BERO: What are you doing to him?

BERO: Keeping him safe. What do you imagine?

SI BERO: I wish to see him.

BERO: I've told you already . . .

SI BERO: I wish to see him.

BERO: You had your chance. No one can see him now.

SI BERO: Why not?

BERO: He's dangerous.

SI BERO: I'll risk it.

BERO: Infectious diseases are isolated. Nothing unusual about it, so
stop making a fuss. I need to work in peace.

SI BERO: What am I to do? I have time on my hands. What can I
do but think!

BERO: I've told you, leave the thinking to me. Stay in your little
world and continue the work I set you.

SI BERO: That's over. And the old women no longer help. They
sit and fold their arms.

BERO: I have no need of them. And you should never have brought them here. Throw them out.

SI BERO: They demand payment.

BERO: Then pay them off.

SI BERO: They won't take money.

BERO: So what do they want?

SI BERO: Nothing. But they refuse to leave until they are paid.

BERO [*looking in that direction.*]: They are asking for death.

SI BERO: They don't seem to be afraid of you, Bero.

BERO: We shall see.

[*He turns to go towards the hut.*]

SI BERO: Wait, Bero, wait!

BERO: Well?

SI BERO: Don't harm them, Bero.

BERO: Either you throw them out or I will. Whose home is it? Theirs? Do they now lay claim to the land?

SI BERO: It belongs to Father.

BERO: Forfeited. Legally, he does not exist. [*He goes into the house.*]

[*The surgery. The Mendicants are picking at the last crumbs of food, licking the last bone of its meat. One or two are humming the 'Ballad of the Disabled'. The Old Man reacts to the sound of singing, listens, then turns away in disgust.*]

OLD MAN: I should have known better.

AAFAA [*stops.*]: What, Old Man?

OLD MAN: For a moment I would have sworn I heard singing.

AAFAA: You heard us.

OLD MAN: I said singing, not cursing.

AAFAA: Perhaps you heard my spasms tuning up. It's like a set of wires Old Man. Something touches them, they hum, and off I go.

OLD MAN: It doesn't bother you much these days, I notice.

AAFAA: That's true. They told me up there when it began, that it was something psy-cho-lo-gi-cal. Something to do with all the things happening around me, and the narrow escape I had. It's not so bad now. I still remember the first time. I was standing there just like this, blessing a group of six just about to go off. They were kneeling before me. Then—well, I can't say I heard the noise at all, because I was deaf for the next hour. So, this thing happened, no signal, no nothing. Six men kneeling in front of me, the next moment they were gone. Disappeared, just like that. That was when I began to shake. Nothing I could do to stop it. My back just went on bending over and snapping back again, like the spirit had taken me. God! What a way for the spirit to mount a man.

OLD MAN: But no revelations? No inspired pronouncements?

AAFAA [*angrily*.]: What of you! I don't see you saving yourself in the situation you're in. [*More to himself.*] Or us.

OLD MAN: There is nothing you can do, of course.

GOYI: Be fair Old Man, how does a man cope with a situation like this? It was all right in the other place.

OLD MAN: So you find it different from the other places?

GOYI: It's not the same.

OLD MAN: There was no madness—then? [*They react, silently.*] You were not maimed then? [*He holds up his hand to stop them.*] And I mean, not merely in body. You were maimed then as now. You have lost the gift of self-disgust.

AAFAA: So have you, Old Man.

OLD MAN: Meaning?

CRIPPLE: I know what he means. I agree with him.

GOYI: So do I.

OLD MAN [*smiling*.]: Explain. I do not understand.

CRIPPLE: You took the cigarette.

AAFAA: A man like me is letting himself down to say he is surprised by anything, but . . . I was surprised at you, Old Man. You may say I was a bit let down. We may be on opposite sides of the camp, but I like to see a man stand up for himself.

OLD MAN: Why?

AAFAA: So I can beat him down.

[*He guffaws but no one joins him. He subsides.*]

OLD MAN: You were disgusted?

AAFAA [*soberly*.]: More than.

[*The Old Man turns silently to each of them in turn.*]

CRIPPLE: Disappointed.

GOYI: Crucified.

OLD MAN: Disgust is cheap. I asked for self-disgust.

AAFAA: Yeah? You took the cigarette—what about that?

OLD MAN: Of course I did. Because I saw your faces.

[*He reaches in his pocket and throws towards them what turns out to be the barely smoked cigarette. All three pounce on it; the Cripple comes out the winner.*]

AAFAA: Only one puff, only one and then you pass it round.

OLD MAN [*watches them with contempt.*]: We'll go on that world tour yet. I'll take your circus round the world, so help me.

CRIPPLE [*slowly releasing a puff of smoke.*]: Oh, that feels good. Haven't had such a good puff since that corpulent First Lady visited us and passed round imported cigarettes.

GOYI: The Old Man was mad for days. Suckers, he called us. Quite right too. Good smoke is a good suck. I wasn't going to throw away that superior brand just to please a crackpot.

AAFAA: Hey, remember the song the Old Man wrote to celebrate the occasion? Visit of the First Lady to the Home for the de-balled.

BLINDMAN: . . . for the Disabled.

AAFAA: Bloody pendant.

BLINDMAN: Pe-dant.

AAFAA [*gives up.*]: Oh Christ!

CRIPPLE [*singing.*]:
    He came smelling of wine and roses, wine and roses

MENDICANTS: . . . wine and roses.

[*Aafaa gradually warms up towards his spastic dance.*]

CRIPPLE: He came smelling of wine and roses.
        On his arm his wife was gushpillating . . .

BLINDMAN: Palpitating.

AAFAA: Oh, can't you shut up? Don't mind him, start all over again.

CRIPPLE: He came smelling of wine and roses.
        On his arm his wife was gushpillating, gushpillating . . .

MENDICANTS: . . . gushpillating.

[*The singing fades out.*]

[*Bero comes out of the house, holstering a revolver. He goes up to the Old Women's hut quietly and tries to peep inside. Iya Agba leans out of the hut and speaks almost directly in his ear.*]

IYA AGBA: Does the specialist have time for a word or two?

[*Bero is startled, leaps aside.*]

Did I scare you?

BERO [*recovering, looks her over carefully.*]: What is a thing like you still doing alive?

IYA AGBA: Can we help you?

BERO: Do what? Just pack up and get out of here before morning.

IYA AGBA: We can help you cure him.

BERO: Who?

IYA AGBA: He's sick, that is what we heard.

BERO: You heard wrong. I am giving you warning to clear out of here. Pick up your lice and rags and get out.

IYA AGBA: Is anyone else sick that we know of?

BERO: By tomorrow I want you out.

IYA AGBA: We want to help him.

BERO: No one needs help from you. Now get out of my way.

IYA AGBA: Maybe you do.

BERO: Do I have to fling you aside!

IYA AGBA [stands aside.]: Pass, then.
[She lets him take a few steps, then.]
Your sister owes us a debt.

BERO [stops, turns slowly.]: If you know what is good for you, you will never let me hear that again.

IYA AGBA: We took her into the fold—did she tell you that? To teach what we know, a pupil must come into the fold.

BERO: What fold? Some filthy thieving cult?

IYA AGBA: It's no light step for man or woman.

BERO: And what . . . cult is this?

IYA AGBA: Not any cult you can destroy. We move as the Earth moves, nothing more. We age as Earth ages.

BERO: But you're afraid to tell me the name.

IYA AGBA: I try to keep fools from temptation.

BERO [instantly angry.]: Watch it, old woman, your age earns no privileges with me.

IYA AGBA: Nothing does from what we hear. So you want to know what cult, do you?

BERO: I can ask your—pupil.
[He turns round to go back to his house.]

IYA AGBA: She won't tell you. Take it from me. She won't.
[Bero stops without turning, waits.]
Your mind has run farther than the truth. I see it searching, going round and round in darkness. Truth is always too simple for a desperate mind.

BERO [going.]: I shall find out.

IYA AGBA: Don't look for the sign of broken bodies or wandering souls. Don't look for the sound of fear or the smell of hate. Don't take a bloodhound with you; we don't mutilate bodies.

BERO: Don't teach me my business.

IYA AGBA: If you do, you may find him circle back to your door.

BERO: Watch your mouth, old hag.

IYA AGBA: You want the name? But how much would it tell you, young man? We put back what we take, in one form or another. Or more than we take. It's the only law. What laws do you obey?

BERO: You are proscribed, whatever you are, you are banned.

IYA AGBA: What can that mean? You'll proscribe Earth itself? How does one do that?

BERO: I offer you a last chance.

IYA AGBA: The fool is still looking for names. How much would it tell you?

BERO: You'll find out when they come for you.

IYA AGBA: What will you step on young fool? Even on the road to damnation a man must rest his foot somewhere.

[Bero marches furiously back to the surgery. He is stopped at the door by the sound coming from the surgery. He listens.]

CRIPPLE: . . . On his arm his wife was gushpillating,
    gushpillating . . .

MENDICANTS: . . . gushpillating . . .

CRIPPLE: You never saw such a gushpillating wife
    Oh, was it gross and was it ugly, was it ugly . . .

MENDICANTS: . . . was it ugly . . .

CRIPPLE: That thing he had clinging onto his arm
    And she knew that all the men did think so, men did
    think so . . .

MENDICANTS: . . . men did think so . . .

CRIPPLE: Did find their own predicaments much prettier.
    So she looked them mean and smiled them dirty,
    smiled them dirty . . .

MENDICANTS: . . . smiled them dirty . . .

CRIPPLE: And her mouth formed silent words
    I may be gross but dears, I'm not beyond it, not beyond
    it . . .

MENDICANTS: . . . not beyond it . . .

CRIPPLE: I may be old but not beyond it.

> While you according to diagnosis, diagnosis . . .

MENDICANTS: . . . diagnosis . . .

CRIPPLE: Will ne . . . ver . . .

> [*He pauses, splutters as if trying to control his mirth, which finally breaks out fully. The Mendicants join in, then at a rallying signal from Aafaa, control themselves long enough to end—*]

ALL: . . . hm-hm-hm . . . no more.

AAFAA: That was the best song you ever wrote for us, Old Man. Ballad of the State Visit to the Home of the De-balled.

CRIPPLE: I prefer the second one.

GOYI: Which one?

CRIPPLE: Pro patria mourir.

MENDICANTS: . . . mourir mourir mourir . . .

CRIPPLE: Dulce et decorum . . .

MENDICANTS: . . . quorum quorum quorum . . .

OLD MAN: Corum, stupes, not quorum.

MENDICANTS: Corum corum corum, not quorum.

OLD MAN: Decorum, Dulce et decorum . . .

MENDICANTS: . . . quorum quorum quorum . . .

OLD MAN: God damn you. Can you learn nothing?—corum, not quorum.

GOYI: No quorum, no quorum, that's the damned trouble.

CRIPPLE: Yes sir, you've banged the hammer on the nail.

OLD MAN [*turning to Aafaa.*]: Will you tell me what these idiots are talking about?

AAFAA: They've lost me.

CRIPPLE: You've gone dense. [*Quoting the Old Man again.*] In ancient Athens . . .

AAFAA: Damn it, you're right. No damned quorum!

BLINDMAN: In ancient Athens they didn't just have a quorum. Everybody was there! That, children, was democracy.

CRIPPLE [*singing, to the tune of 'When the Saints'.*]:
Before I join
The saints above
Before I join
The saints above
I want to sit on that damned quorum
Before I join the saints above

Before I bid
This earth adieu
Before I bid
This earth adieu
I want my dues from that damned quorum
Before I bid this earth adieu
[*The others join in, drumming on the floor, table, etc., with their
crutches, knuckles, etc., repeating the chorus. 'I want my dues . . .
Before adieus' in place of 'Oh when the Saints . . . Go marching in'.
As the tempo warms up Bero enters.*]

BERO [*entering.*]: So you haven't given up your little tricks.

OLD MAN: Does it bother you?

BERO: No. It is bad for you, though.

OLD MAN: It seems to interest you. Spend more time with us.

BERO: What gives you that idea?

OLD MAN: I could hear you listening outside. You were fascinated.

BERO: My interest in you is strictly . . .

OLD MAN: That of a specialist. Proceed.

BERO: How did you do it?

OLD MAN: Do what?

BERO: No more evasions. How did you do it? What made you
do it?

OLD MAN: Prod. Prod. Probe. Probe. Don't you know yet what I
am? [*Dramatic whisper.*] Octopus. Plenty of reach but nothing
to seize on. I re-create my tentacles, so cut away.

BERO: To me you are simply another organism, another mould or
strain under the lens. Sometimes a strain proves malignant and
it becomes dangerous to continue with it. In such a case there
is only one thing to do.

OLD MAN: Are you equipped for that here?

BERO: Even I have no control over accidents. Just now I came
through that room of herbs, I saw something I recognized.

OLD MAN: Something to sap the mind? Or destroy it altogether?

BERO: It depends on the dose. I brought you some. [*He brings
some berries from his pockets and drops them gently over the Old
Man's head.*] If you ever get tired and you feel you need a
nightcap like a certain ancient Greek you were so fond of
quoting, just soak a handful of them in water.

OLD MAN: You've used it before, haven't you? Or something similar. I saw your victims afterwards.

BERO: They were provided a Creed but they talked heresy. Same as you.

OLD MAN: Creed? Heresy? Bread, pleurisy, and what next? Will you try and speak some intelligible language.

BERO: They corrupted unformed minds. That was ba-a-ad.

OLD MAN: Unformed minds in deformed bodies.

BERO: Again you are being evasive.

OLD MAN: I asked to be sent where I would do the most good. I was and I did.

BERO [*smiling.*]: I also was sent where I would do the most good. I was and I did. [*Pause.*] It would appear that we were both efficient volunteers. [*Again, pause.*] What exactly is As, Old Man?

OLD MAN: As?

BERO: You know As, the playword of your convalescents, the pivot of whatever doctrine you used to confuse their minds, your piffling battering ram at the idealism and purpose of this time and history. What is As, Old Man?

OLD MAN: You seem to have described it to your satisfaction.

BERO [*thundering. Moving suddenly, he passes his swagger stick across the Old Man's throat, holding it from behind and pressing.*]: I'm asking you! What is As? Why As!

OLD MAN [*gasps but tries to smile. He cranes up to look him in the face.*]: In a way I should be flattered. You want to borrow my magic key. Yours open only one door at a time.

BERO: WHY AS!

OLD MAN: And rusty? Bent? Worn? Poisonous? When you're through the lock is broken? The room empty?

BERO: What is As?

OLD MAN: But why? Do you want to set up shop against me? Or against . . . others? [*He rolls his eyes towards the Mendicants.*] I think we have a conspiracy.

BERO: What is As?

OLD MAN: As Was, Is, Now, As Ever Shall be . . .

BERO [*quiet menace.*]: Don't play with me, Old Man.

OLD MAN: As doesn't change.

BERO [*increases pressure.*]: From what? To what?

OLD MAN [*choking, tugs at the swagger stick. Bero lets go. The Old Man gets up, chafing his neck.*]: Do you know what one of those men once said? Let's send our gangrenous dressings by post to those sweet-smelling As agencies and homes. He sat down to compile a mailing list.

BERO: Yes?

OLD MAN: I understood.

BERO: What did you understand?

OLD MAN: As.

BERO [*violent reaction. Controls himself.*]: You are certified insane. Your fate creates no anxiety in anyone. Take a look at your companions—your humanity.

OLD MAN: I recognized it. A part of me identifies with every human being.

BERO: You'll be disillusioned soon enough.

OLD MAN: I do not harbour illusions. You do.

BERO [*genuinely astonished.*]: I? You say that of me. I, of all people?

OLD MAN: Oh, you are in good company. Even the cripple who is down-to-earth harbours illusions. Now, that's strange. I would have thought you would find that funny.

BERO: I do not need illusions. I control lives.

OLD MAN: Control—lives? What does that mean? Tell me what is the experience of it. Is it a taste? A smell? A feel? Do you have a testament that vindicates?

BERO: We have nothing that a petty mind can grasp. [*Pause.*] Try if you can, Old Man, to avoid twitching. Control belongs only to a few with the aptitude.

OLD MAN: One should always expect something new from the specialist. [*Contemptuously.*] Control!

BERO: Your old games won't help you. Forget that line.

OLD MAN: Throw me a new line then. Feed the drowning man a line.

BERO: You can swim.

OLD MAN [*turning to the others.*]: See? He's getting good. Swim? How?

BERO [*viciously.*]: We'll flood the place for you.

OLD MAN [*pleased.*]: You're getting very good, very good. It catches, you see. How do I swim? We'll flood the place.

Or . . . is it merely in character? Is that it? Your peculiar little specialization. Perhaps that's it. So. When do you start?

BERO: Perhaps not at all. It would take too long.

OLD MAN [*nodding.*]: Y-e-s. And the place is not waterproof. I noticed rats. That means holes. You should see the rats.

BERO: They'll desert.

OLD MAN [*gazing round at the Mendicants.*]: I suppose so.

BERO: Or smoke you out. You will suffocate, slowly.

OLD MAN: Smoke. Smoke-screen. That's what it all is.

BERO: What?

OLD MAN: The pious pronouncements. Manifestos. Charades. At the bottom of it all humanity choking in silence.

BERO: You think a lot of yourself, don't you?

OLD MAN: Who else shall I think much of? You?

BERO: I control . . .

OLD MAN [*waves it aside.*]: Tell me something new. Or if you won't, these ones will. Aafaa!

AAFAA: What now?

OLD MAN: We are done with the flood. It never came. These midgets try to re-create the Flood but they lack the power. At least God had a reason. A damnable reason but at least he had a reason. And a good pump to clean up the mess. Not like these. What do you offer in place of the Flood?

AAFAA [*challenging.*]: Running water.

OLD MAN [*disgusted tone.*]: Nothing better?

AAFAA: You're dodging.

OLD MAN: Running water! [*He turns to the Cripple.*] You deal with that. It's beneath my intellect.

CRIPPLE: Muddy. How do I get across it?

OLD MAN: God, they're all so self-centred. He means running progress. Faucets, pipes.

CRIPPLE: Can't reach the tap. Too high.

AAFAA: And who cares about you? Just who the hell do you think you are?

CRIPPLE [*stubbornly.*]: Too high.

OLD MAN [*smiles.*]: Like the price. See? Blindman?

BLINDMAN: Running water? Running mouths. Election promises.

OLD MAN [*to Bero.*]: See? Let's have a new one.

AAFAA: Electricity. [*Seeing Blindman about to speak.*] And don't you tell me it's no good to you.

BLINDMAN: And whose fault is that? I wasn't born blind, you know.

CRIPPLE: Ho ho, remember that story of the blind man with a lamp?

GOYI: Don't tell me you went to school too?

AAFAA: What! Same old primer? Reader II or . . . was it Reader III?

CRIPPLE [*complacently.*]: Reader III, Elementary. Lamb and Wool Reader for Schools—well, something like that.

AAFAA: I bet you stopped at III.

CRIPPLE: No. Went up to four. Then I got the call of the road.

GOYI: I'll tell the story. A blind man went walking one day, carrying a lamp. Thereupon he met a neighbour. The neighbour stared, amazed . . .

AAFAA: A born fool.

CRIPPLE: I bet you would have found it queer too.

AAFAA: You forget I am a student of human peculiarities. Human peculiarities.

GOYI: Shut up, let me continue.

AAFAA: The neighbour said, Good blind neighbour, what good on earth is a lamp to you?

GOYI: Whereupon the blind man replied . . .

ALL TOGETHER [*in kindergarten voice.*]: I carry this lamp, good fellow, not that I may see but . . . [*Pause.*]

AAFAA: So that the whole world can see you when you try to rob me. [*He bursts into his maniacal laughter, joined by the others.*]

OLD MAN [*reflectively.*]: A lamp has its uses.

AAFAA: So, electricity.

GOYI: Bleeah! Election promises.

CRIPPLE: What we want is individual manifestos.

AAFAA: Manifesto for every freak? General Electric!

OLD MAN: Electrocutes. Electric chair. Electrodes on the nerve-centres—your favourite pastime, I believe? Tell me something new. What hasn't been abused?

BERO [*has taken out his gun, weighs it significantly.*]: And lightning strikes. What about it?

OLD MAN: The boy learns. The boy learns.

BERO: Don't you dare patronize me. Answer me, what about it?

OLD MAN: That lightning strikes? It could strike you, no?

BERO: Yes.

OLD MAN [*quiet triumphant smile.*]: Then you're not omnipotent. You can't do a flood and you—[*Pause.*]—can't always dodge lightning. Why do you ape the non-existent one who can? Why do you ape nothing?

BERO: You tax my patience. Better watch out in future.

OLD MAN [*quietly.*]: The future?

BERO: The future, yes. The End . . .

OLD MAN: Justifies the meanness.

BERO [*again, angry reaction. He controls himself.*]: Just think of this— you have none.

OLD MAN [*calls after him.*]: Tell me something new. Tell me what is happening in the future. [*They all listen to Bero's footsteps receding.*] If he'd waited, I would have told him what's happening in the future. A faithful woman picking herbs for a smoke-screen on abuse.

[*Lights up sharply in the Old Women's hut. No break in action.*]

IYA AGBA [*screaming.*]: Abuse! Abuse! What do we do? Close our eyes and see nothing?

IYA MATE: Patience now. Patience.

IYA AGBA: What is it then! I see abominations. What do you see?

IYA MATE: The same, but . . .

IYA AGBA: Then what are we waiting for? Get ready the pot of fire.

IYA MATE: Do you think a little more time . . . ?

IYA AGBA: To do worse? To do more? It's a good night for settling accounts.

IYA MATE: She's a good woman.

IYA AGBA: Get it ready. Get it ready. I'll not be a tool in their hands, not in this ripe state—No! Too much has fallen in their hands already, it's time to take it back. They spat on my hands when I held them out bearing gifts. Have you ever known it different?

IYA MATE: We hoped this might be.

IYA AGBA: Hope is dead, I must defend what is mine. Or let it die also. Let it be destroyed.

IYA MATE: Everything?

IYA AGBA: Everything. Everything they took from me.

IYA MATE: I think only of her.

IYA AGBA: She's a good woman and her heart is strong. And it is that kind who tire suddenly in their sleep and pass on to join their ancestors. What happens then?

IYA MATE: We can wait till then.

IYA AGBA: And I? Have you spoken to the ones below and did they tell you I shall still be among the living when her bones are rested.

IYA MATE: You leave me nothing to say.

IYA AGBA: There is nothing more to say. We pay our dues to earth in time, I also take back what is mine.

[*The clinic as last seen. Instant transition as before.*]

CRIPPLE [*singing.*]:
     I want my dues
     Not promises
     I want my dues
     Not promises . . .

AAFAA [*singing.*]: I want my dues. [*Stops.*] How about it, Old Man? I want my world tour. Old Man, you promised. I want that world tour you promised.

CRIPPLE: Promises. What else have we ever got from him?

GOYI: He got us the cigarettes anyway.

AAFAA: Raises a man's hopes for nothing. So where is this world tour you kept promising?

CRIPPLE: A Travelling Exhibition of As Grotesques, I remember.

AAFAA: You should, you illiterate reptile. You flung your crutches at his head because you thought it was an insult didn't you? Said he was making fun of you.

CRIPPLE: Why bring it up? The Blindman explained it. He said Grotesque only meant Greatest and I said I was sorry.

GOYI: He did too, I remember. And the Old Man also promised me top billing. [*Pause.*] I didn't want to ask at the time, but what is top billing, Blindman?

AAFAA: It means the Old Man would see that you got to the top of the ladder.

[*Pause.*]

CRIPPLE: How do *I* get there, Aafaa?

AAFAA: Why ask me foolish questions you persistent little egotist? When the specialist told you you'd soon be doing better than you were when you had both legs, did you come to Aafaa for explanations?

GOYI: So? Are we getting the world tour or not?

CRIPPLE: Nitwit! As if he could even do anything about that now. Better forget it.

AAFAA: Old Man, you shouldn't have promised the travelling show. [*Changing voice.*] Beat all known circuses hollow. I'll take the wrappings off you and leave the world gasping. What else . . . ?

CRIPPLE: You've been pushed in the background too often.

GOYI: Always hidden away.

CRIPPLE [*coyly.*]: Not that we're shy.

GOYI: Always hidden away.

CRIPPLE: We're more decent than most. Hn-hn, than most.

AAFAA: Hidden under pension schemes you are.

GOYI: Tail-of-the-parade outings.

AAFAA: Behind the big drum.

CRIPPLE: Under royalty visits.

AAFAA [*graciously proffering his hand.*]: You may.
   [*Goyi kisses his hand.*]

CRIPPLE: Imperial commendations.
   [*Aafaa unfurls the scrolls, slaps his tongue up and down.*]

CRIPPLE: Unveiling of the plaque . . .

GOYI: Commemoration occasion . . .

AAFAA: Certificates of merit . . .

GOYI: Long-service medals . . .
   [*The Cripple dashes forward to the feet of Aafaa who takes medals from an invisible aide. His eyes roll from side to side, seeing no one. Goyi goes to him, taps him, and points to the Cripple. Aafaa tries but cannot make it. Finally he kisses Goyi on both cheeks, who then kisses the Cripple on both cheeks. He pins the medal on Goyi's left shoulder, who then pins medal on the Cripple's chest. All three cry: 'Speech' 'Speech' 'We want Him' 'We want Him' 'We want Him' rising to a crescendo. Finally Blindman gets up, walks slowly downstage.*]

BLINDMAN [*The speech should be varied with the topicality and locale of the time.*]: It was our duty and a historical necessity. It is our

duty and a historical beauty. It shall always be. What we have,
we hold. What though the wind of change is blowing over
this entire continent, our principles and traditions—yes, must
be maintained. For we are threatened, yes, we are indeed
threatened. Excuse me, please, but we are entitled to match
you history for history to the nearest half-million souls. Look
at the hordes, I implore you. They stink. They eat garlic.
What on earth have we in common with *them*? Understand
me, please, understand me and do not misinterpret my
intentions. The copper is quite incidental. Manganese? I don't
know what it means. I always thought it was female for
Katangese. As for oil, I can't tell which is the margarine. If we
don't stop them now, who knows but it may be our turn
next moment. I ask you, do you want to wake up murdered
in your beds? [*The others laugh.*] I assure you it's quite possible.
No, please, it's no laughing matter. I mean . . . oh, I beg
your pardon. You know what I mean, of course, do you want
to wake up and find you've been . . . no I suppose that is also
unlikely; better simply say . . . oh, well, look, strictly between
you and me, all it boils down to is—would you want your
daughter married to one of them? . . . It may happen, believe
me, it may happen—if we're lucky. Rape is more natural to
them than marriage. Even Confucius said it—if it must be, lie
back and enjoy it. That coming from their greatest—er—er—
atomic scientist is not a statement to be taken lightly. The
black menace is no figment of my father's imagination. Look
here . . . have you had the experience of watching them—
breed? No no, I mean . . . I don't mean being actually *there*
. . . please please please, I was referring to statistics, statistics.
We feed those statistics into a computer and here is what they
say . . . What we have, we hold. What though the wind of
change is blowing over this entire continent, our principles and
traditions—yes, must be maintained. For we are threatened.
Yes, we are indeed threatened. Excuse me, but we are
entitled to match you history for history to the nearest
half-million souls. Look at the hordes, I implore you. They
stink. They eat garlic . . .
[*As Blindman begins the re-run, the other Mendicants commence
their chant, Aafaa taking the lead. The song goes faster and faster*

and louder and they clap him down until Blindman gives up and
bows.]
As Is Was Now
As Ever Shall Be

Bi o ti wa   etc. etc.
Ni yio se wa
Bi o ti wa
Ni yio se wa
[*They give Blindman a round of applause while he feels his way*
towards the Old Man.]

BLINDMAN: I hope I didn't do too badly.

OLD MAN [*sighs, turns to face him.*]: No. It was quite a good effort.

BLINDMAN: It was rather like old times.

OLD MAN: Very much like old times.

CRIPPLE: Hey, listen. The Old Man was pleased.

AAFAA: I should bloody well hope so. It was just like old times.

CRIPPLE: My feelings exactly. Just like old times.

GOYI: It . . . was . . . just . . . like old times.

AAFAA: Yes. So why risk putting us here together?

OLD MAN: Because. . . we are together in As. [*He rises slowly.*] As
Is, and the System is its mainstay though it wear a hundred
masks and a thousand outward forms. And because you are
within the System, the cyst in the System that irritates, the
foul gurgle of the cistern, the expiring function of a faulty
cistern and are part of the material for re-formulating the
mind of a man into the necessity of the moment's political As,
the moment's scientific As, metaphysic As, sociologic As,
economic, recreative, ethical As, you–cannot–es–cape! There is
but one constant in the life of the System and that constant is
AS. And what can you pit against the priesthood of that
constant deity, its gospellers, its enforcement agency? And
even if you say unto them, do I not know you, did I not
know you in rompers, with leaky nose and smutty face? Did I
not know you thereafter, know you in the haunt of cat-houses,
did I not know you rifling the poor-boxes in the local church,
did I not know you dissolving the night in fumes of human
self-indulgence simply simply simply did I not know you, do
you not defecate, fornicate, prevaricate when heaven and

earth implore you to abdicate and are you not prey to
headaches, indigestion, colds, disc displacement, ingrowing
toe-nail, dysentery, malaria, flat-foot, corns and childblains?
Simply simply, do I not know you Man like me? Then shall
they say unto you, I am chosen, restored, re-designated, and
re-destined and further further shall they say unto you, you
heresiarchs of the System arguing questioning querying
weighing puzzling insisting rejecting upon you all shall we
practise, without passion—

MENDICANTS: Practise . . .

OLD MAN: With no ill-will . . .

MENDICANTS: Practise . . .

OLD MAN: With good conscience . . .

MENDICANTS: Practise . . .

OLD MAN: That the end shall . . .

MENDICANTS: Practise . . .

OLD MAN: Justify the meanness . . .

MENDICANTS: Practise . . .

OLD MAN: Without emotion . . .

MENDICANTS: Practise . . .

OLD MAN: Without human ties . . .

MENDICANTS: Practise . . .

OLD MAN: Without—no—Lest there be self-doubting . . .

MENDICANTS: Practise . . . As Was the Beginning, As Is, Now,
As Ever Shall Be, World Without.

[*As the Old Man slowly resumes his seat, Aafaa rises, speaking.*]

AAFAA: In the beginning was the Priesthood, and the Priesthood
was one. Then came schism after schism by a parcel of
schismatic ticks in the One Body of Priesthood, the political
priesthood went right the spiritual priesthood went left or vice
versa the political priesthood went back the spiritual
priesthood went fore and vice versa the political priesthood
went down the spiritual priesthood went up or vice versa the
loyalty of homo sapiens was never divided for two parts of a
division make a whole and there was no hole in the monolithic
solidarity of two halves of the priesthood. No, there was no
division. The loyalty of homo sapiens regressed into himself,
himself his little tick-tock self, self-ticking, self-tickling,
self-tackling problems that belonged to the priesthood

spiritual and political while they remained the sole and indivisible one. Oh, look at him, Monsieur l'homme sapiens, look at the lone usurper of the ancient rights and privileges of the priesthood [*The Cripple makes an obscene gesture. Aafaa registers shock.*], look at the dog in dogma raising his hindquarters to cast the scent of his individuality on the lamp-post of Destiny! On him practise Practise! Practise! As was the Beginning—

MENDICANTS: Practise . . .

AAFAA: As Is . . .

MENDICANTS: Practise . . .

AAFAA: Now . . .

MENDICANTS: Practise . . .

AAFAA: As Ever Shall Be . . .

MENDICANTS: Practise . . .

AAFAA: World without . . .

MENDICANTS: Practise! Practise! Practise!

[*From the chorus of 'Practise' they slip into their chant, softly.*]

OLD MAN [*rising again.*]: On the cyst in the system, you cysts, you damnable warts . . . [*He freezes with his arm raised towards the next scene as if in benediction.*]

[*The 'Bi o ti wa' chant continues underneath and Aafaa continues with his spastic dance somewhat muted all through the next scene.*]

[*Iya Agba and Iya Mate have arrived in front of Si Bero's house, the latter carrying the pot of glowing coals. She places it on the ground.*]

IYA AGBA: Call her name.

IYA MATE: Si Bero!

[*Si Bero comes out a few moments later, obviously roused from sleep. She notices first the pot of coals, then makes out figures of the two women in the dark. She shrinks back.*]

Don't be afraid, daughter. No harm will come to you.

IYA AGBA: We thought it was time for a visit. Bid us welcome so we can go about our business.

SI BERO: It's . . . it's an unusual time for earth-mothers to visit their daughters.

IYA AGBA: Not if they have debts to collect. Say how you want it done, woman.

SI BERO: Debts! No, not him. Don't touch him, my mothers.

IYA AGBA: I waste no strength on carrion. I leave him to earth's rejection.

SI BERO: Give me more time. I have the power of a mother with him.

IYA MATE [*gently.*]: We waited as long as we could, daughter.

IYA AGBA: Time has run out. Do you think time favours us? Can I sleep easy when my head is gathering mould on your shelves?

SI BERO: You said yourself nothing goes to waste.

IYA AGBA: What is used for evil is also put to use. Have I not sat with the knowledge of abuse these many days and kept the eyes of my mind open?

IYA MATE: It cannot wait, daughter. Evil hands soon find a use for the best of things.

SI BERO: Let it wait my mothers, let it wait.

IYA AGBA [*angrily.*]: Rain falls and seasons turn. Night comes and goes—do you think they wait for the likes of you? I warned you when we took you in the fold . . .

SI BERO: I'll repay it all I promise . . .

IYA AGBA: I said this gift is not one you gather in one hand. If your other hand is fouled the first withers also.

IYA MATE: That is how we met it. No one can change that.

SI BERO [*clutching Iya Mate around the knees.*]: Not you too. You were never as hard as she.

IYA MATE: Nothing we can do, daughter, nothing but follow the way as we met it.

SI BERO: And the good that is here? Does that count for nothing?

IYA AGBA: We'll put that into the test. Let us see how it takes to fire.

SI BERO: Fire?

IYA AGBA: It is only the dying embers of an old woman's life. The dying embers of earth as we knew it. Is that anything to fear?

SI BERO: We laboured hard together.

IYA AGBA: So does the earth on which I stand. And on which your house stands, woman. If you want the droppings of rodents on your mat I can only look on. But my head still fills your room from wall to wall and dirty hands touch it . . .

SI BERO: No, no, nobody but myself . . .

IYA AGBA: I need to sleep in peace . . .

[*She raises the pot suddenly to throw the embers into the store. Bero steps out at that moment, gun in hand, bearing down on Iya Agba.*]

Does that thing never leave your hand? I can hear termites in your cellar—why not go and use it on them?

OLD MAN [*his voice has risen to a frenzy.*]: Practise, Practise, Practise . . . on the cyst in the system . . .

[*Bero is checked in stride by the voice. He now hesitates between the two distractions.*]

. . . you cyst, you cyst, you splint in the arrow of arrogance, the dog in dogma, tick of a heretic, the tick in politics, the mock of democracy, the mar of marxism, a tic of the fanatic, the boo in buddhism, the ham in Mohammed, the dash in the criss-cross of Christ, a dot on the i of ego an ass in the mass, the ash in ashram, a boot in kibbutz, the pee of priesthood, the peepee of perfect priesthood, oh how dare you raise your hindquarters you dog of dogma and cast the scent of your existence on the lamp-post of Destiny you HOLE IN THE ZERO of NOTHING!

CRIPPLE: I have a question.

OLD MAN [*turns slowly towards the interruption.*]: It's the dreamer.

CRIPPLE: I have a question.

OLD MAN: Black that Zero! [*Aafaa, Goyi and Blindman begin to converge on the Cripple.*]

CRIPPLE: I have a question.

OLD MAN: Shut that gaping hole or we fall through it.

CRIPPLE: I have a question.

[*The Mendicants chorus 'Practise' as they beat him.*]

OLD MAN: Stop him cold, stop him dead! Let me hear the expiring suction of an imperfect system.

CRIPPLE: My question is . . .

[*Aafaa snatches one of Goyi's crutches. In the background the sound of Bero breaking down the door. Aafaa brings down crutch on the Cripple's head.*]

OLD MAN: Stop him! Fire! Fire! Riot! Hot line! Armageddon!

[*As he shouts, the Old Man snatches the Surgeon's coat from where it is hanging, puts it on, dons cap, pulls on the gloves and picks up a scalpel.*]

OLD MAN [*at the top of his voice.*]: Bring him over here. [*He dons mask.*] Bring him over here. Lay him out. Stretch him flat. Strip him bare. Bare! Bare! Bare his soul! Light the stove! [*They heave him onto the table and hold him down while the Old Man rips the shirt open to bare the Cripple's chest. Bero rushes in and takes in the scene, raises his pistol and aims at the Old Man.*]

OLD MAN: Let us taste just what makes a heretic tick.
[*He raises the scalpel in a motion for incision. Bero fires. The Old Man spins, falls face upwards on the table as the Cripple slides to the ground from under him. A momentary freeze on stage. Then Si Bero rushes from the Old Women towards the surgery. Instantly Iya Agba hurls the embers into the store and thick smoke belches out from the doorway gradually filling the stage. Both women walk calmly away as Si Bero reappears in the doorway of the surgery. The Mendicants turn to look at her, break gleefully into their favourite song. The Old Women walk past their hut, stop at the spot where the Mendicants were first seen and look back towards the surgery. The song stops in mid-word and the lights snap out simultaneously.*]

Bi o ti wa
Ni yio se wa
Bi o ti wa
Ni yio se wa
Bi o ti wa l'atete ko.

THE END